Europe, America, Bush

The transatlantic partnership has been one of the most enduring of all international alliances. Even after the Cold War ended, the United States and its European partners intensified their economic and foreign policy cooperation, with Europe increasingly seeking to be a united, single partner acting through the European Union.

However, long before war in Iraq threatened to rupture both the transatlantic alliance and the EU's common foreign policy, two landmark events – the election of George W. Bush and the terrorist attacks of 11 September 2001 – raised profound new questions about US–European relations. The new Bush Administration quickly showed itself to be sharply at odds with both its predecessor and its European allies on issues such as missile defence, climate change and relations with Russia and China. The policy focus of transatlantic relations was then suddenly transformed by the 11 September terrorist attacks and the declaration of a War on Terrorism.

In this book, American and European experts assess transatlantic relations on matters of foreign and security policy, economic diplomacy, justice and internal security cooperation, environmental policy and relations with Russia, the Balkans and the Middle East. *Europe, America, Bush* is the first study of underlying elements of continuity in the transatlantic relationship, as well as new and powerful forces for change. It offers a definitive assessment of whether, and how much, the election of George W. Bush, the events of 11 September and conflict over Iraq mark genuine and lasting change in transatlantic relations.

John Peterson is Jean Monnet Professor of European Politics at the University of Glasgow. His recent publications include the co-edited volumes *Integration in an Expanding European Union* and *The Institutions of the European Union*.

Mark A. Pollack is Associate Professor of Political Science and European Studies at the University of Wisconsin, Madison. He is the author of *The Engines of European Integration* and co-editor of *Transatlantic Governance in the Global Economy*.

Europe, America, Bush

Transatlantic relations in the
twenty-first century

**Edited by John Peterson and
Mark A. Pollack**

Routledge
Taylor & Francis Group

LONDON AND NEW YORK

First published 2003
by Routledge
11 New Fetter Lane, London EC4P 4EE

Simultaneously published in the USA and Canada
by Routledge
29 West 35th Street, New York, NY 10001

Routledge is an imprint of the Taylor & Francis Group

Typeset in Baskerville by GreenGate Publishing Services, Tonbridge, Kent
Printed and bound in Great Britain by The Cromwell Press, Trowbridge,
Wiltshire

British Library Cataloguing in Publication Data
A catalogue record for this book is available from the British Library

Library of Congress Cataloguing in Publication Data
Europe, America, Bush : transatlantic relations in the twenty first
century / edited by John Peterson and Mark A. Pollack.
     p. cm.
Includes bibliographical references and index.
  1. Europe, Western--Foreign relations--United States. 2. United States--
Foreign relations--Europe, Western. 3. United States--Foreign economic
relations--Europe, Western 4. Europe, Western--Foreign economic rela-
tions--United States. 5. United States--Foreign relations--2001- 6. United
States--Military policy. 7. European Union. 8. North Atlantic Treaty
Organization. 9. International relations. 10. Globalization--Political
aspects. I. Peterson, John. II. Pollack, Mark A.
     D1065.U6 E97 2003
     327.7304'09'0511--dc21

                                                            2003003594

ISBN 0-415-30942-5 (hbk)
ISBN 0-415-30943-3 (pbk)

Contents

Illustrations

Figures

Contributors

Matthew Baldwin	European Commission
Daniel Bodansky	University of Georgia
Jolyon Howorth	University of Bath
Margot Light	London School of Economics
Costanza Musu	London School of Economics
John Peterson	University of Glasgow
Mark A. Pollack	University of Wisconsin-Madison
Wyn Rees	University of Nottingham
Bruce Stokes	*The National Journal*
William Wallace	London School of Economics

Preface and acknowledgements

At various points during this book's gestation, one or the other of us has mentioned *Europe, America, Bush* while speaking publicly on transatlantic relations, out of genuine excitement about the book and its line-up as much as the usual inclination to talk about (and plug) whatever work one has in the pipeline. In doing so, and to give a sense of the book's unusually straightforward purpose, we sometimes borrowed a line from a British television advertisement for woodcare products made by a company called Ronseal (which itself is owned by Sherwin-Williams, and so is very much a transatlantic concern). 'This book', we promised our audiences (and prospective readers), would do 'exactly what it says on the tin'[1] (or 'can', in US parlance). That is, *Europe, America, Bush* would really do what it claimed to do: assess the impact of George W. Bush on transatlantic relations. It would focus on a single, if a complex, question: would the change of government in the US change the tenor of the relationship – possibly leading to a 'divorce' between America and Europe – or would intense transatlantic interdependence in security and economic affairs ensure continuity in the relationship?

No sooner had we posed this question to ourselves and our contributors than the events of 11 September 2001 intervened to complicate – and possibly overshadow – this book's original task. No sooner had our manuscript gone to press than the war with Iraq began, thus further complicating any assessment of the Bush administration's impact on transatlantic relations. In the end, this volume grapples just as much with the effects of '9/11' and transatlantic tensions over Iraq as it grapples with the Bush factor. Neither we nor our contributors would pretend that it is possible to isolate the effects of one of these factors from the other, for obvious reasons. It has been a difficult, as well as exhilarating and disturbing time to study relations between Europe and America.

The book emerged out of a workshop organised under the auspices of the BP Chair in Transatlantic Relations, based at the Robert Schuman Centre for Advanced Studies of the European University Institute in San Domenico di Fiesole, Italy. We are grateful to the BP Chair and Schuman Centre at the EUI,

---

[1] The phrase even merits an entry in the *Oxford Idioms Dictionary for Learners of English*, which (according to Oxford University Press) also 'does exactly what it says on the tin'. See <http://www1.oup.co.uk/elt/oald/buzz_words/tin.htm> (accessed 25 January 2003).

which provided funding and a meeting place for our debates, and to our colleagues Helen Wallace, Ernst-Ulrich Petersmann, Jan Zielonka and (especially) Stan Sloan, all of whom contributed significantly as participants to our discussions in Florence.

On a personal note, Mark Pollack would like to thank both his wife Rita Krueger, who did more than her fair share of childcare for his newborn daughter Fiona during the final preparation of this book, and John Peterson, who did more than his fair share of writing and editing during the same period. John Peterson is grateful to his family for allowing him to be a stranger in the house for several weeks so that the book could get done, as well as to organisers of conferences held in autumn 2002 in Belfast, Cambridge, Brussels, and London for invitations to share and debate ideas that fed into the book.

Finally, we are in debt to our stalwart yet genial cast of contributors, each of whom dutifully produced multiple drafts of their paper and cheerfully (well, most of the time) put up with our intrusive editorship, all the while analysing a target that continued to move even as the book went to press.

John Peterson and Mark A. Pollack
Scotland and Madison, June 2003

Abbreviations

ABM	Anti-Ballistic Missile
AIDS	Acquired Immune Deficiency Syndrome
AWACs	Advanced Warning and Control System (aircraft)
BMD	Ballistic Missile Defence
CAP	Common Agricultural Policy
CEE	Central and Eastern European countries
CENTO	Central Treaty Organisation
CFSP	Common Foreign and Security Policy
CJTF	Common Joint Task Forces
COG	Chief of Government
EABC	European–American Business Council
EC	European Community
ECHO	European Community Humanitarian Office
ECSC	European Coal and Steel Community
EEC	European Economic Community
EMU	Economic and Monetary Union
ERRF	European Rapid Reaction Force
ESDI	European Security and Defence Identity
ESDP	European Security and Defence Policy
EU	European Union
FARC	Revolutionary Armed Forces of Colombia
FBI	Federal Bureau of Investigation (US)
FSC	Foreign Sales Corporations
FTA	Free Trade Area
FTAA	Free Trade Area of the Americas
GATT	General Agreement on Trade and Tariffs
GDP	Gross Domestic Product
G8	Group of Eight (Industrialised Countries)
G77	Group of 77 (Developing Countries)
GM	Genetically Modified (seeds, crops or foods)
GMOs	Genetically Modified Organisms
ICG	International Crisis Group
ICT	International Criminal Tribunal

IISS	International Institute for Strategic Studies
ISAF	International Security Assistance Force (Afghanistan)
ITC	International Trade Commission
JHA	Justice and Home Affairs
KFOR	Kosovo Force (NATO)
KLA	Kosovo Liberation Army
LDCs	Less Developed Countries
MFN	Most-Favoured Nation
MLATs	Mutual Legal Assistance Treaties
NAFTA	North American Free Trade Agreement
NATO	North Atlantic Treaty Organisation
NGO	Non-Governmental Organisation
NRC	NATO–Russia Council
NRF	NATO Response Force
NTA	New Transatlantic Agenda
NTM	New Transatlantic Marketplace
OECD	Organisation for Economic Cooperation and Development
OPEC	Organisation of Petroleum Exporting Countries
OSCE	Organisation for Security and Cooperation in Europe
PCA	Partnership and Cooperation Agreement
PfP	Partnership for Peace
PHARE	Poland and Hungary: Aid for the Restructuring of Economies
SAA	Stabilisation and Association Agreements
SEED	Support for East European Democracy
SLG	Senior Level Group
START	Strategic Arms Reductions Talks
TABD	Transatlantic Business Dialogue
TACIS	Technical Assistance to the Commonwealth of Independent States
TAFTA	Transatlantic Free Trade Area
TPA	Trade Promotion Authority
TREVI	Terrorisme, Radicalisme et Violence Internationale
UK	United Kingdom
UN	United Nations
UNCTAD	United Nations Conference on Trade and Development
UNESCO	United Nations Educational, Scientific and Cultural Organisation
UNFCCC	United Nations Framework Convention on Climate Change
UNFPA	United Nations Fund for Population Activities
US	United States
USTR	United States Trade Representative
WCT	War Crimes Tribunal
WEU	Western European Union
WHO	World Health Organisation
WMD	Weapons of Mass Destruction
WTO	World Trade Organisation

1 Introduction

Europe, America, Bush

John Peterson and Mark A. Pollack

The defining feature of transatlantic relations in the post-war period has been mutual dependence between the United States (US) and western Europe. Under the conditions of the Cold War, their interdependence in the security realm was particularly salient, with both sides responding to powerful incentives to cooperate and avoid discord in the face of a monolithic Soviet threat. Economic interdependence intensified over time, but economic conflict and cooperation were generally second-order concerns. The term 'transatlantic' was rarely used to describe European–American relations because the *Atlantic* Alliance – the North Atlantic Treaty Organisation (NATO) – was the primary channel for the most important exchanges.

It is often forgotten that the Cold War ended almost simultaneously with the final stages of a dramatic effort by the member states of (what became) the European Union (EU) to enhance their economic solidarity and power by creating a single European market. Subsequently, the EU emerged as the United States' most important partner in terms of trade and investment. Before but especially after the collapse of the Soviet Union in 1991, economic and political reform in central and eastern Europe became an urgent and shared western concern. The US under the Clinton administration thus found itself with new incentives to broaden and intensify economic and foreign policy cooperation, and to seek new channels of diplomatic exchange with a Europe increasingly seeking to be a united, single partner by acting through the EU. A formal US–EU dialogue had been sought by the Bush (Senior) administration and agreed via the Transatlantic Declaration in 1990. But it was upgraded under Bill Clinton and given significantly more policy substance through the 1995 New Transatlantic Agenda (NTA).

The EU remained very much a work in progress, especially in foreign or security policy, as revealed by its humiliation as an aspiring peacemaker in the former Yugoslavia. Still, Europe and America seemed closer than ever before to something like a strategic partnership by the late 1990s (see Featherstone and Ginsberg 1996; Peterson 1996; Smith 1998; Monar 1998). Even sceptics admitted that 'the potential for the EU and the United States to raise their relationship to a new level of cooperation remained' as the decade ended (Allen 2002: 45).

The year 2001, however, witnessed two landmark events, each with potential to augur a substantial change in the tenor and substance of transatlantic relations.

First, after a long and bitterly contested electoral dispute, George W. Bush was inaugurated as US President. The Bush administration included a number of well-respected diplomats with extensive transatlantic experience, including the US Trade Representative, Robert Zoellick, who had been a main architect of the Transatlantic Declaration (Featherstone and Ginsberg 1996: 89). Nevertheless, the new administration showed itself to be sharply at odds with both the Clinton administration and its European allies on issues such as missile defence, climate change, relations with Russia, and the Balkans.

Second, on 11 September 2001 (9/11) the policy focus of transatlantic relations – and international relations more generally – was transformed by the terrorist attacks on the World Trade Centre and the Pentagon, and the subsequent declaration of a war on terror by the Bush administration. The initial effect of the attacks was to unite the US and Europe in a common struggle against terrorism as well as in other international endeavours, such as the successful launch of a new round of world trade talks under the auspices of the World Trade Organisation (WTO). Yet the forceful American campaign against terrorism, together with European anxieties about US unilateralism and assertions of an 'axis of evil' linking so-called rogue states, provoked further and powerful transatlantic tensions. These tensions culminated in one of the most serious transatlantic ruptures seen since the Suez crisis of 1956 – over the Anglo-American attack on Iraq in 2003 – even if the rupture between the US and Europe obscured even more serious divisions *within* Europe. The war ended with a decisive 'allied' victory, even if winning the post-war peace looked an even more formidable challenge than winning the war. In any event, attention quickly turned to healing the transatlantic split, even if (perhaps because) grave questions remained about how much and how permanent was the damage done by the war to the US–European alliance.

This book has a simple (if ambitious) purpose: to identify both what changed in transatlantic relations after the 2000 US election, 9/11 and Iraq; *and* what remained the same. Rather than accept truisms such as the idea that 'the transatlantic alliance is finished', we have asked our authors to identify areas where the underlying interests and strategies of the US and Europe remain fundamentally unchanged, and those where the election of George W. Bush, 9/11 and the war in Iraq have provoked genuine, durable changes in transatlantic relations. The chapters that follow offer analysis of a broad cross-section of issue-areas. Revealingly, 'Europe' is most often considered to be the EU in most chapters, but not exclusively and not because of any injunction from editors to authors. More generally, by taking a hard look at hard evidence, this book aims to make it possible for its readers to judge for themselves whether the transatlantic relationship is now brittle or remains durable, and ultimately whether it will move in the direction of convergence or divergence as a consequence of the dramatic events of the past several years.

We begin here with a brief overview of transatlantic relations as they evolved up until 2000. We then focus on the relationship between Europe and the George W. Bush administration, before confronting how and how much the events of 9/11 and war with Iraq altered the relationship. Our conclusion previews the chapters that follow.

The transatlantic alliance: the story so far

The post-war history of relations between Europe and America has been analysed extensively elsewhere (see Featherstone and Ginsberg 1996; Peterson 1996: 35–54; Lundestad 1997; Pollack and Shaffer 2001b: 7–17). Here it suffices to consider Lundestad's (1997) three main claims about the evolution of the relationship. First, US support has been crucial to the post-war success of European integration. Second, this support has often been rooted in rather naïve ideas about replicating a 'United States of Europe' modelled on the US. Third, American support for European unity has remained broadly consistent over time.

In the early post-war period, with the US in a position of political and economic dominance, the Marshall Plan transferred around 5 per cent of American gross domestic product (GDP) to Europe in aid – an entirely unimaginable act today. The Marshall Plan was less an act of altruistic generosity than an anti-Communist measure designed to keep socialist ideas from spreading in Europe. US support for European unity was similarly calculated and purposeful: substantial financial backing in the late 1940s for the fledgling political group, the European Movement, came from the US Central Intelligence Agency (Aldrich 2001). Yet, whatever American motives, it mattered that Marshall Plan aid came with the condition that mechanisms be created to promote cooperation between its recipients. These mechanisms (mainly the Organisation for European Economic Cooperation) did not amount to much. However, the European Coal and Steel Community (ECSC), launched in 1951 with firm American political support, did.

The ECSC was designed with the narrow purpose of combining the war-making industries of Germany and France, thus making it impossible for them ever again to wage war on one another. Few could have foreseen that the ECSC would put Europe on a path, if by no means a straight one, towards locking in cooperative intergovernmental agreements with supra-national rules and institutions. The European Economic Community (EEC), born in 1957 to extend the common market for coal and steel to most other products, at first seemed a modest step along this path. It seemed entirely moribund at multiple points in the 1960s and 70s. But a series of heroic, but often barely-noticed judgements by its supra-national European Court of Justice (see Weiler 1999) laid the groundwork for a major relaunch of the 'European project' via the Single European Act and single market programme in the 1980s. Arguably, these in turn led to the launch of the euro by the late 1990s, by which time the EEC had morphed into the EU.

A curious side effect of European economic integration was the gradual equipping of the EU with the external policy *accoutrements* usually associated exclusively with nation-states. Logically, Europe could not have a common market without a common commercial policy, so the EEC was given one soon after its creation. But decolonisation in Africa and elsewhere, and French requests for German help in managing it, meant that 'Europe' quickly became a donor of aid to the less-developed world. By 1970, with the war in Vietnam violating many European sensibilities, EEC member states began to look for scope to coordinate their foreign policies and speak with a single voice, especially to speak truth (or at least dissent) to power (the US). In the 1980s, the single market programme and the expansion of Community competences to, especially, environmental policy and border controls had powerful consequences for the EU's relations with the non-European world, and not least the US. Ultimately, the 1992 Maastricht Treaty gave the EU, in theory at least, something no other international organisation had ever aspired to have: a 'common foreign and security policy'. The Union even began work on a defence policy in 1998.

Especially during the Cold War, most US policymakers took a 'NATO-first' view of Europe: NATO, of which the US was a member, was the key forum for the most important transatlantic exchanges. For every attempt to boost the role of what eventually became the EU, such as Kennedy's 1962 'Declaration of Interdependence', one could find instances when US administrations – especially those of Nixon and Reagan – showed disdain or neglect towards the EU. Yet, especially when the Cold War ended, suddenly and amidst rapid and wrenching geopolitical change, the instinctive US view that a politically united Europe was desirable re-emerged. Even the most committed American Eurosceptics could but show grudging respect for the EU's success in creating the euro and exporting its model of democracy and capitalism to the former Soviet bloc.

American policy has both determined and been determined by the process of European integration. There is no question that US support was crucial to the earliest post-war attempts at European institution-building. Many Europeans would deny that the US has had much of an impact on the most recent steps forward in European integration, such as the internal market project, the euro, or enlargement. But that America had the power to shape, and indeed did shape, all of these policies is difficult to deny. The perceived political need to cure the US of its phobia about a 'fortress Europe' helped ensure that the internal market did not raise external barriers to the EU's market. The US maintained its position of passive support, at least, for economic and monetary union (EMU) even when it seemed a drag on global growth (Henning and Padoan 2000: 12–17), and even intervened to support the euro during a US election campaign when its weakness became a global concern in 2000. The American push to enlarge NATO by 1999 set a political precedent for the EU's eastern enlargement in 2004.

At the same time, US policy has been shaped by the emergence of the EU as regional power and potential global partner. The Union's emergence as a unified economic bloc, as well as America's most important trading and investment partner, meant a bilateral negotiation on trade liberalisation effectively ended up being 'exported' to the multilateral level via the Uruguay Round, yielding an overall agreement that was breathtakingly radical and barely acceptable in US domestic political terms. Increasing transatlantic economic interdependence manifested itself in a growing number of trade and regulatory disputes over issues such as bananas, hormone-treated beef, genetically modified foods, and the tax treatment of US exports, management of which required direct diplomatic contact between the US and EU.

Meanwhile, closer EU cooperation on matters of foreign policy, while exposing (often brutally) the gap between European rhetoric and action, together with the thawing of the Soviet bloc further convinced both the Bush (Senior) and Clinton administrations that US–EU relations needed to be upgraded. The 1990 Transatlantic Declaration mandated regular US–EU summits at the highest political level and the 1995 NTA sought to make them more substantive. Even if neither was a major success in terms of concrete policy achievements, American policy towards Europe became considerably more EU-focused in the 1990s.

The Clinton administration – while by no means uncritical of the EU (see Holbrooke 1999) – liked to claim that it was more supportive of European integration than any since Kennedy's. By the time that Clinton left office, the US dealt with the EU – as opposed to its individual member states or NATO Europe – on a far broader array of issues, ranging from market regulation to environmental protection to police cooperation, than it did when it assumed office. The days when European hands in the State Department would, in preparation for a visit from the European Commission, ask each other, 'What in the world are we going to talk about with them?', were certainly over. What was unclear was whether the election of George W. Bush in 2000 marked the death of the idea that the US and EU could become strategic partners.

Europe and George W. Bush

In June 2000, Bill Clinton was awarded the Charlemagne Prize, an honour bestowed annually on a leading figure who has worked for the unification of Europe. Clinton was the first American President to win the award. In December 2000, when the identity of Clinton's successor as US president had just recently become clear, Chris Patten, the EU Commissioner for External Affairs, declared 'Europe will miss Bill Clinton. He has been a good friend to this continent' (quoted in Everts 2002: 9).

Patten probably never foresaw how prescient his remark would sometimes seem in the first years of the presidency of George W. Bush. The new administration's foreign policy team included, alongside moderates such as Colin Powell, a group of more hawkish or ideological officials, including Vice President Richard Cheney, Deputy Secretary of Defence Paul Wolfowitz, Defence Policy Board Chairman Richard Perle, and Deputy Secretary of State Richard Armitage. As the Republicans had not held the White House for eight years, very few had much appreciation of the EU's recent emergence as a global actor. Bush's Secretary of Defence, Donald Rumsfeld, had last served in the Ford and Reagan administrations. As such, perhaps it was to be expected that his first major address on European security after his appointment, to the New York Council of Foreign Relations, did not mention the EU once.

Bush and his team made it clear that theirs would be a 'realist' foreign policy based on cool calculation of US interests, a significant military build-up, and little or no interest in multilateral agreements. Bush's National Security Adviser, Condoleezza Rice (2000), was resolute that the new administration would eschew 'romanticism', presumably of the kind that had been the basis of Clinton's foreign policy. Academic opinion dismissed a 'realist' foreign policy, based on 'simple solutions to policy dilemmas', as 'misguided' (Legro and Moravcsik 2001), but that made Rice's signals no less disturbing to Europeans: 'multilateral agreements and institutions should not be ends in themselves ... American values are universal ... Military readiness will have to take center stage' (Rice 2000: 47–51).

The first point of strain between Europe and the Bush administration was over missile defence, which Clinton had tried to keep on a back burner. In contrast, Bush announced that his administration would press ahead with full testing of a comprehensive missile defence system, thus abrogating the 1972 Anti-Ballistic Missile Treaty, which many governments (especially in Europe) viewed as a cornerstone of arms control. A second clash was over the Kyoto Protocol: the Bush administration announced that it was pulling out of international negotiations on the reduction of emissions that were suspected of causing global warming. The timing of the announcement, on the eve of a visit by German Chancellor (and strong supporter of the Kyoto process), Gerhard Schröder, suggested disdain for Europe and European views. A third source of friction was the International Criminal Court. The Bush administration refused to accept the jurisdiction of the court – universally supported by EU member governments – or the idea that any American might be judged by it. Later, of course, it would explicitly threaten to cancel US aid to Yugoslavia unless its government turned over Slobodan Milosevic for prosecution by the International Criminal Tribunal (ICT) in The Hague, in a particularly blatant case of double standards (Hassner 2002: 46).

In economic relations, the Bush administration at least seemed to want to strike a better tone after the bitterness of the bananas and beef hormones disputes and collapse of the Seattle WTO summit in the latter part of the Clinton era. The appointment of Robert Zoellick, a senior State Department official for European affairs during the Bush (Senior) administration, as US Trade Representative was warmly welcomed in Europe. Zoellick visited the European Parliament in May 2001 and expressed the new administration's interest in launching a new WTO trade round, while telling MEPs: 'Make no mistake, we are back at the table of free trade'.[1] Yet, the administration also began to signal that it would endorse highly protectionist measures to assist its beleaguered agricultural and steel industries. When new duties on foreign steel and a new farm bill were eventually unveiled in 2002, European officials were shocked at how blatantly protectionist they were, and how directly they trod on European interests.

Amidst all the ideologues in the Bush administration, Europeans could at least take comfort in the appointment of Colin Powell, a committed multilateralist, as Secretary of State. Powell worked closely with the EU to help resolve a simmering domestic conflict in Macedonia in mid-2001 and appeared to welcome European assistance in an effort to restart peace talks in the Middle East. Yet, over time it became clear that foreign policy hard-liners in the administration were attempting – with considerable success – to isolate or marginalise Powell in policy debates. The 10 September 2001 issue of *Time* magazine featured the cover story headline, 'Where have you gone, Colin Powell?'[2] It was on American news-stands the next day when hijacked planes slammed into the World Trade Centre and the Pentagon, thus dramatically recasting foreign policy debates within the Bush administration.

Europe, America, 11 September

At least initially, the terrorist attacks of 9/11 made transatlantic frictions over missile defence or the Kyoto protocol seem trivial. Thousands of ordinary people
from 26 countries – including hundreds of Europeans – were killed on 9/11 in the
first 'military' attack on continental US soil since the war of 1812. The initial
European response was unified, empathetic, and poignant (Peterson 2002: 26).
Even in France, the hothouse of European anti-Americanism and antipathy
towards the Bush administration, the top headline in *Le Monde* on 13 September
2001 was (in English), 'We are all Americans'. Two leading figures from America's
closest European ally, Tony Blair and Lord (George) Robertson (the latter
Secretary-General of NATO), were primarily responsible for invoking NATO's
Article 5 the day after the attack, making it clear that this attack and any further
ones were considered an attack on all members of the Atlantic Alliance.

The first days and weeks after the attacks saw the Bush administration refrain
from lashing out at any real or perceived perpetrator. Instead it began to work –
with Powell taking a lead – to lay the foundations for an international coalition
against terrorism, including via the United Nations (UN). It also reached out to
the EU, by providing a list of specific measures that it requested be taken by the
Union to assist in the war on terrorism. The EU's response was to convene an
emergency summit within ten days of 9/11 and thereafter to lead diplomatic
efforts to win over 'front-line' states, including Iran, Syria, Egypt and Pakistan, to
the international anti-terrorist coalition.

Yet the solidarity of the coalition was soon strained by the war in Afghanistan,
which began in October 2001. It quickly became clear that the longer the war
went on, the more that Europeans were turning against the war (Peterson 2002:
27–8). Fortunately for the transatlantic alliance, the Taliban regime in
Afghanistan collapsed far more quickly than even the most optimistic calculations
had predicted. With only a minimal European military contribution (much more
was offered than was accepted[3]), the Bush administration appeared to have won
the first major battle in the war on terrorism.

According to Robert Zoellick, the war's next battle was to be played out in
Doha, the capital of the tiny Middle Eastern state of Qatar, where the first post-
Seattle WTO ministerial was scheduled for November. Controversially, Zoellick
began to argue that the launch of a new trade round was one of the best ways to
fight back against the terrorists, since one of the aims of the 9/11 attacks was to
disrupt cross-border trade and plunge the world economy into recession. Arguably,
the successful launch of the WTO's Doha Development Agenda showed that the
amorphous 'international community', with the US *and* the EU (at least in the economic realm) providing leadership, was capable of collective action in response to
a monolithic international threat. To some, the 'Development Agenda' label was a
ruse designed to cover up how many developing countries simply caved into US
pressure to be 'with us or against us', and signed up to the new trade round despite
grave reservations. To others, the agreement at Doha – especially on the politically
loaded issue of the pricing of drugs to counter Acquired Immune Deficiency

Syndrome (AIDS) and other epidemics – showed a new western acceptance of the legitimacy of developing country concerns.

Any European optimism inspired by the successful launch of the Doha Development Agenda quickly dissipated. In retrospect, a defining moment in transatlantic relations came on 29 January 2002 when George W. Bush delivered his annual State of the Union speech to a joint session of Congress. If we are to believe the memoir of one contributor to the address – a 42-year-old Canadian speechwriter named David Frum (2003) – it was not the product of careful reflection or deliberation within the White House, let alone any discussion with US allies. Asked to think of a phrase which equated Iraq with the enemies of the west in World War II, Frum claims to have conjured up the idea of an 'axis of hatred'. The 'axis' was then altered to one of 'evil' (to make it more 'biblical') as the speech was redrafted at upper echelons of the White House command. It also was extended to Iran (and, apparently at the last possible minute, to North Korea).

The speech shocked many in European diplomatic circles (see for example Patten 2002). Despite some claims to the contrary (Gedman 2002: 15–16), little hard evidence linked Saddam Hussein to Al-Qaeda or other international terrorist networks; in fact, staunch US ally Saudi Arabia was sometimes alleged to be a more important state sponsor of terrorism. Considerable European diplomatic energy was being invested in encouraging secular moderates in Iran, and negotiations had begun on an EU–Iranian Trade and Cooperation Agreement. After the Bush administration had announced its disengagement from North Korea, an EU delegation had visited Pyongyang to try to coax the regime of Kim Jong Il away from its nuclear ambitions. From a European perspective, the effect of the axis of evil speech was 'to elide the war on terrorism with the previous United States campaign against rogue states, proliferation of weapons of mass destruction, and the resulting need for Ballistic Missile Defence' (Peel 2002: 23). Suddenly, the US seemed determined to fight the war on terrorism 'via an all-military doctrine' (Gnesotto 2002: 26), in direct violation of Europe's instinctive predisposition to 'civilian power' methods: patient diplomacy, aid and trade instruments, reinforcing multilateralism. More generally, Bush's speech appeared to signal a shift from the measured, restrained, and coalition-focused language and behaviour shown by his administration in the first days after 9/11 to a new brand of headstrong American unilateralism. For the administration's critics, the US decision to launch an invasion of Iraq in early 2003 – as part of a military 'coalition' with the UK but in defiance of France, Germany, Russia, most of the United Nations (UN) and much of world opinion – was almost an inevitable consequence of Bush's 2002 State of the Union address.

Taking a step back from the drama and emotionalism of 9/11, it was clear that the broad contours of the power equation in the international political system had changed in the 1990s. While most defence budgets had fallen, especially in Europe, US defence spending had declined only marginally. The post-9/11 spending increases announced by the Bush administration – the largest in 20 years – meant that annual US defence expenditure would climb to two and half times that of the 15 EU member states. Economically, extraordinary growth during the Clinton-era boom had effectively stapled an economy the size of the UK's onto the existing American economy in the space of a few years. While the American economy grew by 27 per cent between 1990 and 1998, the EU settled for 15 per cent. In these circumstances, and especially after 9/11, it was plausible to think that 'the United States is too powerful to be anything other than unilateral … Thus, America has to make a choice – broad unilateralism or narrow unilateralism' (Lindley-French 2002: 80–2).

Nevertheless, America's European allies found the Bush administration's new foreign policy injunction, that the 'mission would determine the coalition, not vice versa', to be particularly hard to swallow. Different voices in the Bush administration phrased the message in different ways. But Donald Rumsfeld, the Secretary of Defence, was the most blunt in describing the international coalition against terrorism as a 'shifting alliance' that will be 'opportunistic' and 'temporary', with the US always prepared to 'abandon [certain allies] along the way out of sheer pragmatism, just as they will abandon us' (quoted in Dockrill 2002: 10). The effect was to shatter any notion that the transatlantic alliance was special, time-honoured, and permanent, bound together by a shared history and common values. It was widely agreed that NATO was a 'prime victim of 9/11' (Haftendorn 2002: 29; see also Talbott 2002). It was less clear that the US could 'win' a war on terrorism without the EU, especially given its growing competence on justice and home affairs questions and ability to seize or block the assets of international terrorist organisations. But the rise of a new common enemy in the form of international terrorism often seemed to have almost the opposite effect on transatlantic cohesion as did the Soviet threat during the Cold War.

In general, there was much the world could agree on as basic lessons of 9/11: 'violence has been privatised, insecurity has globalized, terrorism threatens all nations, and the line separating internal from external security is now blurred' (Delpech 2002: 3). The consensus about the effects of 9/11 on the transatlantic relationship was somewhat less clear but mainly gloomy:

> American policy-makers see no reason to listen to their European allies; the American debate about foreign policy is self-contained and self-confident. September 11 may be seen in retrospect to have weakened the transatlantic partnership, not strengthened it.
>
> (Wallace 2002a: 285)

> The long-term trends of divergence between American and European cultures, interests, and political systems, skilfully slowed down by diplomacy and a fear of a common enemy, may paradoxically speed up now that an external force has dealt a physical blow across the Atlantic.
>
> (Hill 2002a: 260)

> In sum, the US and Europe are increasingly drifting apart, both militarily and politically.
>
> (Gnesotto 2002: 27)

The expansion of the US campaign to Iraq seemed to drive a final wedge into the transatlantic alliance, while also bitterly dividing the UN Security Council, isolating the vaunted Franco-German alliance within the EU and NATO, and even prompting a US consumer boycott of French products. Nevertheless, predictions of a permanent transatlantic split seemd premature, particularly when both sides appeared to step back and look for new ways to renew the alliance.[4] As this book makes clear, the transatlantic relationship operates on many levels and in a diverse variety of regions and issue-areas. Our contributors offer a broad overview of the relationship but one that does justice to the rich, nuanced, and multidimensional nature of the relationship. Only when the relationship is considered in all its complexity can one judge how and how much it has been changed by the election of George W. Bush, the attacks of 9/11 and the invasion of Iraq.

A roadmap to this volume

This volume begins and ends by tackling broad themes, and narrows its focus in between to examine specific issues central to transatlantic relations in considerable depth. In Chapter 2, Jolyon Howorth examines the state of the transatlantic relationship on matters of foreign and defence policy. He judges the emergent transatlantic division of labour – America fights the wars, Europe reconstructs and/or keeps the peace – to be unsustainable and a recipe for rupture. Howorth is trenchant in arguing that the EU needs to develop its own source of 'hard power' (read: a European Security and Defence Policy, or ESDP, with teeth) but that the US must learn from Europe about how to exercise soft power – the ability to get others voluntarily to do what you want them to do – particularly in the war on terrorism.

In Chapter 3, Matthew Baldwin, John Peterson, and Bruce Stokes offer a similarly broad overview of transatlantic economic relations. They argue that the fundamentals of the economic relationship are mostly immune to political change, such as the transition from Clinton to Bush or transatlantic tensions over Iraq, but that the trade relationship remains highly politicised regardless of who holds political power on either side of the Atlantic, and whatever the state of diplomatic relations. This paradox is one of several at the heart of the relationship. Another is that the US–EU relationship is the most comprehensive yet bitterly contested two-way trade and investment relationship in the world. Moreover, it is a prime focus of media and academic analysis, even though multilateral governance of an increasingly globalised economy is now both far more important and more difficult for the US and EU to provide. That said, even if the days are gone when Europe and America could dictate the terms of global trade, effective global governance without their leadership remains unimaginable.

Chapter 4 shifts the focus to transatlantic cooperation on justice and internal security issues. Wyn Rees demonstrates that a good amount of US–EU cooperation on internal security matters was already occurring before 9/11, but also that the threat of terrorism has provided a major spur both to the internal development of the Union's policies on police and judicial cooperation as well as to transatlantic intelligence and law-enforcement efforts. While both sides are making strenuous efforts to work together, justice and internal security cooperation remains a decidedly 'fragile flower', and a true litmus test for the transatlantic relationship.

Daniel Bodansky's treatment of transatlantic relations on matters of environmental diplomacy in Chapter 5 is, if anything, even more sobering. For reasons examined in detail by Bodansky, there was no meeting of minds on key environmental protection initiatives such as the Kyoto Protocol even when the Clinton administration was in office. The election of George W. Bush and the new, all-out focus on international terrorism both make joint leadership in international environmental diplomacy an even more remote prospect.

The three chapters that follow focus on three regions of great significance to both the US and EU: Russia, the Balkans, and the Middle East. In Chapter 6, Margot Light contrasts Russia's relationship with the US, based very much on 'high politics', with its ties to Europe, which mostly focus on far more nitty-gritty matters. She finds that both the US and EU want much the same sort of relationship with Russia but naturally approach that country in very different ways.

In Chapter 7, John Peterson argues that the US has become a junior partner to the EU in the post-war Balkans, not least because it prefers to let Europe take the lead in its own backyard. The EU faces enormous challenges in the region but has, thus far, achieved considerable success in convincing former combatants that there is little or no place for ethnic nationalism in the New Europe it is creating. The Balkans case contrasts sharply with Iraq: it is perhaps the only case where the EU, as an institution, has enjoyed a clear foreign policy success, but only after a lot of humiliating failure.

In the Middle East, according to Costanza Musu and William Wallace in Chapter 8, the EU has persisted with its dogged multilateralism despite resistance from Israel and, frequently, the United States. Iraq will be the true test of whether the European case for multilateralism and working via the UN can continue to shape US policy or not. Musu and Wallace insist that the US and Europe share a powerful, common interest in preventing disorder from infecting the region. However, it is unclear whether joint US–European efforts to secure agreement on a 'road map' to a Palestinian state and, hopefully, bring peace to the region, could succeed even if the initiative became a true symbol of transatlantic reconciliation following the war in Iraq.

Chapter 9 pulls back to examine the historical record of the US and the EU as foreign policy actors, and particularly their support for multilateralism in the post-war period. Mark Pollack finds that the popular image of 'unilateral America' and 'multilateral Europe' is not entirely without basis in reality, but is an oversimplification. In fact, both the US and the EU have supported multinational rules and institutions selectively throughout their history, reflecting their substantive and issue-specific preferences. Hence, EU countries have differed amongst themselves about the desirability of a multilateral foreign policy, and have varied in their support for multilateral rules in areas such as trade and the environment. Similarly, the US has lent its support most of the time to the construction of today's most important multilateral institutions, yet successive US administrations have grown increasingly wary of multilateral commitments, as illustrated by the muscular unilateralism of the George W. Bush administration.

Chapter 10 concludes by sifting through the evidence presented throughout the book about how and how much the transatlantic relationship was changed by the election of George W. Bush in autumn 2000, the terrorist atrocities that occurred in the US less than a year later, and the Iraqi war of early 2003. We find that, contrary to what is often claimed, much that is fundamental about the transatlantic relationship did not change, or did not change much, despite the sudden appearance of three new 'monster variables'. The general picture is one of an enlarging EU seeking to maintain its unity and often failing, but succeeding more often than usual when it was pushed by the Americans. It is also one of an America whose vulnerability is as clear as its hegemony, and which will struggle to live peacefully with both unless it can rely on its allies, including – we suspect – ones that are more than 'temporary' or 'opportunistic'.

Notes

1   Quoted in *Financial Times*, 16 May 2001, p.10.
2   See <http://www.time.com/time/magazine/0,9263,1101010910,00.html> (accessed 17 January 2003).
3   In fact, the military force which launched Operation Enduring Freedom in Afghanistan was a more multilateral force, consisting of 16,000 troops from 17 countries, than was often appreciated (Dockrill 2002).
4   The efforts to organise a US consumer boycott of products produced in France – seen, by some distance, in America as the country most responsible for transatlantic split over Iraq – were, in some respects, impressive. See *inter alia* http://www.metrospy. com/; http://www.boycottfrenchproducts.org/; and http://howtobuyamerican. leethost.com/ (which also includes a list of German products that Americans were urged to boycott; all accessed 18 May 2003). Some polls showed that no fewer than 84% of Americans favoured a boycott of French products after the war in Iraq (see http://www.vote.com/vResults/index.phtml?voteID=60061059&cat=4075633 (accessed 18 May 2003)). However, it was difficult for US consumers to grasp that they should boycott Dannon yoghurt but not Yoplait (because the latter was made by US-owned General Mills) and Evian bottled water, but not Perrier (since it had been bought up by Nestlé, which was Swiss). Meanwhile, Bush administration officials continued to stress the importance of renewing transatlantic ties. See 'US Official Says Ties to Europe Remain Strong', available at www.useu.be/TransAtlantic/ Mar1303JonesUSEU.html; 'Treasury Official Reviews Scope of US–EU Economic Relations', available at www.useu/be/Categories/Tax%20Finances/Feb1303 DamUSEU.html; and 'US Undersecretary Larson on the Transatlantic Partnership', available at www.useu.be/TransAtlantic/Mar2703LarsonTransatlanticRelations. html (all accessed 13 April 2003). Within a few weeks of the end of military conflict in Iraq, France surprised diplomatic and journalistic opinion by proposing that sanctions on Iraq be suspended. See Mark Turner and Jean Eaglesham, 'France calls for sanctions on Iraq to be suspended', *Financial Times*, 23 April 2003, p.1.

2 Foreign and defence policy cooperation

Jolyon Howorth

The recent literature on US–European security relations is as abundant as its substantive message is contradictory. Analysts emphasising overall and increasing divergence are as numerous as those insisting that convergence remains solid. While 'pessimists' appear to dominate in the media (Pfaff 1998/99), elsewhere this is not true. Academia remains deeply split between pessimists (Walt 1999) and optimists (Nye 2002). Policy think-tanks reflect this divide (Pryce-Jones 1999; Daalder 2001). Chronologically, the picture is no clearer. After 1989, analyses stressing divergence had the edge over those detecting continuity. In the mid-1990s, as the dust settled on the post-Cold War world, the balance swung back again towards convergence. But this trend was reversed as the Clinton era came to an end and a new Republican administration seemed prepared to ride roughshod over the finely-tuned processes of the bilateral relationship. Shortly after 9/11, analysts once again stressed the potential for a new transatlantic understanding. However, divergence soon seemed more serious than ever. In spring 2002, Robert Kagan (2002; see also Kagan 2003) appeared to have delivered the ultimate in pessimistic verdicts: 'When it comes to setting national priorities, determining threats, defining challenges, and fashioning and implementing foreign and defense policies, the United States and Europe have parted ways'. Past tense. The 2003 Iraq War merely appeared to confirm Kagan's prediction. Verdict beyond recall?

A further problem is the shortfall between perceptions and reality (Wallace 2001: 17). While transatlantic problems continue to multiply – thereby aggravating perceptions of drift – so, too, do the solutions, which invariably attract less comment. To illustrate the point, a recent analysis of 24 issues of contention between the EU and the US has shown that in only eight cases did the Americans retain a unilateralist stance, while in all the others bilateral or multilateral negotiations succeeded in reaching workable arrangements (Ginsberg 2002).

While on the surface the world is changing rapidly, deep down at the level of core structures and values, much appears to remain permanent. Even here, differences – not only of perception but also of interest – have a long pedigree. Twenty years ago, Lawrence Freedman noted that: 'the strains facing the Alliance reflect fundamental changes in the international system and cannot be eased simply by a reassertion of the Atlantic spirit.' (Freedman 1982: 398).

Since Freedman wrote those words, 'fundamental changes' have included the Intermediate Nuclear Force crisis of the early 1980s, the rise of Gorbachev, the end of the Cold War and of the Soviet Union, the Gulf War, the Balkan Wars and the rise of Al-Qaeda. A new transatlantic security bargain has been on the agenda since at least 1989. Much recent debate about the transatlantic relationship has focused on the new strategic environment engendered by the post-1989 world, and on its understanding. First, it is a world in which a single 'hyperpower' exercises unrivalled influence in virtually every field outside economics. Second, it is a world in which the Europeans have sought to take advantage of the relative freedom from constraint offered by the end of the Cold War to maximise their international role and impact. This involves a growing bid for global influence. This new European ambition is asymmetrically matched on the US side by strategic disinterest in the European theatre and a shift in focus towards Asia. These first two contrasts are accentuated by a third: the growing disparity between the international behaviour of the two sides. The Europeans have a 50-year apprenticeship in structured multilateralism, and instinctively perceive the international system as a process of genuine institutional bargaining, informed by accepted rules, in which the pooling of sovereignty is recognised as offering more positive rewards than can be obtained through its jealous retention or mere assertion. The US, on the other hand, sees multilateralism as one approach among many, only to be entered into if it clearly yields greater rewards than are attainable by going it alone. Otherwise, unilateralism remains the default position (Boniface 2000; Miller 2002). A fourth feature of the current strategic environment is the growing disparity between the two sides' preferred instruments of international policy: for the US, the stick ('hard power') is significantly more important than the carrot ('soft power'); for the EU, the opposite is the case. Nowhere is this more dramatically illustrated than in the Middle East. But policy towards Russia, China, Korea and South Asia reflects the same pattern. The disparity is also evident in threat assessment, defence spending, and military procurement.[1] This chapter concentrates on the underlying tensions in the US–European security relationship since the end of the Cold War.

The Clinton presidency: 'it's the economy, stupid!'

The Clinton administration's reversal of Bush Senior's prioritisation of US global strategic hegemony in favour of an approach to international policy structured essentially by trade and economic relations produced mixed reactions in Europe. Although Clinton's approach led to constructive new partnerships in a range of fields under the 1995 NTA, in the field of security and defence the picture was more complex. On the one hand, US openness to discussion of burden-sharing solutions and its willingness to endorse a European security and defence identity (ESDI) were warmly welcomed in Europe. On the other hand, perspectives for NATO enlargement, via what was to be called Partnership for Peace (PfP), carried contradictory implications. While enlargement constituted a welcome breakthrough for collective security in central and eastern Europe, it also implied extended US hegemony in the region, a prospect that meshed uneasily with the autonomist implications of ESDI. Moreover, Clinton's initial carry-over of Bush's reluctance to become militarily involved in the Balkans, followed by his brief but alarming flirtation with a policy of arming the Croatians and Bosnians and bombing the Serbs ('Lift and Strike'), were viewed with concern by countries such as the UK and France, heavily committed on the ground and struggling hard to contain the Balkan crisis.

Clinton's cooperative style nevertheless bore fruit. France's *rapprochement* with NATO, driven both by the necessities of interoperability and by a growing fear of US isolationism, was discreetly facilitated by British diplomatic activity in Washington. While London had few illusions that Paris would meekly rejoin NATO's integrated military structure, continental instability and the self-disqualification of Germany from military engagement led Britain to optimise French engagement. In an apparent breakthrough at NATO's June 1996 Berlin ministerial meeting, the nuts and bolts of ESDI and the mechanics of Combined Joint Task Forces (CJTFs) were spelled out in principle, and tacit agreement reached. France would reintegrate into NATO's military structure in exchange for genuine restructuring of the Alliance, including more European commands. This package appeared to solve the burden-sharing stand-off by facilitating greater European military engagement via access to NATO (predominantly US) assets. The meeting in Berlin has been described as a 'watershed in the development of US and NATO policy toward creation of a more coherent European role in the Alliance'.[2] But Berlin turned out to be a double illusion. First, despite repeated official Alliance assurances that the 'Berlin Plus'[3] process was making headway, the opposite was true. The US military objected to allowing the Europeans access to crucial but sensitive American assets. Second, the first real test of 'Europeanisation' of the Alliance structures – the French bid for NATO's southern command (AFSouth) – saw the whole house of cards come tumbling down (Parmentier 2002).

Despite the mishandling of the AFSouth crisis by Paris, the incident also revealed the real limits of US political flexibility over transatlantic leadership. Task-sharing in the field (risking US equipment and European lives) was one thing. Sharing leadership, especially in an area as sensitive for US policy as the eastern Mediterranean, was quite another. The final straw for the inchoate ESDI project seemed to come at the June 1997 EU summit in Amsterdam. Citing the primacy of NATO, the newly elected Blair government, in its first major security policy decision, vetoed a proposal by nine EU member states to merge the EU with the Western European Union (WEU) – as a means of conferring upon the former some of the military attributes of the latter.[4] In late 1997, it seemed that security relations between the two sides of the Atlantic were as unstable and as unsatisfactory as they had been when Clinton first took office. Hegemony was unacceptable; balance unattainable.

From Pörstchach to Göteborg

The final years of the Clinton administration and the first nine months of the George W. Bush administration reveal a period of rapid change in European security policy, yet relative stability in US policy developments. Change in Europe included the switch from ESDI to ESDP[5], the creation of four new security and defence institutions in Brussels,[6] the launch of a European Rapid Reaction Force (ERRF), the parallel emergence of a range of civilian instruments such as police, judicial and administrative services for post-conflict reconstruction, consolidated under the Swedish presidency (June 2001) and the wholesale rationalisation of the EU defence industry to create just three big companies (Schmitt 2000). Irrespective of the change of US administration, the Europeans, to their consternation, encountered ongoing ambivalence towards ESDP, reluctance to engage in genuine multilateralism, a military policy based on the 'Powell doctrine' of selective engagement and the use of overwhelming firepower for rapid results, and a recalibration of threat assessment prioritising territorial protection against missile attack. European governments disagreed with virtually all of these key US approaches.

In Europe, change came in the summer of 1998. As the crisis in Kosovo gathered steam, Tony Blair discovered that appropriate EU military capacity was wanting. Blair simultaneously received an unambiguous message from Washington: unless the EU equipped itself with the military capacity to underwrite regional security, the Atlantic Alliance itself was in serious trouble. For some time already, the small transgovernmental community of French and British officials formulating defence and security policy had been rallying to the view that the only viable means of creating a European security capacity was by situating it directly within the EU itself. The various alternative schemes for transformation of the WEU were perceived as offering more problems than solutions.

The story of Blair's crossing of the European Rubicon, first at the informal EU summit in Pörtschach (Austria) in October 1998 and then at the Franco-British summit in Saint-Malo in December 1998, is well known. The Saint-Malo Declaration is remarkable both for its brevity and for its strategic ambiguity. From the perspective of transatlantic relations, it immediately posed several problems. The first and most significant was the strategic relationship between the two sides of the Atlantic. Would Saint-Malo, at first modestly dubbed the 'European security initiative', provoke further US–EU tensions, even strategic rivalry and eventual decoupling?[7] Or could it be managed as a process of transatlantic rebalancing and mutual reinforcement (Quinlan 2001; Hunter 2002)? The answer was not immediately obvious. That France should pursue European autonomy was only to be expected. That Britain was also involved could be seen in Washington as either reassuring or alarming. Hence Madeleine Albright's immediate '3-D' reaction[8] of guarded conditionality, subsequently to be echoed in many different forums by spokespersons for both the Clinton and the Bush administrations. This was dubbed by Stanley Sloan the 'Yes, but ...' approach (Sloan 2000). Clinton's challenge was to find the right balance between support and conditionality. Blair's challenge was to tread a fine line between reassuring Washington and disillusioning Paris. Chirac's challenge was to maximise European autonomy without undermining the Alliance.

Albright's '3-Ds' reflected genuine worries in DC. Would the existing cosy networks of transgovernmental security officials linking Washington to the various EU national capitals be superseded by some new institutional bureaucracy in Brussels, leading to 'decoupling'? As the EU sought to define its 'autonomous' security needs, would NATO experts be properly involved in the discussions? Would NATO enjoy a 'right of first refusal' in the management of any regional European security crisis? What were to be the implications for the 'Berlin Plus' process? ESDP was clearly a very different project from ESDI. Were the two compatible? The problem for the Europeans in providing answers to these crucial questions was that they did not agree among themselves (Howorth 2000a). The problem for the US in confronting ESDP was that, in its longstanding support for a 'European Pillar' in NATO, the US had never imagined that autonomy might one day be on the agenda. A second major source of tension concerned 'discrimination' against 'third countries'. Under WEU arrangements since 1992, non-EU NATO members[9] had acquired important consultative rights. Under ESDP, key allies such as Norway and Turkey were to be replaced in the inner decision-making sanctum by four former neutrals. For Washington, this was unacceptable and pressure was exerted on the Europeans to allow Turkey in particular a special place in decision making.[10]

A third source of tension concerned projected EU procurement needs. The initial US fear of 'duplication' was that the EU would create a rival military arsenal – a fundamentally political concern disguised as a resources issue (wasting money recreating assets already available in NATO). Behind the apparent rationality of Alliance resource allocation lay a multibillion dollar defence industrial base which, from Washington's perspective, had to be protected against European incursions by a series of restrictive controls over export licences and technology transfer. From the European perspective, it had to be strengthened both by European rationalisation and by penetration of the American market (Schmitt 2000, 2001). In reality, there existed a good case for strengthening the Alliance by building up European capability in areas where US assets were in short strategic supply, a process dubbed 'constructive duplication' (Schake 2002). However, US fears of European over-ambition were rapidly replaced by the opposite fear: that the projected ERRF would fall seriously short of what was required for operationality, thereby creating a potential situation in which the US could, once again, be sucked into a European crisis which was going badly wrong (IISS 2001).

All these tensions were heightened by the Europeans' collective inability, owing to their own internal divisions, to lay US fears to rest. Throughout the years 1999–2000, there remained a number of fundamental ambivalences within the ESDP project. For the Atlanticist members of the EU (Netherlands, UK, Portugal, Denmark), ESDP was essentially geared to solving a serious burden-sharing crisis in the Alliance. For a group of countries less focused on Alliance primacy (France, Belgium, Spain, Luxemburg), the project responded to an essentially European logic. Ultimately, these two perspectives are not inevitably incompatible, but that was not clear at the time. A second ambivalence derived from the choice of policy instruments. One of the major contributions to ESDP of the smaller, neutral countries was to promote a range of civilian instruments, emphasising the EU's role in peacekeeping, nation-building and 'softer' policy objectives. While some analysts optimistically interpreted this move as leading to an appropriate division of labour within the Alliance (Grant 2000; Everts 2001),[11] others stressed its increasingly negative effects on interoperability and military planning (de Durand 2001). A third source of European ambivalence arose from the institutional/political realities behind ESDP. Was this project, despite the relative lack of involvement of the European Commission, nevertheless destined to follow a more centralised, Brussels-based dynamic (a prospect which again invited contradictory interpretations in the US)? Or would European security policy, despite the new institutions in Brussels, remain firmly anchored in two or three national capitals (Howorth 2001; Howorth and Keeler 2003)?

The European member states faced a triple challenge as Clinton handed over to Bush: reaching a modicum of agreement internally on the nature of the project, selling this agreed package to the US administration, and responding to US security policy priorities with which most EU members disagreed. The first challenge was relatively successfully resolved. Throughout 2001, the practical requirements of ESDP took over from ideology, and commonality was forged through day-to-day experience. The EU institutions began to work. Negotiations with NATO proved constructive and unproblematic (apart from Turkish objections). Work started on the ERRF. As for the second challenge, however, the bitterly critical comments of outgoing Defence Secretary William Cohen in December 2000 and of incoming Secretary Donald Rumsfeld in February 2001 indicated that little genuine progress had been made in persuading Washington of the necessity or desirability of greater partnership in leadership.[12] EU officials discovered that, whatever progress may have been made since 1998 in convincing Democrat officials of the merits of ESDP, the Sisyphus task had to be started afresh with the Republican team, many of whom had been out of touch with European realities for as long as a decade.

But the real quarrel with the Bush team was over the tone and style underlying its foreign policy approach. This exacerbated three existing sets of problems. The first set – the US role in the Balkans and reticence about ESDP – had been faced before under Clinton (Dassù and Whyte 2001–2002). The second – missile defence and US military doctrine – were intensified versions of Clinton's policies (Tertrais 2001; *Survival* 2001). The third set of problems – such as a unilateral refusal to be bound by international treaties and conventions (Everts 2001; Wallace 2001) – revived an 'America first' conservatism redolent of the early days of the Reagan presidency. In addition, the partisan or ideological disparities between such a conservative mindset and the 'third way' social-democracy dominant in Paris, London and Berlin suggested a relationship moving inexorably towards stalemate (Ramet 2002; Cooper 2002).

The first set of problems was defused – although not resolved – in the early months of the Bush administration. Reassurances, especially from Secretary of

State Colin Powell, that there would be no rapid or unilateral US withdrawal from the Balkans ('in together, out together') were welcomed in Europe. A February 2001 visit to Camp David by Tony Blair appeared to have reassured Bush that the Europeans were not hell-bent on destroying NATO. Following that meeting, the new administration appeared to settle into a relatively passive approach toward ESDP, perhaps in the belief that nothing dramatic affecting US interests was likely to happen in the near term.

The more urgent priority for the US was to intensify policy toward ballistic missile defence and sell it to the allies as well as to build up American military muscle. This second set of problems rapidly shifted gear. The orchestrated European campaign against missile defence, previously aimed at influencing the internal US debate, was subsequently refocused as it became clear that the new administration would not be deterred on the principle, and as Bush began to assure both the allies and the Russians that they might be included in the scheme. Long-term prospects for missile technology cooperation seemed set to break down European resistance. On the other hand, the forthcoming US Quadrennial Defense Review seemed set to widen the already yawning gap between the military capacities of the two parties in ways which seemed likely to compromise interoperability and to pose a threat to the coherence of the Alliance itself (Yost 2000; Thomas 2000).

The third set of problems was more deep-rooted since it derived from a growing divergence of politico-cultural attitudes and perceptions, indeed of the socialisation processes informing the mindsets of political leaders. The post-war leaders weaned on an instinctive sense of shared geopolitical interest had been replaced during the 1990s by a new generation which saw the world in fundamentally different terms. On the US side, supremacy in all non-economic domains, combined with an awareness of the jealousies such a situation arouses, produced a complex self-image as victor and victim, increasing the feeling that the costs of alliances were doubled by their inconvenience. On the EU side, the end of superpower confrontation had removed the main source of European diffidence. This process was accompanied by a growing assertiveness in world affairs arising out of the accelerating integration project. This growing divergence of mindset made the management of contentious issues more sensitive. One study concluded, in August 2001, that the 'real threat to continued good relations is not so much in individual issues, but in the style and language with which they are treated and the effect this has on mutual perceptions'.[13] This disparity of overall perceptions – of the world, of foreign policy and of the principles informing the 'international community' – augured badly for US–EU relations in the medium term. Then along came Bin Laden.

From Ground Zero to Prague: change and continuity

In the immediate aftermath of 9/11, there were dramatic – and asymmetrical – shifts on both sides of the Atlantic. While the US appeared momentarily to have embraced multilateralism, European responses appeared to betoken a re-nationalisation of security and defence policy. National leaders expressed solidarity with the US on behalf of their respective countries. Each pledged national military assets to the US administration – which Washington, for the most part, politely ignored. Most European leaders insisted that the emerging campaign against Al-Qaeda was not a 'war', and that attention had to be paid to the root causes of terrorism. Most EU leaders also expressed their respect for Islam and Muslim nations. Yet there was something of a cacophony between those insisting that US military retaliation should be tightly 'targeted' and those (including, surprisingly, Germany) who offered 'unlimited' support to the US military effort. Some managed to articulate both. This heterogeneity of response was epitomised by Blair's invitation to Schröder, Chirac and Jospin to dinner in Downing Street on 5 November 2001. The attempt to create an EU leadership *Directoire* was gate-crashed by Silvio Berlusconi, Jose Maria Aznar, Javier Solana, Guy Verhofstadt and Wim Kok, highlighting the disorderly EU ranks of first, second, and third division players, allies and neutrals.[14] These divisions enormously complicated the ESDP work of the Belgian presidency, struggling to impose its authority in the context of high profile solo diplomacy on the part of Europe's big three. Above all, it was Tony Blair's crusading leadership style which, while commanding respect, also fostered divisions. As UK Prime Minister, Blair threw himself into personal shuttle diplomacy on behalf of the US administration. NATO's 12 September invocation of Article 5 emanated from a telephone conversation between Blair and the Alliance's Secretary-General Lord Robertson. Did this amount to unconditional EU alignment on US policy?

Paradoxically, NATO's invocation of Article 5, high in political symbolism, could prove to be the historical swan-song of the Alliance in its traditional guise (van Ham 2002). It also helps explain why, despite the short-term disorder of European responses to 9/11, the longer-term dynamics of ESDP seemed likely to be reinforced (Gnesotto 2001). Although in mid-September 2001 NATO adopted a series of measures to enhance intelligence sharing, to increase security of Alliance facilities, to guarantee blanket over-flight for allied aircraft and to re-deploy certain naval assets to the eastern Mediterranean, these had to be regarded as the bare minimum given the gravity of the crisis. The US, while re-engaging tentatively with a number of multilateral institutions (particularly the UN), preferred to discuss military cooperation via multiple bilateralisms rather than through the framework of the Alliance itself. Washington had learned the lessons of Kosovo and had no intention of allowing the American war against the Taliban to be held up by ill-equipped and politically fractious Europeans.[15] Moreover, throughout the 1990s, several US leaders had been calling for NATO to go 'out of area or out of business' (Gompert and Larrabee 1997). The Europeans, preoccupied with their own backyard, had remained uninterested. On 7 October 2001, in the skies over Afghanistan, the US went 'out of area' – unilaterally. Although Washington eventually associated with its military efforts small numbers of cherry-picked European forces, and although NATO's contribution in terms of logistics and infrastructure was not insignificant, the Afghan war was anything but a NATO operation (O'Hanlon 2002; Bennett 2001/02). In the context of dire predictions by military experts in many countries, who warned that the Afghan war would be long-drawn-out and much bloodier than expected, the US military successes seemed swift and relatively painless. Yet fear of losing US lives resulted in the failure of the Tora Bora operation and the apparent 'escape' of Bin Laden. Moreover while the US Air Force 'softened up' Taliban targets from a distance, it was Russian military hardware, from Kalashnikovs to T-55 tanks, which allowed the Northern Alliance to secure victory on the ground.

European nations, in proffering their troops, may well have hoped to lock the US into a multilateral campaign legitimised by the UN. The reality was that, despite the coalition-building efforts of the State Department, US instincts and practice remained deeply unilateral. This was especially so on the military front. Moreover, US spokespersons made it clear that, once Bin Laden had been brought to justice or killed, Washington had no intention of remaining long in Afghanistan to engage in 'nation-building' (Woodward 2002). The US was planning for an extended war on terrorism and refused to acknowledge any connection between the escalating crisis in the Middle East and the events of 9/11. By mid-November 2001, transatlantic tensions were already multiplying. The Europeans, for their part, prioritised the political over the military, humanitarian relief over further escalation of the war on terrorism, the quest for a balanced Middle East settlement over blanket support for Israel, and a long-term commitment to stabilisation in Afghanistan over the hunt for Bin Laden. Did the unilateral US shift to 'out of area' therefore imply that NATO was destined to go 'out of business'? That was the big debate which occupied the transatlantic defence establishment throughout most of 2002. NATO will undoubtedly survive. At one level it will be further transformed from an essentially military organisation to an essentially political one (Forster and Wallace 2001/02). Enlargement to seven states from central and eastern Europe, announced at the Prague summit in November 2002, will accelerate the Alliance's transformation from a collective defence to a collective security agency. The new, upgraded relationship with Russia will intensify and accelerate that development. In the war against terrorism, the campaign against weapons of mass destruction (WMD), and in regional peacekeeping tasks, Russia is likely to share centre stage with the US and the EU. An Alliance with less US military involvement and more participation from former Warsaw Pact members will be a very different actor from the body founded in 1949.[16] On the other hand, plans to develop a NATO Response Force (NRF), deployable anywhere in the world, could well give NATO's military activities a new lease of life. Whatever form the NRF eventually assumes, there are likely to be further tensions with military developments in ESDP. Many see the NRF as a type of 'cream-skimming' which will divert the best military assets in Europe away from the EU's own military planning. At the end of the day, NATO's survival – and the form that might take – depends as much on the US administration's seriousness of purpose about properly involving the Allies in military planning (Talbott 2002) as it does on the EU's ability to engineer a more differentiated bilateral relationship (van Ham 2002).

This brings ESDP even more prominently into the spotlight. Despite the short-term phenomenon of re-nationalisation of European defence, most analysts and actors agree that, in the longer term, 9/11 appears to have made the case for ESDP more compelling. Beyond the probe of the cameras, significant elements of integration have emerged. After 9/11, ESDP institutional turf wars were set aside and the complex EU nexus of agencies and actors worked seamlessly together to develop a coherent political approach to the crisis. Within ten days, the main outlines had been agreed and were articulated at the extraordinary meeting of the European Council on 21 September. Beyond the expression of 'total support' for the American people and recognition that UN Security Council resolution 1368 made a US military riposte 'legitimate', a relatively distinct EU political agenda suggested a longer-term approach to the global crisis. It involved, first, the creation of the 'broadest possible global coalition against terrorism *under United Nations aegis*' [my stress]. Second, a major political emphasis would be reactivating the Middle East peace process on the basis of the Mitchell and Tenet reports and the 'road map' drawn up by the US, EU, UN and Russia, which was finally made public in April 2003.[17] Third, the EU would seek the 'integration of all countries into a fair world system of security, prosperity and improved development'. Humanitarian relief for Afghanistan and its neighbours became a number one priority. Europe's leaders (in various combinations) embarked on an unprecedented round of shuttle diplomacy, repeatedly visiting most countries of Central and South Asia and the Middle East in a relentless quest for dialogue. The EU also intensified overtures towards its neighbours, with heightened diplomatic activity towards Russia, the Mediterranean and Turkey, coordinated efforts which bore real fruit. The EU, despite its obvious shortcomings, was slowly emerging as an international actor (Duke 2002; Grant 2002). Christopher Hill (2002b: 31) has concluded that the EU responded to 9/11 'in as effective a manner as could have been hoped for'.

However, throughout 2002, new and serious clashes with the US arose over Middle East policy and over US policy towards Iraq. As violence on the West Bank escalated in the spring and as the Bush administration appeared reluctant to re-engage with the peace process, notably by putting serious pressure on Tel Aviv, the EU intensified its activism, issuing the 'Declaration of Barcelona on the Middle East' (15 March 2002) which posited that there could be no military 'solution' to the crisis and that the security, political and economic aspects of the situation were 'inseparable and interdependent elements of a single process'. Even Germany, Israel's staunchest EU supporter, joined in the pressure on Tel Aviv. EU governments, including the various representatives of the Common Foreign and Security Policy (CFSP), spoke with a single voice. Faced with a decision about whether to challenge openly Washington's centrality to the peace process or give the US yet another chance to broker a deal, the EU collectively deferred to Secretary Powell. But the divergence between US and EU approaches to the Israel–Palestine conflict was yet another symptom of a deeper transatlantic malaise. This was to become a major trial of strength between the two camps after the end of the Iraq War and the long-delayed publication of the road map for the Middle East. On the issue of prioritising the Israeli–Palestinian peace settlement, the UK aligned itself with the rest of Europe in pressing the Bush administration to act.

On Iraq, the bellicose rhetoric of President Bush's State of the Union address on 29 January 2002 (the 'axis of evil' speech)[18] provoked general condemnation in Europe. Europeans inferred from a range of statements emanating from Washington that Baghdad had emerged as the next – and possibly even imminent – target. Certainly Bush was under pressure from conservatives to complete the job his father had left undone, a job henceforth labelled 'regime change'. The presence or absence of European allies in any military strike on Iraq seemed of little significance to Washington hawks. During the summer of 2002, a new doctrine of 'pre-emptive strike' emerged which then took centre-stage in the September National Security Strategy document: 'To forestall or prevent hostile acts by our adversaries, the United States will, if necessary, act pre-emptively' (p.15 pdf version). European rejection of this doctrine was virtually universal. Schröder, Chirac and even Blair drew Bush's attention to the wider implications of flouting international law and to the risk that US unilateral action would destabilise the entire Gulf and Middle East regions. This pressure was sufficiently coordinated and robust to induce a change of US tack. On 12 September, before the United Nations General Assembly, Bush announced that:

> My nation will work with the UN Security Council to meet our common challenge. If Iraq's regime defies us again, the world must move deliberately, decisively to hold Iraq to account. We will work with the UN Security Council for the necessary resolutions ... [But] the purposes of the United States should not be doubted. The Security Council resolutions will be enforced – the just demands of peace and security will be met – or action will be unavoidable. And a regime that has lost its legitimacy will also lose its power.[19]

The transatlantic crisis provoked by the 2003 Iraq War was without doubt the most severe since the end of the Cold War. It was a crisis at several levels. At the level of international institutions and law, the November 2002 agreement on United Nations Security Council Resolution 1441, calling upon Iraq to submit to a new regime of weapons inspectors or face 'serious consequences', seemed initially to be a triumph of transatlantic diplomacy. What most analysts failed to recognise was that Resolution 1441 contained two contradictory logics: it was both a *legitimisation* of military action should inspections prove to be a dead end, and an *alternative* to military action for those who saw war as a last resort. The fact that the war was eventually fought without an explicit UN mandate arising from a follow-on resolution to 1441 constituted a major blow to the authority of the United Nations. The second level of crisis arose from the fact that, progressively, all nations allowed themselves to be corralled into two seemingly irreconcilable camps: 'pro-war' and 'pro-peace'. In reality, these labels, like all political shorthand, were – in most cases – misleading. There seems little doubt that the Bush administration had decided, as early as the spring of 2002, that war with Iraq was both inevitable and desirable. Chancellor Schröder of Germany on the other hand, partly for reasons of electoral opportunism, decided in the summer of 2002 to oppose war under any circumstances. These two nations defined the polarised extremes of the international community. All other countries (including France and the UK) situated themselves somewhere on a continuum between these polarised positions. However, under pressure of the rapidly escalating crisis, all were forced to join one or other of the two basic 'camps'. At a third crisis level, this had the effect of artificially splitting the European Union down the middle. In January 2003, the leaders of the UK, Spain, Italy, Portugal, Denmark, Poland, the Czech Republic and Hungary signed a letter stressing the 'community of values' between Europe and the United States which was widely – but erroneously – interpreted as being tantamount to alignment with the Bush 'war camp'. Yet, arguably, the differences within Europe were vastly overblown by the crisis. All EU nations were able to endorse the conclusions of the Extraordinary European Council meeting in Brussels on 17 February 2003, which insisted on five main points:

- EU determination to deal effectively with the threat of WMD proliferation.
- Commitment to the UN remaining at the centre of the international order.
- Commitment to full and effective disarmament of Iraq in accordance with Resolution 1441.
- Full support for the UN inspectors who should be given the time and resources they need, without continuing indefinitely in the absence of Iraqi cooperation.
- Force should only be used as a last resort.

The major basis of disagreement among the EU member states and accession candidates hinged largely around the *timing* of that last point. On that crucial issue, their margin of negotiation was abruptly removed when the US went to war with Iraq on 19 March.

A final victim of the Iraq conflict was NATO, which appeared to have sprung back to life at its Prague summit in November 2002, announcing the creation of its new 'response force' – with a global remit. Yet it failed at the first hurdle in its new global guise when, in January 2003, several European allies (namely, France, Germany and Belgium) refused to endorse American proposals to offer security guarantees to Turkey in the event of a threat from Iraq. Thereafter, officials and commentators on both sides of the Atlantic busied themselves once again with hammers and coffin nails.

After the cessation of hostilities in Iraq in May 2003, attempts were made, mainly on the European side,[20] at damage-repair. But the war had highlighted in its starkest form the underlying difference between US and 'European' approaches to international crises. Urgently needed was a debate on the meaning of and criteria for the 'pre-emptive' and the 'preventive' use of military force in the post-9/11 world. Without a constructive international dialogue on this issue, the prospects for the future management of similar crises are poor.

Robert Kagan (2002; 2003) has argued that the Europeans prefer multilateral and diplomatic methods because they are weak (rather than because of the superiority of those methods), while the US favours military instruments because it is strong. By the summer of 2003, the debate between the two sides had become so intense that these two approaches appeared to be incompatible and even contradictory – coming, as Kagan put it, from 'different planets'. Yet the new and dangerous world which dawned on 9/11 clearly required a combination of these two approaches. The key to the future of transatlantic relations thus became the issue of the division of labour between the two sides.

'The US fights, the UN feeds, the EU funds'?

A *de facto* division of labour currently exists, with the US prioritising 'hard' power, the EU 'soft' power. Some feel that this is a logical arrangement, playing to both parties' strengths. Yet in its absolute form, it is unsustainable. A military 'alliance' featuring the absence of interoperability among its constituent forces is little more than a charade. Assuming a mission continuum ranging from low-intensity humanitarian tasks to high-intensity warfare, there is a middle range including peace-support and peacekeeping operations where the US and the EU *must* work together. Interoperability is as crucial as ever. The EU collectively needs to follow the example set in the summer of 2002 by the UK and France in raising and rationalising defence spending. But, by the same token, there are serious risks in soft power becoming an EU monopoly. It is in part through engagement with problems on the ground that the international community can hope to avoid having to address them from the air. The Bush administration came to power expressing contempt for 'nation-building'. Yet, as the Bush administration was soon to discover once the guns were silenced in Iraq, military power alone does nothing to address deep-rooted social and economic (*ergo* political) problems. It merely exacerbates them. The US needs to take soft power more seriously. Each side must move in the other's general direction.

The EU's problem has been military capacity. The 'Force Catalogue', constituting a pool of earmarked EU military assets assembled on the eve of 2003, corresponded fairly accurately to the target set by the 1999 Helsinki Headline Goal (roughly 100,000 troops, 100 warships and 400 military aircraft). The problem lay not so much in the generation of these forces. Everything that was eventually pledged by the member states already existed at the time of Helsinki; it simply required ear-marking for the ERRF. Some such capacity remained essential. As the Afghan and Iraqi campaigns showed unequivocally, the EU would be unwise to make any assumptions about the availability of US assets in the new strategic climate. The prospect of military autonomy ceased after 9/11 to be a simple political aspiration and became a functional necessity. A trickier problem was that of combining pursuit of the classic procurement objectives of the Headline Goal with the requirements of the EU's October 2001 priority focus on the 'war on terrorism'.[21] On one side of the debate were those who suggested that, while thinking through the military requirements for combating terrorism (which are not immediately obvious – Freedman 2002), the EU should concentrate on delivery of the Headline Goal since the need for conventional intervention capabilities into the medium term will remain (scenarios usually conjured up involve Africa, the Maghreb or even the Middle East). On the other side are those who suggest that the sort of military campaign witnessed in Kosovo could well prove to be both the first and the last of that type that will ever be fought in the European theatre. What the EU *per se* is more likely to require, according to this analysis, are small, high intensity, élite combat units to carry out limited missions such as those engaged by British commandos and special forces in Afghanistan in early 2002 (Clarke and Cornish 2002). And masses of intelligence. Deciding how much the Union needs is something of a theoretical discussion since nobody knows for sure what it might be used for. However, the EU, collectively, is the second largest military power on earth, spending over $150 billion – approximately three times that of the third power – Russia. What is required is the coordination and rationalisation of that expenditure.

And what of the mix of hard and soft instruments? The war against terrorism may well be more effectively conducted through civilian, police and intelligence instruments than through smart bombs. Cheque-book diplomacy and a concentration on development aid and the reconstruction of civil society are appropriate foreign and security priorities for an EU not seeking to become a military superpower. In order to maximise the effectiveness of soft power, the EU has learned that it cannot dispense altogether with hard power. But the US is also learning that, in the real post-9/11 world, military power alone cannot solve the problems that led to Ground Zero (Nye 2002). The Bush administration was forced, by the very complexity of the situation in Afghanistan, to recognise that a policy of bomb-and-withdraw was a non-viable option. Iraq could not simply be zapped. It also had to be helped to reconstruct itself.

Hard power, in order to be really effective, requires the concurrent or subsequent application of considerable doses of soft power. In this, the US is discovering an EU with much relevant experience. True statesmanship consists in addressing root causes. In Vietnam, a generation ago, the US attempted – inappropriately and futilely – to 'win hearts and minds'. In the war on terrorism, by contrast, *influencing* hearts and minds – particularly in the Islamic world – will be crucial to the outcome. The EU will not become a military superpower. It would not wish to and the US would not allow it. The US will not cease to be a global hegemon. But, in order to achieve their foreign and security policy objectives, each side will have to operate in closer cooperation with the other. This will require not so much a new division of labour as new equilibrium in the old division of labour. Mars and Venus must re-write their marriage contract.

The problems confronting the international community at the dawn of the twenty-first century pose infinitely more complex questions than mankind has faced hitherto. The construction of a sustainable, stable, secure, just – and terror-free – world requires every ounce of cooperative energy the two sides of the Atlantic can bring to bear. Hanging together is not just an option. It is an imperative.

Notes

1   These differences are presented in somewhat polemical mode by Kagan (2003: 3) 'Europe is [...] moving beyond power into a self-contained world of laws and rules and transnational negotiation and cooperation. It is entering a post-historical paradise of peace and relative prosperity, the realization of Kant's "Perpetual Peace". The United States, meanwhile, remains mired in history, exercising power in the anarchic Hobbesian world where international laws and rules are unreliable and where true security and the defense and promotion of a liberal order still depend on the possession and use of military might'.

2   Stanley Sloan, 'European Foreign and Defense Policy Cooperation: an American Perspective', Paper given at EUI Conference on 'Change and Continuity in Transatlantic Relations', 8–9 February 2002. Sloan was one of the original architects of the 'Berlin approach' in a Congressional Research Service Report entitled 'NATO's Future: Beyond Collective Defense' (CRS Report 95–979 S). Similar policy evolutions were taking place simultaneously in London and (to a lesser extent) in Paris.

3   The term describes discussions, post-Berlin, on the detailed procedures for ESDI/CJTFs in three main chapters: assured access to NATO planning facilities, presumed access to NATO assets and capabilities, and the identification of a distinct European command chain.

4   The WEU (founded in 1955) was an intergovernmental organisation comprising the main NATO states of the EEC/EC/EU. It served primarily as a European forum for the exchange of ideas on defence and security. After the end of the Cold War, its small secretariat moved from London to Brussels, the better to coordinate its thinking with that of NATO. It organised some European naval operations during the Gulf and Balkan Wars and, in 1992, at a meeting at Petersberg near Bonn, defined the 'Petersberg tasks' ('humanitarian and rescue tasks; peacekeeping tasks; tasks of combat forces in crisis management, including peacemaking') as being appropriate military objectives for the EU. Since WEU was the only intra-European organisation with a defence remit, it was designated, under the terms of the Maastricht Treaty in 1992, as the 'defence arm' of the EU. Article 17.3. of the Treaty of Amsterdam (1997) stated that '[t]he Union will avail itself of the WEU to elaborate and implement decisions and actions of the Union which have defence implications'. However, WEU was too small, underfunded and above all institutionally anomalous (its membership excluded the EU neutrals, one EU NATO member – Denmark – and all non-EU NATO allies) to carry out such a mission.

5   ESDP – an acronym for the common European Security and Defence Policy – launched at the Helsinki European Council in December 1999 – is a sub-set of the Common Foreign and Security Policy (CFSP) launched at Maastricht in 1991.

6   The post of High-Representative for the Common Foreign and Security Policy (HR-CFSP) and its associated Policy Unit, the Political and Security Committee (PSC) commonly referred to by its French acronym (COPS), the European Union Military Committee (EUMC) comprising the 15 Chiefs of the Defence Staffs or their representatives, and the European Union Military Staff (EUMS) totalling some 150 senior officers.

7   The classic statement of this concern was that of Assistant Secretary of State Strobe Talbott: 'We would not want to see an ESDI that comes into being first within NATO, but then grows out of NATO and finally grows away from NATO, since that would lead to an ESDI that initially duplicates NATO but that could eventually compete with NATO.' (Talbott 1999).

8   Albright warned that there should be no decoupling (of the EU and the US), no discrimination (against non-EU NATO members – particularly Turkey and Norway) and no duplication (of existing NATO assets) (Albright 1998).

9   These were known as 'associate members'. Non-NATO EU members were offered 'observer' status and EU/NATO accession candidates from CEE were offered 'associate partnership'.

10   Turkey was a special case since most of NATO's scenarios for crisis in the European theatre were in the proximity of Turkey and the involvement of Turkish forces in those crises was likely. See, on this subject, Webber *et al.* 2002.

11   A division of labour which allowed the US to concentrate on major campaigns, while the EU 'mopped up' afterwards had been a campaign pledge on the part of the Bush team (Gordon 2000).

12   Cohen remarked at a NATO meeting in December 2000 that, if ESDP were not carefully managed, the Alliance could become a 'relic of the past'. At the *Wehrkunde* meeting in Munich in February 2001, Rumsfeld said he was 'worried' about ESDP's potential to destabilise NATO. By March, he was of the opinion that ESDP could 'put at risk something that is very special' (NATO, quoted in the *Sunday Telegraph* 18 March 2001).

13   *Oxford Analytica* 29 August 2001.

14   The crashers were, respectively, the Prime Ministers of Italy and Spain, the High Representative for the CFSP, and the Prime Ministers of Belgium and the Netherlands.

15   After Kosovo, both the US and the EU vowed 'never again': the US never to fight a 'war by committee', the EU never to be forced into such a secondary role. On the US war in Afghanistan, see O'Hanlon 2002; IISS, *Strategic Survey 2001–2002*, pp.229–253; and Charles Grant, 'Does this war show that NATO no longer has a serious military role?', *Independent*, 16 October 2001.

16   On NATO's future, see Sloan and van Ham 2002; Hunter 2002; Sloan 2003; Eisenhower 2002; Lindley-French 2002. On the implications of Prague, see Szabo 2002; Kay 2002; Joffe 2002.

17   Former US Senator George Mitchell presented a plan to end the *Intifada* in May 2001 which met with reservations from Israel. George Tenet, Director of the CIA, then refined the plan with concrete proposals for a ceasefire and withdrawal to positions held in September 2000.

18   'Some governments will be timid in the face of terror. And make no mistake about it: If they do not act, America will […] America will do what is necessary to ensure our nation's security. We'll be deliberate, yet time is not on our side. I will not wait on events, while dangers gather. I will not stand by, as peril draws closer and closer. […]. Our war on terror is well begun, but it is only begun. This campaign may not be finished on our watch – yet it must be and it will be waged on our watch. We can't stop short.[…] History has called America and our allies to action, and it is both our responsibility and our privilege to fight freedom's fight'. <http://www.whitehouse.gov/news/releases/2002/01/20020129-11.html>

19   <http://www.whitehouse.gov/news/releases/2002/09/20020912-1.html>

20   The US, for its part, embarked on a policy of 'punishing France, ignoring Germany and forgiving Russia'. This did not assist the process of transatlantic reconciliation.

21   The Seville European Council in June 2002 published a 'Draft Declaration on the Contribution of CFSP, including ESDP, in the Fight against Terrorism' (<http://www.europa.eu.int>).

3 Trade and economic relations

Matthew Baldwin, John Peterson and Bruce Stokes

The transatlantic relationship is by far the world's most complex trade and economic relationship. At its heart lie three basic paradoxes. First, it is mostly immune to political changes – the transition from the Clinton to the Bush administrations changed nothing about its underlying fundamentals – but the relationship has become highly and increasingly politicised. Second, the EU and US have the biggest and most comprehensive two-way trade and investment relationship in existence, yet they often appear to be engaged in a bloody fight unto death. Third, while much debate focuses on their bilateral ties, a key question – arguably *the* key question – is what the transatlantic partners can contribute to multilateral stewardship of an increasingly globalised world economy.

We begin by sketching the broad economic context that defines, in crucial ways, the politics of the transatlantic relationship. We then consider the effects on the US–EU relationship of globalisation and the emergence of new players in international economic diplomacy. Most of the chapter offers an historical narrative of the post-war evolution of US–European economic relations, with emphases on the transitions from Bush (Senior) to Clinton, and later from Clinton to George W. Bush, as well as the effects of 9/11 on the diplomacy that launched the Doha Development Agenda. Before concluding, we offer case studies of two very different but equally tense transatlantic trade disputes: an old-fashioned, twentieth-century-style clash over steel and a very new age row over genetically modified (GM) foods.

Conflict or cooperation?

The EU and the US are by far the biggest players in the global economic system (see Table 1). There is no denying that the US is the more economically dynamic of the two, and that it still carries more political weight in the transatlantic relationship. Yet, even before the EU's eastern enlargement makes it a considerably bigger player, the Union is 'an economic hegemon in its own right, even if an immature or schizophrenic hegemon' (Peterson 2001c: 51).

The transatlantic trade and investment relationship has become a super highway. In 2000, the US accounted for about 22 per cent of EU trade, and the EU for around 19 per cent of US trade. Transatlantic trade deficits and surpluses

Table 1 Basic statistics for the EU and the US in 2000

	EU-15	US
Population	377.6 million	284.2 million
Gross Domestic Product (GDP)	7,836.7 (US$ bn)	9,896.4 (US$ bn)
Share of global exports (%)	17.2	15.7
Share of global imports (%)	18.2	23.9
Imports as % of GDP	12.2	12.9
Exports as % of GDP	10.9	7.9

Source: Delegation of the European Commision in the US (available at<http://www.eurunion.org/profile/facts.htm>)

generally do what economic textbooks suggest they should do – that is, they follow underlying economic trends. When the US economy is strong and the EU economy weak, as it has been in recent years, the US runs a trade deficit with Europe. History shows that the converse is also true. There is no transatlantic 'structural deficit', as is claimed to exist in, say, US–Japanese trade relations (see Figure 1).

In investment, the figures are even more startling. In 2000, US investors accounted for no less than 77 per cent of new foreign direct investment in Europe. Meanwhile the US was the destination for nearly two thirds of all foreign investment by Europeans (EABC 2002). Europe invests more annually in Texas than Japanese investors invest in all 50 US states combined (see Figure 2). US investment in Europe is nearly equivalent to total American investment in the rest of

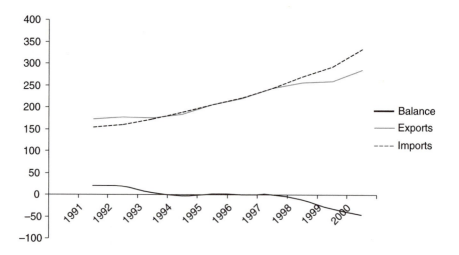

Figure 1   US exports, imports and balance of trade (goods and services) with Europe, 1991–2000 (US$ billion)

Source: EABC 2002

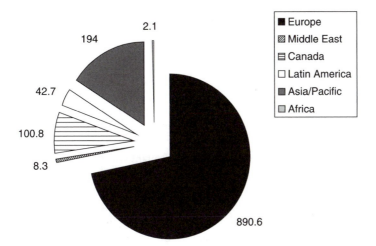

Figure 2 Volume of foreign direct investment in the US by region, for 2000 (US$ billion)
Source: EABC 2002

the non-European world. The result is a staggering degree of interdependence between the two economies, not least because the fabled US and European multinationals are now so thoroughly intertwined by mergers and cross-fertilisation. Something close to a quarter of all US–EU 'trade' simply consists of transactions *within* firms with investments on either side of the Atlantic.

Moreover, the two economies exert tremendous strength outside the relationship. Each is the other's largest single trade and investment partner, but one or the other is also the largest trade and investment partner for nearly every other country. The EU and US, acting both individually and together, play a leading role in global economic governance – agreeing rules to control or steer globalisation – not least within the WTO.

There is much common ground to be found even in areas of traditional disagreement. On agriculture, public support systems are slightly different, and each side accuses the other of distorting markets to the detriment of their own farmers, and those of developing countries. But the reality is that both the US and EU support agriculture to a roughly similar extent.[1] In any case, exceptions tend to prove the rule: conflict tends to breed where there is little transatlantic integration, such as in steel or airline services.

The enormity of the bilateral economic relationship effectively condemns the US and EU to work together (Wallace 2002a: 283). Nonetheless, transatlantic tensions over trade and (especially) other issues following the election of George W. Bush in 2000 prompted fears that Europe and America were heading for collision or even 'divorce' (see Daalder 2001; Matthews 2001). Even allowing for journalistic hyperbole, trade disputes are often vigorously pursued, whoever is in the White House, whether they are bilateral spats played out at the WTO or broader differences on how and how fast to pursue multilateral trade agreements. In any event, our three paradoxes remain unresolved. Vast amounts of economic exchange are untouched by political change, yet specific disputes are highly politicised. Transatlantic economic interdependence generates huge wealth, but it is also a source of bitter conflict. And while the US and Europe can accomplish a lot together, their economic fortunes are ever more dependent on their ability to contribute to the governance of an increasingly globalised economy.

Globalisation and new players

Regardless of its breadth and depth, the transatlantic trade relationship is far too often studied in a vacuum. Some commentators argue that if only the global economy could look more like the transatlantic economy, and be governed in a similar way, all would gain (Atlantic Council 2001). But such a prescription is blind to both the power of galloping globalisation and the emergence of new and far more diverse players in global economic governance.

Neither Europeans nor Americans appear to be 'sold' on globalisation. Majorities of Americans (usually around 60 per cent) tell pollsters that they are in favour of globalisation and free trade. However, the majority shrinks to barely more than half at the lower end of the income scale, and Americans consistently state that the protection of US jobs should be the top priority of American trade policy.[2] Meanwhile, there are vast differences between the views of different European peoples, with 87 per cent of Dutch people believing the effects of globalisation to be positive, as compared to only about a third of French and Spanish citizens.[3] If there is anything genuine contained in warnings about rising anti-Americanism in Europe, it is that some Europeans, at least, 'equate globalization with Americanization' (Blinken 2001: 35), and do not like either one.

Increased trade and international investment have spurred fabulous levels of wealth creation in both the US and Europe, but have also unleashed disruptive social and economic forces. By many estimates, inequality rates are growing again – and not just between rich and poor states, but also within them. Who could blame ordinary citizens for being concerned when, for example, 'child labour in Honduras displaces workers in South Carolina or when pension benefits are cut in Europe in response to the requirements of the Maastricht Treaty' (Rodrik 1997: 18)? There is no question that for every dollar or euro of new wealth created when trade is freed, a considerably larger amount must be redistributed between economic actors – a lot of disruption for limited gain. It is no wonder that a diverse array of new players (or stake-holders, in today's jargon) – including non-governmental organisations (NGOs), trades unions, and consumer groups – are demanding a say in political decision making about trade policy.

Moreover, with 146 members, the days are long gone when the WTO could be run as a rich man's club, dominated by the US and EU. China is a new and assertive WTO member, and is likely to be followed by Russia. Brazil and India have been forceful and weighty players from the origins of the WTO. Others, including African states, have more recently taken places at the top table.

Both globalisation and the emergence of a more pluralistic group of players have consequences for global governance. Everyone seems to agree on the need for a stronger, rules-based, multilateral trading system in which bilateral conflicts are mitigated or curtailed. Few doubt that such a system can only be constructed with large doses of US–European leadership, regardless of their declining grip on global economic diplomacy. If no longer sufficient, the US–EU partnership is clearly still necessary.

How they got here

If the average anti-globalisation activist (assuming one exists) were asked, they would say – after decrying the 'World Takeover Organisation' as the ultimate capitalist plot – that the WTO was designed by the US and Europe for their own use. The fact is that the first years after the WTO was created in 1995 saw the US and EU disagree repeatedly and fundamentally on a range of questions of trade diplomacy.

If there was any general trend, it was towards growing European confidence in the multilateral trade system, and growing US hesitations and doubts about the very same system. It was not always like this. The US took the lead in post-war multilateral trade policy, partly as a reflection of simple economic interests after 1945. As Krueger (1995: 26) makes clear, the US emerged from the war with its productive capacity intact and a relatively open economy compared with Europe. Taking the lead in successive rounds of negotiation, US trade policy was assertively, even aggressively, multilateral in focus.

Meanwhile the EU struggled to maintain its unity through successive enlargements. It was not always easy to agree a single negotiating position for such a large and diverse group, notably on agriculture. As a consequence, the EU tended to follow behind as a somewhat reluctant partner to the US. Europe usually remained ready to take its multilateral trade liberalisation medicine through successive rounds of negotiation, but contributed little beyond that. Arguably, this dynamic was still in place as late as 1986, at the launch of the Uruguay Round, which eventually led to the creation of the WTO. The deal stitched together at Punte del Este was largely, if not exclusively, designed in Washington.

But the pendulum had shown signs of swinging back as early as the 1970s. As the US economy began to suffer from increased foreign competition, and the US trade deficit mounted, Washington began to define its trade interests more narrowly and pursue them through aggressive bilateralism and indeed unilateralism. First the US Congress wrote into domestic trade law provisions for punishing foreign states for alleged 'unfair trade practices' (section 301 laws of the 1974 Trade Act and subsequent 'Super 301' and 'Special 301' variants). The early 1980s saw growing use of these measures in a number of sectors, although mostly not against the EU other than on matters of agriculture (Kahler 1995: 45–6; Pollack and Shaffer 2001b: 11–12).

More generally, post-war American foreign policy had always been underpinned by a basic belief that a united Europe was in America's self interest (Lundestad 1997). But American self-doubt in the 1980s led to growing worries that an economically revitalised Europe, especially one with a 'single' European market by 1992, might pose a challenge to US global economic leadership. In a politically ill-judged moment, Robert Mosbacher, the US Commerce Secretary in the first Bush administration, called for an American 'seat at the table' as Brussels crafted the single market, a remark which many in EU circles found offensive (Peterson 1996: 47). Eventually, US fears of a 'fortress Europe' resulting from the 1992 project were mollified. Attention shifted away from the economic relationship after the post-1989 geopolitical earthquakes rocked Europe.

From Bush to Clinton

The decade when things really changed in Washington on questions of economic doctrine and diplomacy was the 1990s. For the first time, overt public hostility to trade liberalisation emerged in debates over, first, the North American Free Trade Association (NAFTA) and then the end of the Uruguay Round.

Bill Clinton was the first American president born after World War II, and was partly educated in Europe (at Oxford as a Rhodes Scholar). More importantly, he was the first US chief executive to understand the implications of the emerging global economy. Anthony Lake, Clinton's first White House national security adviser, recalls sitting with the President one morning early in Clinton's first year, as he reviewed the summary of overnight world events prepared for him each day by the Central Intelligence Agency. Halfway through his five-page summary, Clinton muttered out loud: 'Oh shit!' A worried Lake immediately wondered what crisis he had somehow missed in his earlier review of the material. Clinton explained that he was responding to a report that Germany's economic growth was expected to slow. He knew this would hurt overall European growth, thus slowing US exports to Europe and stalling an American economic upswing. More generally, even as the US rose to the pinnacle of its global power largely on the back of its strong economy, Clinton understood that the toolbox he had to run the US economy did not give him much control over America's economic destiny, and that a structural shift in power from states to global markets was taking place.

After initial hesitations, the Clinton administration won the battle for NAFTA (Mayer 1998). But the war was by no means over. Passage of the Uruguay Round implementing legislation in 1994 was not a sure thing in the US Congress until relatively late in the day. For the first time, anti-globalisation sentiment started to appear. Despite a president who actively sought to accelerate globalisation, the White House apparently banned the use of the word in its public statements for a time because it showed up badly in focus groups.

In crucial respects, global governance posed even more problems than globalisation itself. Particularly problematic from an American point of view was the idea that the US should be part of a body whose rules bind its members in international law. The notion of global governance was resisted by a growing number of American conservatives in the 1990s who opposed the loss of US sovereignty, as well as some consumer and environmental groups who feared that it would undermine domestic environmental and consumer standards.

Significantly, US 'Fast Track Authority' expired in 1994. The US Constitution grants control over trade to Congress, and Fast Track is the legislative mechanism by which the Congress allows the administration to negotiate trade agreements on its behalf. Crucially, it requires the Congress to vote 'up or down' on the results of those negotiations, without any amendments. Without Fast Track, it is hard for any American administration to be taken seriously by its negotiating partners, and those who want to slow down negotiations have the perfect excuse. Despite desultory efforts by the US administration to get a new Fast Track Authority, it was not renewed until after Clinton had left office (and then under a new name: 'Trade Promotion Authority', or TPA). Opposition amongst trade-concerned NGOs to the inclusion of investment issues in trade negotiations and the desire of many to use trade sanctions to enforce labour and environmental rules both contributed to the political stalemate. Republican opportunism to frustrate a Democratic president and growing doubts amongst Democrats about the virtues of free trade were also key ingredients in Fast Track's long hiatus.

In part because of domestic opposition to his economic agenda, Clinton developed a firm political view that Europe was needed as a partner in economic diplomacy. He and his team saw the EU as America's logical European interlocutor, in a departure from the first Bush administration's distrust of the European Commission and focus on America's traditional national European partners – primarily the UK and Germany. The perception that Europe was central to world and US economic well-being was reflected in Clinton's appointment of Stuart Eizenstat as his first Ambassador to the European Union. Eizenstat, a veteran of the Carter White House and a political heavyweight, was the most experienced and Washington-connected official ever to hold the post.

Clinton's European focus was not initially shared by his first Secretary of State, Warren Christopher. Yet, by 1995 Christopher had embraced the NTA, which revamped transatlantic relations considerably. The NTA invigorated existing consultations that had been launched by the 1990 Transatlantic Declaration, particularly between the European Commission and the US government, and also gave fresh purpose to regular summits at which Clinton met EU leaders. At the same time, US Commerce Secretary Ron Brown, together with the transatlantic activists inside the European Commission, Sir Leon Brittan (responsible for external trade) and Martin Bangemann (Commissioner for the internal market), launched a Transatlantic Business Dialogue (TABD) to try to create a transatlantic lobby for open transatlantic markets. The NTA generally marked an attempt to move beyond mere exchanges to actual policy cooperation.

The NTA's achievements were, by most estimates, modest, and Clinton's interest in Europe eventually waned. The characters changed – Brown died in a plane crash and Eizenstat was promoted and returned to Washington. Clashes between Brittan and US Trade Representatives (USTR), first Mickey Kantor and then Charlene Barshefsky, meant that by the time Brittan came up with a radical proposal for a transformation of trade relations in 1998 ('The New Transatlantic Marketplace' – NTM), he had few (if any) allies in Washington. EU member states, led by France, who thought that the Commission was trying to run too far, too fast, found it easy to block the NTM.

Thereafter, economic relations soured rapidly. The US imposed sanctions on the EU in the banana and beef wars of 1998–9. The early demise of the Commission under Jacques Santer in spring 1999, and the subsequent six-month power vacuum in Brussels were unhelpful to efforts to resolve the disputes. After Pascal Lamy took over the EU's trade portfolio from Brittan, the relationship seemed to become less rancorous, but the beef and banana disputes still raged, and bilateral problems multiplied in the WTO. This period also witnessed a very low moment in transatlantic economic relations: the Seattle WTO summit of December 1999 (see below).

The EU: learning to love liberalisation

For the EU, the pendulum swung in the direction of multilateralism, in a reflection of the Union's greater economic self-confidence and political cohesiveness following the completion of the Single Market in 1992. Perhaps ironically, the EU never had to face the same agonies as the US did over 'Fast Track': Europe was blessed with a simple mechanism by which the Commission proposes a negotiating mandate to the EU's Council of Ministers (representing the member states) which approves it by, if necessary, a qualified majority vote.[4] The Commission then negotiates on behalf of member states, and submits the results for approval, which can be achieved if necessary by the same qualified majority. This mechanism allowed rapid and relatively uncontroversial endorsement of the results of the Uruguay Round in 1994.[5]

In 1999, Lamy discovered that things had become easier since his previous stint in Brussels as head of President Jacques Delors' (1985–95) cabinet. Lamy liked to say that his predecessors had had to spend two thirds of their time negotiating with EU member governments, leaving only one third for negotiations with other countries. Newly discovered EU unity had enabled him to reverse these percentages. By the mid-1990s, the EU slotted comfortably into the WTO, and embraced the idea of binding international rules, particularly in new, uncharted areas such as investment, competition, and the environment. Quite suddenly, the EU had become the leading advocate for a new and comprehensive round of negotiations.

A speech by Clinton in Geneva in May 1998 brought the US administration on board in principle for a new round as well. However, in the intervening 18 months, before the next WTO Ministerial meeting in Seattle, the US failed to agree an agenda with the EU for the new negotiations. Meanwhile, the transatlantic rift was being overtaken by a north–south split of even more serious dimensions.

The débâcle in Seattle

In the run-up to the ill-fated Seattle ministerial in December 1999, the Clinton administration signalled that it wanted essentially more of the same: trade liberalisation, or market access, with a nod in the direction of US labour unions in the form of new rules on 'core labour standards'. It refused outright to discuss renegotiating US trade remedy laws. The EU, by contrast, pushed on with its idea of a comprehensive agenda. The Europeans were also more prepared to respond to the concerns of developing countries about their ability to implement past trade agreements, which was a primary source of their discontent at Seattle.

In pursuing this broad agenda, Europe was self-consciously trying to surf the wave of globalisation. But the EU came under continued heavy fire from the Cairns Group (of agricultural exporters) and the US on what mattered more to them than anything on the EU's proposed agenda: reform of the Common Agricultural Policy (CAP). Agriculture had dominated the Uruguay Round but refused to go away even after the negotiations were complete. The EU and US were still at loggerheads, and both defended their positions on agriculture aggressively. The EU insisted that it had transformed the CAP considerably since the MacSharry reforms of 1992 (Peterson and Bomberg 1999: 132). The US usually retorted that the Union's refusal to commit itself to the elimination of trade distorting farm support was holding up reform elsewhere. Into this cauldron, several years later, came the US Farm Bill of 2002, which reversed the prevailing US policy direction and sharply increased support for American farmers.

What made Seattle such a landmark event was that the transatlantic row coincided with street riots featuring anti-globalisation protestors and fury from developing countries who felt their own interests were being ignored in the discussions on a new trade round. In trade terms, Seattle was the perfect storm. Umbrellas inscribed with 'The Seattle Round' became collectors' items, but for all the wrong reasons: because there was no new Round launched in Seattle.

From Clinton to Bush

Even after Seattle, few believed that it would take two years to re-boot the agenda for the new Round. But successive attempts at US–EU rapprochement in the closing months of the Clinton administration failed. At the end of an administration that had proclaimed itself, with some justification, to be the most pro-trade since Kennedy's, trade was pigeonholed in a pre-election box marked 'too sensitive'.

The multilateral trade system did not figure prominently in George W. Bush's 2000 presidential campaign, in contrast to his extravagant endorsement of a Free Trade Area of the Americas (FTAA). FTAA was an eye-catching, even dramatic extension of NAFTA to the south. It played well to Bush's strong record of working with Latin America when Governor of Texas. To Europe, the idea seemed to reinforce the message that US priorities lay elsewhere.

Once in office, Bush appointed Robert B. Zoellick as US Trade Representative. Zoellick had been a key US negotiator in the first Bush administration, participating in the talks that led to German unification and designing much of the Transatlantic Declaration in 1990. He was a long-time friend of EU Trade Commissioner Lamy, and widely respected in European capitals. But none of the other major Bush economic policy appointees had strong ties with Europe.

The Bush team seemed prone to unilateralism in its foreign policy more generally, quickly torpedoing the Kyoto Protocol on global warming, and notifying its intention to abandon the Anti-Ballistic Missile Treaty. Nevertheless, hopes rose for a new trade round as the date for the next WTO ministerial approached at the end of 2001. Zoellick boldly singled out TPA as a key priority, issuing a call to arms to the US Congress: was the US going to sit meekly back, and allow Europe and Japan to lead the world trade system?

There remained the problem of finding agreement on the scope of the WTO agenda. Lamy set out to convince Zoellick to embrace a broad negotiation covering rules as well as market access. Eventually, Zoellick came to accept the case, although apparently reluctantly and as a tactical means of moving towards an overall agreement. Perhaps above all, both sides agreed that European and American efforts alone would not be enough to launch the Round. Informal gatherings of trade ministers, dubbed 'mini-ministerials', in Mexico City and Singapore during 2001 were crucial to building trust and 'ownership' of the Round, especially amongst developing countries. A formal meeting to try to launch the Round was arranged at Doha (in Qatar) for late 2001, after no other WTO member state offered to host the first post-Seattle ministerial summit. But 9/11 came first.

Assessing the impact of 9/11 on the Doha negotiations is tricky. Zoellick's claim that a new trade round would be an effective anti-terrorist measure, and subsequent attempt to wrap TPA in the American flag, drew criticism but ultimately seemed to help sway support in Congress (which approved TPA in summer 2002). For their part, developing countries were pushed towards agreeing to a new Round, despite lingering reservations, by Bush's injunction that they were either 'with us or against us' in the war on terrorism.[6] And all sides may have been able to make more concessions at Doha than if 9/11 had never 'happened'. One financial journalist argues that 'the spirit of September 11 fathered the Doha compromise' (Beise 2002: 48); two others contend that 9/11 'galvanised decisions in Doha'.[7] One British participant concurred: 'it felt like the whole world was watching us and waiting for some good news after all the bad news. I think that concentrated minds'.[8]

In any case, the outcome of Doha was a classic international compromise. What was given the title of 'the Doha Development Agenda' was sufficiently broad to address European concerns about a balance between liberalisation and regulation, and yet held back until later in the process negotiations on investment and competition (which most worried developing countries) and trade remedy rules (which most worried the US). The agenda addressed classic questions of market access, but also developing country demands for 'special and differential treatment'.

More generally, the Doha Development Agenda revealed a new approach to finding a US–EU *rapprochement* on multilateral issues. This time, the EU and US did not seek to reach bilateral agreement on each and every point, with a view then to presenting an overall deal to others on a take-it-or-leave-it basis. One lesson of Seattle was that the US and EU could no longer lead the WTO by frog-marching developing countries where they did not want to go.

Thus, several major roadblocks to early completion of a new WTO round had been removed. Yet, right at this point, a new set of bilateral disputes emerged, and threatened to overwhelm the new multilateral rapprochement.

Condemned to quarrel?

The Bush White House inherited three major trade disputes with Europe:

- bananas – a longstanding row about the access of US banana processing companies to the EU's banana market;
- hormones – whether the EU could legally ban US imports of beef from hormone-treated cattle;
- Foreign Sales Corporations (FSC) – a huge case centred on whether US companies could legally exempt some of their export earnings from tax by sluicing revenue through an overseas affiliate.

Zoellick and Lamy quickly (in April 2001) found a pragmatic solution to the bananas conflict that had dogged transatlantic relations for ten years. As a signal-sending device, the agreement said that they were ready to wade in and solve problems. But the hormones and FSC cases were to prove deeply intractable, and other disputes were to join the list.

The underlying problem

The EU and US clearly share systemic interests: as the biggest commercial players, they have the most at stake in the multilateral rules-based system. It is in neither side's interest to overload the WTO dispute settlement system to the point of collapse. Moreover, the capacity of each to hurt the other (and transatlantic trade interests more generally) is a powerful disincentive to striding too frequently down the path of dispute settlement.

Again, the swirling tentacles of globalisation complicate matters. EU and US interests are often intertwined and are difficult to separate. As Clinton's Secretary of Labour, Robert Reich (1990), once put it, 'who is us?' Is Daimler-Chrysler a purely European firm or is it a hybrid transatlantic company? Are Ford or General Motors, who have built cars in Europe since before World War I, purely American companies? Such questions complicate internal decision making on both sides, as was demonstrated when the EU struggled in 2001 with the question of whether to impose anti-dumping duties on bicycle gears made by a Japanese company on the basis of a complaint from a US manufacturer producing in Germany (Allen and Smith 2002: 100).

Nonetheless, differences in basic economic interests remain, and the WTO dispute settlement system provides clear leverage to those with a grievance if the other party has violated the rules.[9] The system usually offers only a series of unpalatable choices to losers. Either comply – often by changing domestic legislation in politically charged circumstances – or come up with an acceptable offer of compensation, usually in the form of trade concessions elsewhere, or accept retaliation in the form of trade sanctions.

Strong domestic constituencies frequently push both sides to use the WTO dispute settlement system. The mere existence of the weapon of litigation tends to downplay the importance of the WTO's pre-litigation or consultation phase, as the lawyers rapidly take over. On occasion, it may be politically easier for a defendant government to accept litigation rather than to prod a key constituency to accept a deal, particularly when it is not clear whether the offending practice is WTO incompatible. Once defeated, it can be easier to accept retaliation as punishment, rather than fight domestic battles to come into compliance. Arguably, trade wars remain the template in transatlantic relations because the WTO system – largely US and EU created – is unnecessarily tilted towards conflict.

Not only have the EU and US been heavy users of the system, they have also trained their guns quite frequently on each other. Of the 54 completed cases that went to dispute panels between 1995 and 2001, 16 involved litigation disputes between the EU and US. Even as they launched a number of cases against a third party together, there was a sharp upward trend in US–EU cases, and within that trend, a sharp increase in cases taken by the EU against the US. Of the cases completed in 2002 or already in the panel process, the US was defendant more times (26) than it had been plaintiff (20). The EU was much more often plaintiff (26 times) than defendant (8).

The US was overwhelmingly in the dock in one sector: steel. However, Europe's reluctance to accept genetically modified (GM) foods, feeds and seeds strained American patience and threatened to land the EU with a painful and difficult dispute. We probe these two very different disputes – one in an aging economic sector, the other a 'new age' row – in the section that follows.[10]

Steel – the twentieth century lives on

Having put the bananas dispute to bed, Lamy and Zoellick hoped they could make further progress on hormones and FSC, while preventing simmering conflicts (such as over aircraft subsidies) from boiling over. A return to the limelight for steel was unexpected. Gradually and over a considerable period of time, a global overcapacity problem had emerged in steel markets, with a lot of product swimming around looking for a market, not least because many developing states – South Korea, China and others – viewed a modern steel industry of their own as a prerequisite for entering the club of industrial nations. Anti-dumping measures were used more often against steel than any other product. Domestic industries faced waves of reform and restructuring in a continual search for competitiveness – restructuring in the 1990s resulted in fewer than half as many steel workers in the EU's 15 member states in 2002 as there were in the EU's nine member states 20 years earlier. The EU industry was thus relatively lean, competitive, and concentrated. Of the world's ten largest steel producers in 2002, five were European firms.

In the US, although capacity and numbers of steel workers had both been reduced dramatically since the 1980s, Big Steel (large, integrated and relatively inefficient firms) remained prominent. Very little transatlantic cross-ownership existed in the sector. It was difficult in the US system to take additional capacity out of the market and restructure the big companies because of traditional US government reluctance to step in to pick up the 'legacy' costs – notably for pensions and healthcare – of retired steel workers (costs usually borne in Europe by social security systems, not directly by companies). A powerful coalition of industry and unions, with vociferous Congressional support, had grown up around defence of the status quo and protection of the domestic industry from imports.

In 2001, even with 200 anti-dumping and anti-subsidy measures in place, the US industry and unions felt they needed more protection. Arguing that the effects of the 1997 Asian crisis, which saw millions of tonnes diverted to both US and EU markets, were still crippling the US industry, Big Steel and its allies pushed Congress to take unilateral measures. To pre-empt Congress, the Bush administration asked the US International Trade Commission (ITC) to investigate the possibility of a safeguard action. In early 2002, the ITC called for tariffs of up to 40 per cent to be imposed on foreign steel. In the spring, the Bush administration imposed tariffs of eight to 30 per cent.

US steel prices rocketed upward in late 2002, with prices for key products shooting up 40 per cent. This result was in some ways, of course, the goal of the tariffs: to raise prices so that US firms could avoid bankruptcy and to buy them time to restructure. But whether the US industry, now on a roll, would use the breathing space to restructure, as opposed to producing feverishly to make large, quick profits, was a matter of widespread scepticism in Europe, Asia and on Wall Street.

An unprecedented and outraged coalition of foreign countries responded – taking the US measures to the WTO, enacting (in some cases) their own safeguards to ward off steel diverted from the US market, and threatening to respond with trade sanctions. Short-term retaliation was averted in 2002 as the US administration acted to exempt some European steel products from the measures. But public opinion did not make it easy for either side to compromise; while Americans supported the tariffs on steel imports by nearly two to one, citizens in Germany, Italy, the UK and France (especially, by about eight to one) strongly disapproved.[11]

The political magnitude of the steel crisis threatened to blow both US–EU bilateral relations and even multilateral cooperation off course. Clearly, neither side wanted to lose control of the dispute. EU pressure in 2002 was met with a rapid and generally pragmatic US response, staving off short-term retaliation. But no one believed that this was the end of the story. Steel, a quintessentially old-fashioned product, had become the source of a dispute big enough to plunge modern US–EU trade relations into crisis.

GMOs – the twenty-first century arrives

Alongside the old, traditional trade wars over bananas, agriculture, and steel, a new phenomenon has emerged: international differences over what had previously been considered purely domestic regulatory matters. This group of challenges tests the limits of public acceptance of transatlantic economic integration, and globalisation in general. It exposes different sets of values and sharply divergent attitudes towards the tolerance of risk, and trust in government (and scientists) versus reliance on the marketplace. The most difficult and disputed area in which transatlantic frictions have arisen is biotechnology, and specifically foods made with genetically modified organisms (GMOs).

Both sides faced enormous political difficulties on this issue. Throughout the 1990s, in the wake of a variety of contaminated food scares, European resistance to imports of US corn and soybeans, much of which had been genetically altered to make the crops more resistant to insects and disease, grew steadily. But under pressure from NGOs and ultimately its own consumers, the EU refused to certify many GM products for sale. Meanwhile, genetically engineered crops had become a core US comparative advantage, with US farmers accounting for two thirds of global production of GM crops by 2001, and GMO acreage in the US rising by nearly 20 per cent annually. Any attempt to regulate the sale of GMO products threatened US economic interests, and doubly so if EU restraints were picked up and copied by others, such as the Chinese and others in emerging markets.

Washington's official position on GMOs evolved under the Bush administration. In June 2002, just as the steel dispute threatened to boil over, the US issued a clear warning that it was losing patience and was looking 'more aggressively at what our options are' – a clear signal that it was considering WTO action.[12] However, by the autumn it appeared to rethink its tactics. In another illustration of how globalisation was changing international trade diplomacy, Zoellick declared his intention to 'to pull this out of the US–EU bilateral context and make it into a global issue',[13] specifically by shifting global attitudes towards GM foods and isolating Europe. Amidst signs that other major players, such as China, were softening their opposition to GMOs, the US played on the outrage provoked by famine-ravaged Zambia's refusal to accept American GM corn as emergency food aid. The Bush administration argued that it was morally wrong that countries on the brink of starvation should refuse GM food aid out of concern for their relations with Europe. Many in Europe claimed that US tactics were driven by an ideological determination to advance a case for GM food, or indeed by a need to find outlets for domestic surplus production.

As the European Commission struggled to persuade member states to restart the process of authorising new GM varieties, the idea of building consumer confidence via a system that allowed GM foods to be traced and labelled gathered support. But the devil was in the details. Should goods made with GM seeds, for example, but with no trace of GMOs found in them, still be labelled as a GM product? What, precisely, constituted the 'adventitious presence' of GMOs in foods: 1 per cent of the total product, as proposed by the Commission, or less than that, as many members of the European Parliament and some member states wanted? Were labels indicating that a product 'may contain' GMOs sufficient in terms of informing the consumer? Here, the GMO controversy illustrated that today's trade controversies are often as much (or more) internal disputes as they are US–EU disputes. In this case, the Commission sought to lift the ban and to restart licensing of GM foods in Europe, but was stymied by member states including France, Austria and Luxembourg.

The dispute also highlighted the generic problem of regulating new technologies, often before scientific evidence reaches definitive conclusions about their safety, in the face of conflicting pressures from producers and consumers. Clearly, no government wished to get too far ahead of their voters on GMOs. All were forced to respond to consumer perceptions, regardless of whether or not they were based on sound science.

A more fundamental challenge was overcoming differences in regulatory culture, particularly concerning tolerance of risk. In Europe, after the 'mad cow disease' crisis, the dioxin scare, and a contaminated blood scandal, the plea of European politicians to the effect that we have to 'put our trust in the scientists' had a hollow ring to it. Polls showed that clear majorities of European citizens opposed GMOs. So did a majority of the American public, according to some polls. Yet in the US domestic context, the Bush administration seemed able to argue, successfully most of the time, that regulation should be based solely on science. To no apparent avail in the transatlantic context: a poll of 16,000 EU citizens in late 2001 found that 56.5 per cent rejected scientific claims that GM foods posed no risk to the environment or human health.[14] European consumers seemed to want to keep political control of the decisions, whatever the scientists concluded and at whatever cost to transatlantic relations.

Conclusion

We have seen how transatlantic tensions have erupted, persisted and escalated on matters of multilateral and bilateral trade, but also, paradoxically, how the relationship is largely unaffected by political changes. It is unclear whether the transition from the Clinton to the Bush administration changed bilateral economic relations in any way. The events of 9/11, which threatened to plunge the international economy and trade system into crisis, may have helped to make Doha 'happen'. But clearly they did not mark an 'end' to globalisation (see Guerrieri 2002).

A second paradox sees the US and EU becoming ever more economically interdependent, but often struggling to find workable political compromises when a trade dispute erupts. Does it follow, then, that new initiatives are needed to reinvigorate transatlantic economic relations and inoculate the wider economic relationship from specific trade rows? The recent past is littered with transatlantic initiatives, including the Transatlantic Declaration (1990), the NTA (1995), the NTM (1998), and a successor arrangement that (unlike the NTM) *was* adopted but had little political impact – the Transatlantic Economic Partnership (1998). They have no doubt combined to make US–EU economic relations far more systematic, in stark contrast to the days when officials on one side would sometimes find out that the other side had imposed new trade restrictions by reading about it in a newspaper. Still, while these US–EU initiatives have produced many meetings, they have delivered few (if any) new solutions in the game of economic diplomacy.

When it has come to major trade proposals, such as the NTM or even the periodically floated idea of a Transatlantic Free Trade Area (TAFTA), the ideas always seem aimed at addressing apparent needs rather than achieving actual results. As Schott (1996: 33) argues, the idea of a TAFTA always seems to be proposed as a way of addressing a foreign policy problem – the need to reinforce the transatlantic alliance – or a signal that 'the transatlantic partners were giving increased prominence to their bilateral trade relationship' (see also Frost 1997). Similarly, by the halfway point of its (first) term, the George W. Bush administration seemed increasingly intent on pursuing unabashedly political Free Trade Areas (FTA), particularly with Morocco but perhaps eventually also with Indonesia, Taiwan, Turkey and Afghanistan.

Yet, a TAFTA would be an FTA of an entirely different magnitude. To float, it would have to address the most difficult and contentious issues, such as agriculture, textiles, audiovisual services and product standards. Outside these sectors, market access is rarely a transatlantic trade problem in practice. If agriculture or textiles were excluded, or protected by rules of origin, the positive income effects for developing countries of such massive regional integration would be dwarfed by the adverse effects of trade diversion that would be likely. For a TAFTA to avoid systemic risks of this kind, it would basically have to extend most-favoured nation (MFN) tariff liberalisation to the rest of the world.

Moreover, market access initiatives carry more weight in the context of a multilateral Round. It would have been an oddity, to say the least, if the proposals by both sides on the table in Geneva (by early 2003) had been undercut or devalued by the announcement that the EU and US were ready to extend MFN liberalisation to the rest of the world regardless of what other countries were ready to do. Besides, a TAFTA would not, in and of itself, do much if anything to solve 'new style' regulatory disputes (see European University Institute 2002).

Our third paradox comes into play here: the political economy of transatlantic relations is frequently debated in a vacuum and with little reference to the need for the US and EU to contribute to multilateral governance of the global economy. We have argued that globalisation is changing the terms of the global trade game, and that it has become politically untenable for the US and EU to try to dictate terms to the rest of the world, as both sides now seem to realise. Many argue, moreover, that the dispute settlement system in the WTO is counter-intuitive, in that the only weapon available to enforce the rules is sanctions that hinder trade and shut down markets; an equivalent system in the World Health Organisation (WHO) would find it endorsing the spread of viruses to countries that did not cooperate in international health efforts (see Charnovitz 2001). Moreover, retaliation is a weapon that is clearly hard for a number of developing countries to use effectively.[15]

As a review of the WTO's dispute settlement system dragged on into 2003, where were the real alternatives in terms of governance in the system? US interest in some kind of substitute to sanctions as a means of encouraging compliance was growing by 2003, in part because of the Bush administration's reticence to use sanctions to enforce environment and labour provisions, upon which Congress often insisted. It proposed a system of fines to enforce such provisions in bilateral US free trade agreements being negotiated with Singapore and Chile, thus encouraging speculation that a precedent would be set for the Free Trade Area of the Americas (FTAA) or even the WTO itself.

The EU was less favourable to this and other alternatives to sanctions. Lamy's message was clear:

> It would be good to think that we could find a way of ensuring WTO confor-mity without getting into the business of distorting trade flows which stem from sanctions. That said, the current system is all we have to enforce com-pliance, and I certainly cannot and will not tell you today that we renounce the instrument in the absence of better ideas.[16]

Meanwhile, managing highly politicised trade disagreements in the context of an overly legalistic and generally imperfect WTO dispute settlement system was only one challenge amongst many in transatlantic economic relations, and arguably not even the most difficult one. Tensions between the profusion of bilateral FTAs and management of the multilateral trade system seemed to be growing. The 'new' politics of trade, touching on thorny issues of consumer sovereignty and implicating far more players including developing countries and boisterous NGOs, were far more demanding than the old trade politics. One thing, at least, was clear in transatlantic economic relations after Clinton gave way to Bush. None of the fundamental paradoxes of transatlantic trade were going to become any easier to resolve anytime soon.

Notes

1 OECD (Organisation for Economic Cooperation and Development) figures in 2000 showed that while EU support for its farmers was slightly higher ($104 billion against $92.3 billion), this works out as less per capita ($276 versus $338) and less per full-time farmer ($14,000 versus $20,000). The main difference concerns the size of farms (the average US farm size is 207 hectares, against 18 hectares in the EU), number of farms (almost 7.4 million in the EU and just over 2 million in the US) and the amount of farmland under cultivation (425 million hectares in the US against 134 million hectares in the EU).

2 See for example a Pew Research Centre poll on American attitudes towards the WTO post-Seattle, available at <http://people-press.org/reports/display.php3?ReportID =44> (accessed 10 January 2003).

3 See results of the World Economic Forum Survey of 25,000 citizens across 25 coun-tries taken in February 2001, available at <http://www.weforum.org> (accessed 10 January 2003).

4 The EU's system of qualified majority voting assigns each member state a number of votes based loosely on its population and requires, following the Treaty of Nice, super-majorities of states representing a minimum threshold of the EU's population in order for measures to be passed. In practice, majority voting is rarely used to determine

EU trade policy, where consensus is the norm, but its 'shadow' – that is, the mere possibility that it may be used – encourages recalcitrant member governments to compromise.

5   This despite the uncertainty caused by the European Court of Justice ruling (1/94) which gave the Commission only a weak green light to negotiate trade agreements outside classic trade in goods.

6   There seems little doubt amongst members of the anti-globalisation NGO community that the successful launch of the new Round at Doha was a direct consequence of 9/11 and the reluctance of developing countries to resist the Bush administration's agenda. See for example Aileen Kwa, 'Impact of Sept 11 on WTO negotiations: War on Terrorism weakened South's Opposition to New Trade Round in Doha', *Focus on the Global South*, January 2002, available at <http://www.ourworldisnotforsale. org/acts/act08.htm> (accessed 12 November 2002).

7   Frances Williams and Guy de Jonquieres, 'Stalled in Geneva', *Financial Times*, 19 June 2002, p.22.

8   Interview, British Foreign and Commonwealth Office, 18 January 2002.

9   For a clear explanation of the WTO's dispute settlement system, along with a trenchant analysis of how to avoid overloading it, see Petersmann (2001).

10   We have chosen not to focus on FSC, despite its potential to be the mother of all trade wars, because it actually seemed close to resolution by early 2003 (see below).

11   See Pew Research Center poll, 'Americans and Europeans Differ Widely on Foreign Policy Issues', 17 April 2002, available at <http://people-press.org/reports/display. php3?PageID=453> (accessed 10 January 2003).

12   Allen Johnson, chief US negotiator on agricultural affairs, quoted in *Financial Times*, 21 June 2002.

13   Quoted in *Financial Times*, 15 October 2002.

14   See Eurobarometer poll 55.2, December 2001, 'Europeans, science and technology', available on <http://europa.eu.int/comm/research/press/2001/pr06122en-report.pdf> (accessed 18 November 2002).

15   Even when developing countries win a case, they often find that retaliation hurts them more than the 'loser', since losers often fail to change their illegal trade practices and sanctions simply raise the cost of essential imports. For example, in the bananas case Ecuador did not even bother to apply WTO-authorised sanctions against the EU. No African or least-developed country brought a single case in the first eight years of the WTO's existence.

16   Speech to the Economic Strategy Institute, 7 June 2001, available at <www.europa.eu.int/comm/trade/index_en.htm> (accessed 15 November 2002).

4 Justice and internal security

Wyn Rees

US–European cooperation occurs across the myriad fields of governmental responsibilities. It is said to be rooted in the common values of democratic pluralism, market economies, adherence to human rights and the rule of law. In some fields, such as military security, cooperation has been particularly close in the postwar period because it was built upon a perception of an imminent threat from the former Soviet Union. In others, cooperation has been more modest and patchy. Judicial and internal security cooperation has fallen into the latter category. Such issues have traditionally been approached as closely-guarded matters of national sovereignty and have not experienced significant investments of time or energy from governments on either side of the Atlantic.

However, in the post-Cold War period, the evolving nature of internal security challenges has led states to recognise the need for external assistance. As military threats to the territorial integrity of western countries have diminished, attention has shifted to new concerns. Issues such as terrorism, international organised crime and drug trafficking threaten the internal security of all western countries to varying extents. They are phenomena that are transnational in nature in that they are perpetrated across international boundaries by sub-national actors. They share some similarities in that they involve covert and often highly organised groups, who frequently employ violence (Schmid 1996). They are difficult for states to combat without the help of international cooperation.

The impact on transatlantic internal security cooperation of the inauguration of George W. Bush was negligible. Due to the fact that judicial and law enforcement cooperation has been built up quietly over many years and has not been a high profile political issue, the arrival of a new Republican president in the White House was of little significance. Internal security cooperation, for example, was not a contentious matter in the presidential campaign and received little attention. Unlike controversies over national missile defence, peacekeeping in the Balkans and the future of transatlantic military relations, law enforcement cooperation was a relatively invisible issue in the US–European relationship.

In contrast, the 9/11 terrorist attacks on the twin towers of the World Trade Centre and on the Pentagon had a major impact on US–European judicial and internal security cooperation, catapulting the issue of counter-terrorism to the very top of the transatlantic agenda. The American government searched for ways to respond to the grievous blow that had been inflicted upon it and simultaneously Europe reached out to demonstrate solidarity with the US. One way of demonstrating this solidarity was to enhance judicial and law enforcement cooperation across the Atlantic. In this fight against terrorism, the very instruments that had hitherto been treated as low profile areas for transatlantic efforts, such as the sharing of intelligence and the granting of extradition requests, now became the focus of attention.

This chapter seeks to assess the new importance of judicial and internal security cooperation in transatlantic relations in the light of the events of 9/11. It will argue that the terrorist attacks have provided a massive stimulus to intergovernmental cooperation and overcoming barriers that had stood in the way of US and European attempts to work together. This stimulus has not been confined to countering terrorism but has extended to combating organised crime and drug trafficking. Measures taken against terrorism are also relevant to other non-traditional security challenges. For example, the facilitation of assistance between police agencies, the seizure of criminal assets and the targeting of fundraising capabilities have been just as relevant in the fight against organised crime as in combating terrorism.

Yet a cautionary note will be sounded about the prospects for future cooperation. The goodwill that accompanied European support for the US after 9/11 faded relatively quickly as the US shifted its attention to 'regime change' in rogue states. New fault lines between the US and some of its allies, particularly France and Germany, opened up as a result of the US-led war on Iraq. This new set of transatlantic tensions may well undermine future cooperation in the judicial and law enforcement fields.

Tensions in the post-Cold War relationship

If one looks back to the 1990s to assess the extent of US–European cooperation in internal security, one is struck by its limited nature. The record of the transatlantic allies in working together in this area was limited. This is not to deny that there were some achievements in internal security cooperation (which will be discussed at a later point in this chapter), nor that this sphere was starting from a low base. Nevertheless, three main factors help to account for why there were only modest achievements over the past decade.

First, transatlantic attention remained preoccupied with the traditional military security relationship. With the end of the Cold War and the disorientation that followed from the collapse of the Warsaw Pact and then the disintegration of the former Soviet Union, western countries were preoccupied with ensuring the survival of their security organisations. There were doubts about the continuing relevance of the premier transatlantic organisation, NATO, once the Soviet adversary had disappeared. In actual fact there proved to be plenty of military tasks in the aftermath of the Cold War to preoccupy US–European policymakers. The need to adapt the Alliance to new missions, such as peacemaking and peacekeeping, absorbed considerable energy, as did major crises such as Bosnia and

Kosovo. The Alliance also found that it had to wrestle with internal questions over the balance of power between its American and European halves and the offer of membership to the states of central and eastern Europe.

Whilst it was reassuring to affirm the continuing relevance of NATO, it was exposed as an inappropriate organisation to reconfigure its energies to emerging security threats such as international organised crime and terrorism. NATO remained an organisation preoccupied with military concerns and was reluctant to consider a range of diffuse, non-military tasks. As a result, there was a tendency in the transatlantic relationship to pay lip service to the need to devote more attention to emerging security threats, whilst concentrating in practice on the issues at hand.

An illustration of the transatlantic relationship's concentration on military-security issues and established organisational frameworks was the limited attention accorded to the 1995 New Transatlantic Agenda (NTA). The Clinton administration and its allies solemnly declared their intention to cooperate across a range of international matters including organised crime, terrorism and drug trafficking. In practice, the NTA proved to be a mechanism for conducting a dialogue but it never received the political investment necessary to realise its ambitious objectives. The transatlantic allies continued to focus their relationship on the changed security situation in Europe, rather than looking to an evolving global agenda. One implication of this was a consistently higher level of political and diplomatic investment in NATO and its enlargement, especially on the American side, than in the NTA.

A second factor constraining cooperation was disagreement between the US and Europeans over how to deal with these security challenges. Although the transatlantic allies share the view that international terrorism, organised crime and drug trafficking are menaces that have to be combated, they take different views about the nature of the threats as well as the most appropriate instruments to utilise. These differences of view result partly from the fact that the US and Europe experience different manifestations of these problems. For example, the principal drug problem for America over the last two decades has been cocaine imported from South America through the Caribbean and Mexico and into the US. For the Europeans, their foremost concern in relation to drugs has been the importation of heroin from central and south east Asia.

As well as varying experiences of the problems, differing transatlantic cultures have led to the advocacy of alternative policy approaches. In the case of terrorism, prior to 9/11, the US treated the issue primarily as a foreign policy matter. This reflected the fact that the majority of attacks had been on American personnel and interests overseas. The US regarded terrorism as a multifaceted national security issue that justified drawing upon the resources of all major government agencies. Thus, whereas European countries looked upon terrorist activities as criminal behaviour, the US response was broader than just law enforcement. The American government was willing to draw upon a wide array of instruments including diplomatic channels, economic sanctions, the use of covert activity and the employment of military force (Testimony of J. O'Neill to Permanent Select

Committee on Intelligence, 1996). Each year in its publication *Patterns of Global Terrorism* (Department of State 2001), the US Department of State identified both groups that employed terror and states that it accused of sponsoring them. Legislation, such as Helms-Burton and the Iran–Libya Sanctions Act, was introduced to ban American companies from trading with terrorist sponsors and the laws were extended to apply to the companies of allies who undermined the embargo.

In adopting a hard line against state sponsors of terrorism around the world, recent US administrations have received consistent encouragement from Congress. Both houses of Congress have advocated a tough stance against terrorist activity, particularly where it has threatened US interests and those of close allies. A recent example was the bipartisan US National Commission on Terrorism, which reported to Congress in June 2000. It called for stronger measures to be taken against the threat and advocated the imposition of sanctions against all states supporting terrorists. It also argued that the guidelines restricting the Central Intelligence Agency's use of criminal sources to obtain information on suspected terrorists should be relaxed in the future (Perl 2001).

Many European states, with the frequent exception of the UK, have expressed dismay at the instruments chosen by the US against target states, particularly economic sanctions and the use of force. They have also complained about Washington's predilection to act unilaterally. The Europeans have often argued that American policies are counter-productive, and that modifying the behaviour of state sponsors of terrorism is unlikely to be achieved by punishment. Instead, they have argued for and pursued policies characterised by dialogue and constructive engagement, attempting to influence states by a series of positive inducements. The response from American officials and members of Congress has been to criticise European policies for being driven more by perceptions of selfish commercial interest than by principle. The decision by the Reagan administration to bomb Libya in 1986, in the face of European opposition, clearly illustrated these divergent approaches.

European opposition to the death penalty in the US has been a further irritant to transatlantic counter-terrorism cooperation. Governments and interest groups in Europe have long been critical of the use of capital punishment in parts of the US and this problem was exacerbated in 1996 when the Clinton administration presided over the introduction of the 'Antiterrorism and Effective Death Penalty Act'. European states have been faced with the problem of how to respond to American requests for the extradition of terrorist suspects to the US when these individuals may subsequently be sentenced to death. A route by which this problem has been overcome in the past has been for the US authorities to give an undertaking that they will not press for capital punishment if an individual is extradited from Europe.

It has not just been in the area of counter-terrorism that transatlantic disagreements have constrained cooperation: attempts to combat international organised crime and drug trafficking have also led to tensions. The American government has adopted a national security approach in relation to international crime and illegal narcotics. In October 1995 Presidential Decision Directive 42 (PDD-42) defined illegal drugs as a national security threat and from 1996 to 1998, the US administration developed both an 'International Crime Control Strategy' and passed an 'International Crime Control Act'. These policy initiatives enabled the US to mobilise substantial resources in its 'war' against crime and drugs, and involved a variety of government agencies, including the intelligence services and the military, in its endeavours. In the process of developing this machinery, Washington has looked to its European allies for support and has been disappointed with the response.

For their part, European governments have not been convinced either by American perceptions of the scale of the problems or by the policy responses that emanate from Washington. Whilst international organised crime is undoubtedly a real phenomenon, European analysts have viewed it in more measured terms. They have seen it largely as an opportunistic outgrowth of established domestic crime groups rather than part of an emerging global network. When it comes to strategies for dealing with the problem, the Europeans have preferred low key law enforcement cooperation to the mobilisation of the military-security apparatus of their states. Only in cases such as in Italy, where organised crime has long held a powerful grip, have extraordinary measures and special legislation been drafted to deal with the problem.

Different transatlantic approaches have been evident in relation to the issue of illegal drugs. European countries have focused upon 'harm reduction' and public health matters, which has resulted in policies that include the provision of clean needles and injecting rooms, opiate substitutes such as methadone and the decriminalisation of soft drugs such as cannabis. The US emphasis, in contrast, has been upon punitive penalties for abusers and particularly for suppliers of illegal drugs. The US has been critical of the European 'harm reduction' approach, arguing that it sends out mixed signals regarding the dangers posed by illegal narcotics.

The US has also invested considerable efforts in supply-side reduction. This has led it to conduct an annual certification process of those countries complying with American anti-drugs legislation. Decertification risks the imposition of sanctions and the denial of foreign aid programmes to which the US contributes. The US has focused upon the Andean states of Colombia, Bolivia and Peru, as these are the principal exporters of coca, the raw material for cocaine. Washington has called upon its European allies to participate in crop eradication programmes in South America but has encountered widespread reluctance. States such as Spain, who have close relations with Andean countries, have been unwilling to participate in American-led coercive policies. The EU has preferred to channel funds into development efforts rather crop eradication. In the case of 'Plan Colombia', initiated by the American government in June 2000, a large component of the $1.3 billion appropriated by Congress for that country was to be spent on military assistance to the government for helicopters and training to help defeat guerrillas. The American rationale for this was that the 'Revolutionary Armed Forces of Colombia' (FARC) were benefiting from coca production by taxing it and using the income to support their activities. American requests for the Europeans to support and help to fund Plan Colombia fell on stony ground because the EU felt the plan was too focused on military priorities and because the human rights record of the Colombian military was poor (*Economist* 2000).

The third factor constraining cooperation has been different stages of development of the policy machinery in Europe and the US. The US has been developing policies on international crime, terrorism and drug trafficking for the last 30 years and the severity of some of its problems has encouraged the federal government to accord them a high priority. In contrast, it has been up to individual governments in Europe to develop their own national responses. No substantive, Europe-wide machinery has been available to address the challenges of crime, terrorism and drugs until the last decade. Even then, organisations such as the EU have only been capable of moving into these policy areas at a speed sanctioned by the most conservative of their members because the process has been subject to unanimity. This helps to account for why it has been the US that has been pushing for transatlantic cooperation over the last ten years, often with a clear view of what it has wanted to achieve. But the EU has been at too early a stage of policy development to respond to American demands.

The EU constructed its Third Pillar on 'Justice and Home Affairs' (JHA) as part of the Maastricht Treaty on European Union, which was ratified in November 1993. Prior to this, there had been limited efforts between European states to share information on internal security matters through the mechanism of *Terrorisme, Radicalisme et Violence Internationale* (TREVI), which operated outside the European Community through the intergovernmental channels of 'European Political Cooperation'. Even with the creation of the JHA pillar, the ability of the EU to act collectively in the area of internal security was circumscribed by the absence of clear objectives and the weak instruments that were available in the Treaty. Here was clear evidence of the mixed attitudes amongst the EU membership towards this policy initiative. As in the area of foreign policy cooperation, several member states were wary of the implications for national sovereignty of granting the EU sweeping powers over criminal and judicial issues.

It was not until the 1997 Treaty of Amsterdam that the EU began to establish more ambitious targets for Third Pillar activities. Parts of the JHA portfolio were included in the original European Community pillar, enabling the European Commission, Parliament and Court of Justice to become more fully involved – although this 'communitarisation' did not extend to criminal and judicial issues. At the Special European Council meeting at Tampere in 1999, which was devoted to JHA issues, it became evident that the member states were determined to make the Union a powerful actor in the internal security field. One significant step forward at Tampere was to agree upon the principle of the mutual recognition of each EU member state's laws, thereby enabling cooperation to proceed at the European level. Nevertheless, it will take time for the EU to realise its aspiration of working more closely together in the field of internal security.

Attempts to construct links with 'Europol' (the European Police Agency) illustrate the problems experienced by the US in building cooperation with the EU.

Europol was constructed on the foundations of the European Drugs Unit and promised to be of enormous benefit to the US as a central point of transatlantic contact for criminal intelligence information. Yet attempts to secure collaboration for much of the 1990s were frustrated because the EU member states did not ratify the Europol Convention until 1998. Even at that late stage the capacity of American agencies to interact with Europol remained limited because its breadth of competencies was not fully developed. For instance, Europol did not receive a remit to deal with terrorist issues until 1999. A further problem has been an inability to resolve differences between the transatlantic allies over data protection. Europol has been unable to share information with the US because the latter's data protection legislation has not conformed to European standards.

Transforming cooperation: the impact of 11 September

It would be misleading to convey the impression that there was no transatlantic cooperation in law enforcement and judicial matters prior to 9/11. Nevertheless, much of the substance of cooperation was undertaken on a bilateral basis between individual European countries and the US. Agencies within the American government have built up strong relationships with their European counterparts. In the sphere of counter-narcotics activity, for example, the US has developed cooperative arrangements with the law enforcement communities of France, Italy and Holland. In the sphere of combating organised crime, the US has good relations with the Italian authorities whilst in the field of counter-terrorism, the US has worked closely with the UK.

The US has made strenuous efforts in the past to improve judicial and law enforcement linkages with its European allies through the stationing of relevant personnel overseas. Experience has proved that face-to-face contacts can help to smooth the ability of two countries to work together and to understand the differences between their respective legal systems. The US stations Legal Attachés from the Federal Bureau of Investigation (FBI) in its embassies in Europe to serve as liaison contacts and to facilitate collaboration when complex legal cases arise. It also bases representatives of the Drug Enforcement Agency in major European capitals. The US has negotiated treaties with each of the European states in order to specify the conditions on which people can be extradited for prosecution. The US has Mutual Legal Assistance Treaties (MLATs) with nine EU member states, detailing the information that can be shared across the Atlantic.

Where cooperation has evolved at a multilateral level, it has tended to grow between the European Union and the US. Multilateral cooperation has often taken the form of particular initiatives that have emerged under the system of six-monthly EU presidencies. This has reflected the problems inherent in the EU system: short-term, high profile actions that do not enjoy sustained support. US–EU initiatives have included the combating of 'cyber-crime' and pornographic images on the internet; an information campaign in eastern Europe to warn women against being trafficked to the west; a counter-drugs initiative in the Caribbean and an agreement to control the sale of chemicals used in the production of illegal drugs – the Chemical Precursors Agreement of 1997. Of these different initiatives, only the last two have enjoyed significant political support. Even in the case of the Caribbean initiative, the US was critical of the level of effort made by some of its European partners. Washington complained that EU funding for work in the Caribbean was exceedingly slow and that US bilateral cooperation with countries such as the UK and the Netherlands tended to deliver more rewards than multilateral efforts.

The events of 9/11 transformed the environment in which transatlantic internal security cooperation was conducted. Whereas in the past this area of cooperation had been of low political salience, the enormity of the attacks on New York and Washington and the wave of sympathy it elicited from European countries reversed this priority. There was a European desire to demonstrate support for the US as actively as possible. The US declaration of a 'war on terrorism' had the effect of galvanising US–European cooperation across the spectrum of security threats. Many of the measures that were taken under the aegis of fighting terrorism were also relevant to countering organised crime and drug trafficking.

One result of the aftermath of the attacks was to reinforce the traditional military-security and diplomatic relationship between the transatlantic allies. For the first time in its history the NATO alliance activated its Article 5 collective defence guarantee. This led to Advanced Warning and Control (AWACS) aircraft from Europe being sent to patrol the eastern seaboard of the US and American forces being given the right to use European ports and bases for the prosecution of the war in Afghanistan. European countries offered substantial military contributions to assist the US in fighting against the Taliban. The UK, France, Germany, Italy and the Netherlands all offered assets but, with the exception of some special forces and units from the UK, the US mostly chose to conduct the war alone. European offers of assistance were not taken up until US Central Command was ready to invite the International Security Assistance Force (ISAF) to undertake peacekeeping duties in the capital Kabul. The US expressed its appreciation for the diplomatic support that the Europeans provided over the conflict in Afghanistan, such as the part played in helping to form an interim Afghani government at the Bonn Conference and the mobilisation of financial help for reconstruction at the Tokyo Conference.

Yet the military–diplomatic relationship was just one facet of a re-invigorated transatlantic dialogue. More innovative forms of cooperation were judicial and internal security measures that were agreed between the allies in the weeks and months following the attacks on America. These represented the 'coming of age' of an understated sphere of security cooperation and reflected an appreciation on both sides of the Atlantic that terrorism posed a common challenge. There was evidence of real political will on both sides of the Atlantic to make progress.

Three principal categories of cooperation were taken forward. The first was police and judicial cooperation. Europol was allowed to sign an agreement with the US authorities that facilitated the sharing of intelligence information (European Commission 2001a). The US was allowed to send officials to attend the meetings of working groups that were dealing with terrorist issues. This was of much potential benefit as it offered the US access to the criminal intelligence files and the knowledge base that European states pooled within Europol. At the US–EU Summit in May 2002 discussions were begun over a multilateral legal agreement between the EU and the US that would supplement the bilateral arrangements already in existence. In the lead up to the Summit it was envisaged that judicial cooperation could be extended to joint investigation teams and to the creation of single points of contact for exchanges of information (*Agence Europe* 2002). The EU determined that issues pertaining to extradition and the exchange of criminal evidence with US law enforcement authorities would not take place if the death penalty were involved.

The ability of the EU to offer closer police and judicial cooperation with the US was built upon progress that was agreed amongst the member states in the period following the 9/11 attacks. The EU agreed upon both a common definition of terrorism – a goal that had long proved elusive – and a list of organisations that were regarded as perpetrators of terrorism. The acceptance of an EU-wide arrest warrant was a major step forward. The endorsement of the arrest warrant makes it possible for a suspected offender to be arrested on the territory of one member state based upon a judicial document issued by another. The implications of this went beyond the field of terrorism as it applied to some 32 offences (whose minimum punishment exceeded three years in prison). In addition, the Union agreed to operationalise the concept of 'Eurojust', a body of prosecutors and magistrates from EU member states set up to facilitate cross-border cooperation in significant criminal cases. Such measures as these form the basis of a substantial advance for the EU in police and judicial cooperation from which the US might be able to benefit in the future.

Second, the US and the EU agreed to target terrorist financing. This applied to the suppliers of funds and the accounts by which terrorist organisations move resources around the world. Both sides agreed to freeze the accounts of known groups and sympathisers through a variety of channels. By the middle of 2002 the EU claimed to have suspended accounts worth over €100 million (European Commission 2002). The EU urged its members to ratify the UN Convention for the Suppression of Financing of Terrorism. The EU made clear that states seeking membership of its organisation in the future would be expected to sign up to the full range of measures against terrorist financing and money laundering. The Union also undertook to adopt its Directive on money laundering and to widen its remit from only drug-related proceeds to the laundering of profits from all types of serious crime. This demonstrates once again the 'spill over' effect in which measures taken ostensibly to combat terrorism can have ramifications for many other forms of crime. The process tends to result in a general ratcheting up of security cooperation against all types of criminal activity.

Third, the transatlantic allies committed themselves to improve airline security in the light of the *modus operandi* of the terrorists in the 9/11 attacks. They announced their intentions to improve the safety of ground operations at airports, for example, in closer monitoring and checking of baggage and tighter controls on potential weapons that can be carried onto aircraft. They also agreed to reinforce safety measures in the air, including consideration of limiting access to the flight deck of airliners and to providing armed 'marshals' on long distance flights (Council of the European Union 2002).

The future of cooperation

Since 9/11, transatlantic judicial and internal security cooperation has been accorded a salience and political momentum that it never enjoyed throughout the 1990s. Despite the fact that the measures taken have been relatively modest, there is now the potential for a series of agreements to be rolled out over the next two or three years. However, such an optimistic prospect cannot be taken for granted. Obstacles have arisen to US–European cooperation that may derail these efforts.

The transatlantic allies remain divided over how to respond to transnational threats and these divisions may frustrate their ability to work together. In relation to terrorism, the conduct of the US since its declaration of a war on terrorism has caused consternation in Europe. For example, the way that the US dealt with suspected Al-Qaeda fighters from Afghanistan, transporting them to Camp X-Ray in Guantanamo Bay and incarcerating them as 'unlawful combatants', rather than giving them 'prisoner of war' status, elicited criticism in Europe. The Pentagon responded by saying that the detainees were not subject to the customary rules of war and that they continued to present a possible danger to their guards.

Meanwhile, within the US itself, a whole new government department has been created, the Department of Homeland Security. Its purpose is to coordinate the American response to the threat. Moreover, the US passed legislation in October 2001 which enables the federal authorities to conduct secret house searches of terrorist suspects, tap phones and deport people considered to be undesirable (Dannheisser 2001). The US domestic response to the 9/11 attacks has been much more robust than that of its European allies.

Similarly, in the field of countering international organised crime, the powers of US law enforcement agencies tend to be considerably greater than those of its allies, thereby demonstrating an important difference of approach. American legislation on organised crime enables the authorities to confiscate criminal property, use *agent provocateurs* to trap suspects and employ various forms of electronic surveillance (the Racketeer Influenced and Corrupt Organizations Act). The evidence from these sources would be inadmissible in a European court because they do not recognise the use of such measures. This makes it difficult for US and European law enforcement agencies to collaborate together in some instances. Only a few countries such as Italy have legislation on crime and money laundering that is comparable with that of the US.

A different sort of obstacle to future transatlantic cooperation remains the fractured nature of Europe as a partner of America. Although 9/11 provided a powerful stimulus to push forward with initiatives, once that stimulus fades there is the possibility that Europe will revert to its normal practice of protracted decision making. For example, an extraordinary European Council meeting on 21

September 2001 instructed the JHA council to push forward with the European arrest warrant and the common definition of terrorism. Yet, by the time of the Ghent European Council on 19 October little progress had been made. This caused the heads of state to issue an unusual statement demanding that efforts be redoubled to meet the December deadline. Such evidence is indicative of how detailed negotiations can frustrate a political desire to reach agreement even after an event as important as the terrorist attacks on the US.

Although JHA initiatives have grown at a surprising speed since the Treaty of Amsterdam, there remain internal barriers to more effective policies and in turn, these barriers circumscribe the EU's ability to cooperate with third parties. There are European countries that are wary of enhanced cooperation with the US, fearful that Washington is trying to become too influential in Europe. This is particularly strong in relation to the proposed enlargement of the EU. Here there is a suspicion that the US is trying to compete with the EU to maximise its influence over the development of the central and eastern European countries. For example, in 1995 the FBI negotiated an arrangement with Hungary to open an 'International Law Enforcement Academy' in Budapest to train officers from central Europe in modern policing techniques. The US offered the EU the opportunity to work with them in the venture but France vetoed the proposed cooperation on the grounds that America was trying to dominate Europe's back yard.

A final determining factor of future transatlantic cooperation will be how the aftermath of the US-led war on Iraq is handled in the context of the wider war on terrorism. The US decision to attack Iraq led to a major rupture with several of its allies, particularly France and Germany, which actively sought to frustrate military action and made it clear that they regarded it as illegitimate. It remained unclear whether and how much the transatlantic rupture over Iraq would impact on judicial and internal security cooperation.

Conclusion

Transatlantic cooperation on judicial and internal security matters was an objective pushed mainly by the US during the 1990s. The US sought cooperation with a Europe that was struggling to put the necessary policy machinery in place and as a result Washington frequently experienced frustration. The effect of 9/11 was to generate the political momentum needed to transform the nature of cooperation and place it upon a new level. The rush of new transatlantic agreements that followed the attacks on the US attest to this change. These US–European agreements have been justified under the mantle of countering terrorism but they have implications for combating various forms of international crime and drug trafficking.

The events of 9/11 have also served to enhance the legitimacy of the American approach to fighting terrorism and international crime. Whilst the US and the Europeans exhibited differing approaches to these problems during the 1990s, the fact that it was America that was attacked enabled Washington to imprint its priorities on the response. The predisposition of the US to confront and threaten to punish suspected state sponsors of terrorism has overshadowed the European approach of dialogue and engagement. It remains to be seen whether the dominant American perspective will continue in the future or whether a rebalancing of approaches will evolve.

Judicial and internal security cooperation has become a new dimension within the US–European relationship. It is still a relatively fragile flower and it will need to be carefully nurtured if it is to continue to grow. Nevertheless, this aspect of the transatlantic relationship has the potential to be of increasing importance. In a relationship that is experiencing a period of considerable turbulence, it will represent a useful litmus test.

5 Transatlantic environmental relations

Daniel Bodansky

At the heart of transatlantic environmental relations is a puzzle. On the one hand, Europe and the US share many features that one would expect to produce broad agreement on environmental policy. But, in fact, US–European environmental relations are characterised more by conflict and even antagonism than by cooperation. This chapter explores this puzzle and seeks to explain the divergence between the US and the EU on environmental issues, focusing in particular on climate change.

Several factors make the environment appear a strong candidate for positive transatlantic relations. The US and Europe are both advanced economies, with comparable standards of living and a shared commitment to democracy. As one would expect, given these commonalities, American and European domestic environmental standards are roughly comparable. The US has led in some areas, such as eliminating leaded gasoline and phasing out ozone-depleting substances, while Europe has been ahead in others such as pollution taxes. In a recent global environmental index, the US and European states scored roughly the same. The US ranked a bit below some Scandinavian countries but above Germany and the UK (Global Leaders 2002).

Despite these broad similarities, the environment has been more a source of conflict than cooperation in transatlantic relations. On virtually every prominent issue – GMOs, persistent chemicals and, above all, climate change – the US and the EU have lined up on different sides.

Given the Bush administration's weak record on many environmental issues, including climate change, the current conflict between the US and EU is perhaps not surprising. But the present antagonism between the US and Europe predated the Bush administration. The split on issues such as bio-engineering, chemicals, trade and climate change emerged during the Clinton administration, which ostensibly had a strong environmental orientation.

Related to this central puzzle are two additional puzzles.

- Why do non-governmental groups seem so much more influential in Europe than in America? Membership in environmental organisations in the US is as high as, or higher than, in Europe. And the Clinton administration was populated by numerous officials from the non-governmental community. But, in contrast to their European counterparts, American environmental groups have had an influence only at the margins, and have been unable to persuade the US to join either the Kyoto Protocol or the Biological Diversity Convention.

- Conversely, why hasn't European business exercised more of a moderating influence on the EU's environmental positions? Why has there been so much less transatlantic cooperation among business than among environmental NGOs, despite the increasing internationalisation of economic production and sales?

What was particularly surprising to me, when I entered the Clinton administration in the summer of 1999, was the antipathy felt towards the EU on climate change, a feeling that I sensed was reciprocated on the European side. It was not simply that we disagreed. On the American side, the EU was seen as hypocritical, making pious pronouncements with no real intention of taking serious action. And, on the European side, America was seen as immoral, evading its responsibility to address climate change. Of course, at the personal level, the negotiators generally liked each other and tended to work well together. But this did not override the tendency to denigrate the other side.

Perhaps the hostility between the two sides should not have been surprising. Darwinian theory teaches that the struggle for survival is usually fiercest among closely-related species, who share a common niche. The same seems to be true in politics, where nothing is as bitter as an internecine fight. On most environmental issues, including climate change, American and EU positions tended to be much closer together than either was to other blocs such as the Group of 77 (the developing-country negotiating group). But, despite US overtures, the EU remained reluctant to reach a settlement in advance of the final negotiations, so that the US and Europe could present a unified front to other countries. Instead, serious US–EU negotiations did not begin until literally the eleventh hour, when insufficient time remained to close the deal.

In exploring the divergence between the US and EU on environmental issues, three initial caveats are in order. First, to contrast 'Europe' and 'the United States' is of course an oversimplification, since each embraces a wide spectrum of views, which overlap to a significant degree. In contrasting Europe and the US, I am contrasting official positions rather than the full distribution of views. Second, despite the general perception that the EU is more environmentally-oriented than the US, this is not always true. On the stratospheric ozone issue, for example, the US took domestic action earlier and pushed for stronger international measures in the Montreal Protocol negotiations than did Europe (Benedick 1998). Similarly, US export credit agencies have had stronger environmental requirements than their European counterparts. Third, the search for general explanations should not obscure the fact that often the rift in transatlantic environmental relations may have issue-specific rather than generic causes. Economic interests, for example, vary from one environmental issue to another. On some issues, such as stratospheric ozone depletion, these interests have led the US to be more environmentally oriented; on others such as biotechnology, they have led Europe to take the more 'environmental' position. Regulatory approaches also differ between issues. Although Europe is often seen as the more regulated economy, on some issues such as food safety the situation is reversed: the US developed a regulatory system much earlier, through the Food and Drug Administration, leading to greater public trust of government regulators than in Europe, where the 'mad cow' episode and other food scares have created deep mistrust of government and has led to greater emphasis on 'precaution' (Pollack and Shaffer 2001c).

Climate change: the background

With these general observations and caveats in mind, consider the issue of climate change. The US and Europe have disagreed significantly since climate change first emerged as a political issue in 1988. Through four US presidencies and numerous changes of government in Europe, the basic dynamic of US–EU relations has remained remarkably consistent.

In the first phase of the negotiations, from 1988 to 1992, the debate between Europe and the US centered on whether to establish binding 'targets and timetables' to reduce national greenhouse gas emissions (see generally Bodansky 1994). The EU wanted to do so, following the model used to combat acid rain and ozone depletion. In response, the US argued that targets are merely rhetorical and that what really matters is the adoption and implementation of national policies and measures to reduce emissions. On this view, the role of the international regime should be to exert peer pressure on countries by requiring them to report on what they are doing and then subjecting those reports to international review, rather than to impose requirements on countries from the top down.

Initially, many people attributed the US position against binding targets and timetables to John Sununu, the White House Chief of Staff under the first President Bush. But when he left office in early 1992, the US position remained unchanged, illustrating that while individual personalities may play a role in determining national positions, those positions usually reflect deeper political and economic factors.

The first round of negotiations resulted in the 1992 United Nations Framework Convention on Climate Change (UNFCCC), which contains two paragraphs on targets and timetables. Although these paragraphs are masterpieces of obscurity, they suggest that countries should aim to return their emissions to 1990 levels by 2000, even if this does not appear to be a legal requirement, and the Convention says nothing about what should be done after the year 2000. Interestingly, the political deal between the US and EU on targets and timetables was brokered by the UK prior to the final round of negotiations and was successfully presented to other countries as a *fait accompli*, with no possibility of change. The satisfactory resolution of this core issue for the US allowed President Bush to sign the UNFCCC at the Rio Summit. In October 1992, the US became the first industrialised country to ratify the convention.

Although the Clinton–Gore administration brought less change in US climate change policy than many people had expected, there were still several significant shifts. First, in 1995, the US accepted the so-called Berlin Mandate, which found that the 'commitments' in the UNFCCC were inadequate and that an additional legal instrument – ultimately the Kyoto Protocol – was necessary. The following year, the US made an even bigger shift, accepting that the new legal instrument should set forth legally-binding emission targets – exactly the approach that the first Bush administration had successfully opposed in the UNFCCC negotiations back in 1992.

Nevertheless, US–EU relations continued to be marked by conflict. The EU wanted the new agreement to require significant emission reductions, while the US was willing to accept, at most, a commitment to stabilise emissions (since even stabilisation would amount to a significant reduction below the business-as-usual forecasts, which projected large increases in emissions).[1] The Kyoto Protocol represents a compromise between these positions. The US accepted a tougher target than it wanted – a 7 per cent reduction below 1990 levels – but won provisions allowing countries considerable flexibility in achieving that target, including a five-year commitment period, emissions trading and the possibility of credit for carbon dioxide taken out of the atmosphere by forests and farmlands (so-called carbon 'sinks').

Most of the negotiations since Kyoto have concerned the rules for how these 'flexibility mechanisms' will work. The US wanted the flexibility mechanisms to be unfettered, so that countries could achieve their targets in the cheapest manner possible – for example by undertaking emission reduction projects in other countries (including developing countries), acquiring credits from countries with a surplus (such as Russia, whose economic collapse has caused emissions to decline), and pursuing forest and agricultural activities that remove carbon dioxide from the atmosphere. The EU, in contrast, sought to impose restrictions on the use of the flexibility mechanisms, arguing that industrialised countries – in particular, the US – needed to change their ways by reducing domestic emissions of carbon dioxide.

From a broader perspective, these differences, although significant, were second order. Both sides accepted the need for legally binding emission targets, involving significant reductions in emissions from business as usual, backed by a strong system to monitor emissions and assess compliance. Nevertheless, the differences rather than the commonalities tended to dominate the post-Kyoto negotiations. Indeed, suspicions were so great that, as late as 1 October 2000, a month before The Hague conference (at which the negotiations were scheduled to conclude), arranging a high level meeting between the US and EU proved difficult. At The Hague, real negotiations did not begin until the wee hours of the morning on the final night of the conference and ultimately fell apart due to lack of time. Although the 2001 Bonn and Marrakech accords – which generally tracked the US–EU discussions in The Hague – illustrated that a deal should have been possible, the George W. Bush administration's subsequent repudiation of the Kyoto Protocol rendered the issues moot. And, of course, even had The Hague negotiations ended successfully, the fate of the Kyoto Protocol in the US Senate would have been, at best, an uphill struggle.

Explaining transatlantic divergence

What explains the divergence between the US and the EU on the climate change issue? Each side had its own favourite theories. On the American side, a common view was that the Europeans were simply hypocrites. The EU talked a good game but, when push came to shove, it was not prepared to take serious action to reduce emissions; it was simply engaged in rhetoric. On this view, the US took a more cautious approach because, unlike Europe, it takes its international commitments seriously. It views them as binding law and is therefore unwilling to ratify a treaty unless it knows how it will comply. EU countries, in contrast, regard commitments 'as targets that they will seek to achieve, rather than obligations they will have to fulfill' (Jacobson 2002; see also Levy and Newell 2000). The mixed record of treaty compliance by the US in recent years makes this argument somewhat questionable[2] – although US compliance with environmental agreements in particular has been quite good. Nevertheless, at least in the climate change negotiations, this view was strongly held by some US negotiators.

A related explanation was that, for the EU, compliance with the Kyoto targets was easy, since the EU could rely on East German 'hot air'[3] and the reduced emissions in the UK resulting from energy deregulation and the consequent shift away from coal. According to this view, the EU's main goal was to make the Kyoto Protocol as expensive as possible for the US, in order to give Europe a competitive advantage (or at least reduce the competitive advantage that the US currently enjoys in energy prices). In essence, Europe wanted to use Kyoto to force the US to adopt the types of inefficient, costly energy policies that the EU had already undertaken – hence, the EU's focus on the need to harmonise domestic policies and measures and its efforts to hamstring market mechanisms (which would have allowed the US to avoid imposing costly domestic policies).

Again, this explanation has a grain of truth, but generally seems wide of the mark. Even taking into account German hot air and the reduced emissions in the UK resulting from non-climate policies, some economic models project that the EU will have to reduce its emissions significantly in order to meet its Kyoto target and might even face higher compliance costs than the US (Viguier *et al.* 2001). And although, as the US never tired of repeating, many European countries have not yet adopted policies ensuring that they will meet their Kyoto targets, many are considerably further along in their policy development than the US. There is no particular reason to think that Europe will not adopt sufficient policies in time to comply with Kyoto.

The explanations usually given by Europeans to explain their rift with the US are closer to the mark, but are based on simplistic stereotypes contrasting progressive, socially-oriented, civilised Europe with individualistic, selfish, recalcitrant America (see Levy and Newell 2000, Wiener and Rogers 2001). According to one view, the divergence in government positions reflects a divergence in public opinion: Europeans have a stronger environmental consciousness than Americans, perhaps because of Europe's higher population density and lack of open spaces (in contrast to the American experience of seemingly inexhaustible natural resources).

Specific differences in public attitudes that are often emphasised include:

- *Attitudes towards risk* – A common view, usually cited to explain the European emphasis on the 'precautionary principle,' is that Europeans are more risk averse and suspicious of technology than Americans, and therefore more willing to take action even when the scientific evidence is uncertain.
- *Attitudes about government* – Another claim is that Europeans have a stronger tradition and are more accepting of government intervention in the market than Americans, and that this translates into a greater willingness to accept environmental regulation (Wiener and Rogers 2001: 3).
- *Attitudes about lifestyles* – Europeans are also said to have a greater sense of responsibility towards future generations – a greater sense of stewardship – which makes them approach environmental issues from a moral and not just an economic standpoint.
- *Attitudes towards developing countries* – Finally, Europeans are said to feel a greater sense of responsibility towards developing countries, possibly out of a sense of colonial guilt.

How accurate are these stereotypes? Certainly, they all have elements of truth. In some cases, Europe has indeed manifested greater risk aversion than the US – for example with respect to biotechnology. And the US often tends to be more pragmatic and instrumental in its approach to international environmental problems, whereas Europe tends to be more moralistic. In the climate change negotiations, for example, the Clinton administration believed that, if technology can solve the problem, fine. Europeans, in contrast, seem to feel that, regardless of technology, we consume too much and need to change our lifestyles. The difference between the American and European approaches was most evident in the debate about international emissions trading. The US argued that if emissions can be reduced more cheaply in India or China than in the US, then the US should be able to buy emission reductions from abroad rather than making the reductions at home. Any other approach would simply promote economic inefficiency, leading to fewer overall reductions. In contrast, Europeans tended to see the emissions trading debate as, in part, a moral issue, arguing that people in rich industrialised countries need to change their way of life, rather than being permitted to buy their way out.

But, while there are often important differences between European and American public attitudes towards the environment, the situation is more complex than the simple claims described above. Polling data, for example, suggests that Americans rate environmental protection as highly as Europeans. Concern about stewardship and natural resource conservation has a long tradition in the US dating back to the early twentieth century. Moreover, although the US is less precautionary than Europe in some cases, in others it takes the more precautionary approach. For example, the US has stricter food safety controls than Europe, which have helped the US avoid a 'mad cow' scare. Similarly, Americans have typically shown greater risk aversion than Europeans on a variety of important issues including smoking, highway safety, and child product safety. Although the US has questioned the utility of the so-called precautionary principle in international instruments, its domestic regulation often reflects a precautionary approach, as have its positions on international issues such as protection of the stratospheric ozone layer and whaling. One recent study found that 'the conventional wisdom that Europe is now the more precautionary regulator is oversimplified and largely incorrect' and concluded that 'the notion of a great transatlantic struggle over risk and precaution is misleading' (Wiener and Rogers 2002: 3).

Another often-cited difference between the EU and US is that Europe is more committed to multilateral approaches than the US, which due to its history, size and geography has traditionally tended to go its own way. Again, there is an element of truth in this characterisation. The Bush administration in particular – even after 9/11 – instinctually seems to favour unilateral approaches. Its decision to repudiate Kyoto, for example, was taken without consulting even key allies and was driven largely by domestic politics.[4]

Again, however, the full story is more complex. While the US has resisted multilateral approaches to climate change and the protection of biological diversity, in other areas it has pushed for multilateral regulation to protect the ozone layer (Benedick 1998), prevent oil pollution from tankers (McGonigle and Zacher 1979), and protect endangered wildlife such as elephants and whales. To some degree, the difference between the US and Europe results less from attitudes about multilateralism itself than from the fact that the US and Europe are at different phases of the regulatory process. Because the US tended to regulate environmental protection early on, vested interests have grown up around its environmental laws, making them difficult to change. The EU, by contrast, is still in the standard-setting phase, resulting from EU integration. In developing new regulations, it recognises that, for trade purposes, there is an advantage to having its standards accepted as the recognised global standards.

What is clear is that – whatever differences exist in attitudes towards risk, sustainable development and multilateralism – they are magnified by the very different domestic political processes in Europe and the US. In my view, understanding these differences provides a key to solving the puzzle of why American and EU environmental positions have tended to diverge so widely. On the one hand, the recent tradition of divided government between the President and Congress in the US has produced a least-common denominator effect. Whichever branch is environmentally the most conservative tends to prevail. This is particularly true in the case of treaties, where the two thirds majority requirement in the Senate means that, to be ratified, an agreement must enjoy significant bipartisan support. As a result, despite the Clinton–Gore administration's desire to take strong action on climate change, it had to cater to the Senate, whose support it needed in order to ratify the Kyoto Protocol. Although its climate change team included many former members of the environmental NGO community, its policy diverged widely from the NGO and European positions. Indeed, ironically, it tended to work more closely with the moderate business community than with the environmental groups that one would have expected to be its natural allies.

In contrast, the political economy in Europe of coalition governments has tended to produce exactly the opposite effect – what could be called a greenest denominator rather than a least-common denominator. Green parties care most about the environment and demand Green positions as a condition of supporting the government. In several key European countries, including Germany, France, Denmark, Italy, Finland and Belgium, Green parties held the environment portfolio during at least part of the post-Kyoto negotiations (see Rudig 2002). Although the total vote for Green parties has not been so different in Europe than the vote for Ralph Nader in the 2000 US presidential election, the result in Europe has been Green environment ministers; the result in the US was the election of George W. Bush.[5] In dealing with the EU, it is not always clear who is in charge (a fact that can make negotiating with the EU difficult). However, the breakdown of negotiations in The Hague suggest that, within the EU coordination process, the Greens carry significant weight.

This fundamental difference in the structure of government combines with another difference between American and European government: in the US, the president is the only elected official in the Executive branch and Cabinet members serve at his pleasure. In Europe, ministers are elected officials with their own political bases. The effect is that whereas the White House serves as a unifying influence, helping to constrain ministries and to ensure that policies reflect interagency input, environment ministries tend to call the shots in Europe.

In the US, the Department of State rather than the Environmental Protection Agency has had the negotiating lead on climate change since at least 1989, in part to ensure that US climate policy reflects broad interagency input. Indeed, during the first Bush administration and again during the policy review undertaken at the outset of the second Bush administration, climate policy was run out of the White House directly. As a result, US climate policy has never been driven by an environmental agenda. Instead, economic and energy considerations have played an important role from the start, reflecting the input of the President's Council of Economic Advisers, the Treasury Department and the Energy Department. Moreover, even the US heads of delegation are sub-cabinet officials who operate on the basis of careful negotiating instructions rather than as independent political operators. In contrast, European delegations have typically been led by environment ministers, who often have their own political power base and who, even when not from the Green party, tend to emphasise environmental over economic considerations. Only when it comes to domestic implementation do other ministries have an important say. In some cases, this leads to a disjunction – and to charges of hypocrisy by the US – between the Green positions of EU negotiators internationally and the less environmental decisions taken domestically.[6]

The effect of both of these factors has been to make the divergence between Europe and America appear much wider than is actually the case. My experience in the climate change negotiations was that other parts of EU governments were often sympathetic with the US positions on issues such as emissions trading and carbon sinks. One reason why they may have been willing to allow their environment ministries to call the shots was that they counted on the US to ensure that the final results were not too Green and reflected economic as well as environmental factors. In essence, finance and energy ministries in Europe could afford to play the good cop because they knew that the US would play the bad cop.

Recent developments

Thus far I have been attempting to explain the rift in transatlantic environmental relations during the Clinton administration. But it is important to bear in mind that, although US–EU relations were often conflictual, at least the two sides shared broadly compatible goals. There was always a sense that, in the end, one should be able to reach an agreement with the other side. Indeed, it was this sense that helped create a greater sense of tension and disappointment when agreement proved elusive.

The election of George W. Bush changed the equation dramatically. The Bush administration had a fundamentally different view on climate change to that of Europe. Initially, it was unconvinced that climate change is a serious problem requiring a serious response. Even after a National Academy of Sciences study concluded that the climate change issue was not merely a figment of 'UN science', as some Bush administration officials originally believed, the Bush administration remained adamantly opposed to Kyoto. It took a while for the EU to comprehend the degree to which Kyoto has become an ideological symbol to American conservatives – much as biotechnology has become an anathema to Europeans – and therefore outside the realm of rational persuasion. It is, I think, particularly galling to Europeans that what they regard as a major international issue, which has been the subject of years of international negotiations, is now being driven by US electoral politics – and nothing they say or do can change that.

Initially, some commentators thought that 9/11 might change the Bush administration's approach to multilateral issues such as climate change. But, as with many other issues, the attacks on the World Trade Centre and Pentagon have changed much less than people anticipated. The Bush administration has not become significantly more multilateral in its orientation. Indeed, even in the fight against terrorism, its approach has been that America should lead and others should assist. Beginning with its decision not to seek UN Security Council authorisation to use military force against Afghanistan, and continuing with its decisions to prosecute members of the Taliban and Al-Qaeda in national rather than international tribunals and, in 2003, to invade Iraq, the US has not been willing to accept significant multilateral decision making. On the European side, although 9/11 initially muted European criticism of the US, the EU position on Kyoto has remained unchanged and criticism of the US has recently revived.

One thing that 9/11 did show is that, for all the rhetoric by the EU about the importance of climate change, it remains a second-tier issue internationally. In the aftermath of President Bush's decision to repudiate the Kyoto Protocol, EU representatives initially said that the decision would undermine transatlantic relations and was therefore not in America's interest. The Bush administration's response, in essence, was, 'get real': the transatlantic relationship is built on much more fundamental economic and security interests than climate change, interests that Europe would not want to jeopardise. And 9/11, at least initially, seemed to prove Bush right. Despite Europe's huffing and puffing over climate change, Europe was still at America's side in responding to the threat posed by international terrorism. In the longer term, however, the Bush administration's rejection of Kyoto – while itself not enough to cause a transatlantic breach – contributed to a fraying of relations that preceded the rift over Iraq.

Interestingly, the withdrawal of the Bush administration from the climate change negotiations has created a vacuum that EU representatives have quite self-consciously sought to fill. Their success in saving the Kyoto Protocol at the Bonn and Marrakech meetings in 2001, despite predictions of its demise, was seen as one of their most significant diplomatic triumphs to date. Assuming that the Protocol enters into force (which remained uncertain due to conflicting signals about whether Russia would ratify Kyoto), the Kyoto process will provide an ongoing opportunity for Europe to exercise leadership internationally.

At the same time, Europe understands that it cannot go its own way entirely. The US accounts for about a quarter of global greenhouse gas emissions. So a climate change treaty without the US cannot, in the long run, succeed. This means that, while Europe and the US are now going their separate ways, the last chapter in transatlantic climate change relations has yet to be written.

Notes

1   The other principal issue in the Kyoto Protocol negotiations concerned developing country participation. The US and the EU agreed that, in the long run, developing countries would need to accept binding emission targets. The difference concerned timing. The US, for domestic political reasons, wanted a decision at Kyoto that would have given developing countries at least the option of accepting binding emission targets now. In contrast, the EU was unwilling to push developing countries on this issue, fearing that doing so would jeopardise the overall deal and arguing that industrialised countries had a moral responsibility to act first.

2   See, for example, the failure by the US to pay its UN dues, or its violations of the duty of consular notification under the Vienna Convention on Consular Relations.

3   'Hot air' refers to Kyoto emission allowances that are in excess of a country's business-as-usual emissions and that are therefore available to trade, even if the country does nothing to reduce its emissions. In the case of East Germany, the collapse of the East German economy reduced emissions by a greater amount than required by Kyoto, leaving surplus allowances that Germany could use to meet its Kyoto target.

4   The Bush camp knew that, without the support of the coal industry, Bush might not have won West Virginia and hence the presidential election.

5   The Greens receive about 5 per cent of the vote in Germany (although 8.6 per cent in the 2002 federal election for the Bundestag) and 1 to 2 per cent in Italy, compared to 2.74% for Nader in the 2000 presidential election.

6   The inability of the EU to adopt a carbon tax is a good example, reflecting the fact that although finance ministries have little say in the international negotiations, their agreement is necessary to adopt an EU carbon tax.

6 US and European perspectives on Russia

Margot Light

Throughout the Cold War, but particularly from the 1960s onwards, there were intermittent differences between the US and the major west European countries with regard to Soviet policy. Although they shared a common perception of the nature of the Soviet threat, they did not always agree on the best means of dealing with it. At one level, it was simply that the geographic proximity of the USSR made the Europeans aware of the need to find some kind of *modus vivendi*, and wary of the kind of confrontation the US sometimes seemed to court. But Europeans also tended, in general, to be less ideological in their policy pronouncements than Americans and more pragmatic in their policies. For example, they responded to détente earlier, but with less enthusiasm than the US and they were less affected when it broke down in the middle of the 1970s (Garthoff 1985; Gori and Pons 1996). Since they had not subscribed to President Ronald Reagan's portrayal of the Soviet Union as an 'evil empire', Europeans were also quicker to accept the 'new political thinking' introduced by Mikhail Gorbachev after 1984. But they were more tempered than the US in their response to it (Garthoff 1994). These differences were carried forward into the post-Cold War period but they were not immediately apparent in the euphoria that accompanied the end of the Cold War and the confusion about how best to construct a new international system.

By the eve of the transition from the Clinton to the Bush administration, however, differences in US and European Union (EU) relations with the Russian Federation had become more obvious. EU member states were preoccupied with the enlargement process and intent on ensuring that exclusion from EU and NATO enlargement did not turn Russia into a troublemaker on Europe's new border. They were, therefore, careful in the way they dealt with the Russian leadership. Americans had initially responded enthusiastically and uncritically to the development of a market economy in Russia. However, the US Senate Foreign Relations Committee, in particular, became critical of the Clinton administration's aid programmes to Russia. A widely publicised money-laundering scandal involving the Bank of New York fuelled the criticism. Since Al Gore had chaired the Gore–Chernomyrdin Commission which had presided over US–Russian economic relations, US–Russian relations became a contentious issue during the 2000 presidential election campaign.[1]

As far as the incoming Bush administration was concerned, political and economic weakness had deprived Russia of the ability to influence western policy. For their part, Russians were convinced that the perceived disregard for Russia's views about air strikes on Iraq, for example, or NATO's intervention in Serbia, indicated that the US intended to construct a unipolar world. Russian attitudes towards the US became quite hostile. The relationship between Russia and the US had, therefore, become rather uncertain. President Yeltsin's unexpected resignation at the end of 1999 and the accession to the presidency of Vladimir Putin, a man with as little foreign policy experience as president-elect George W. Bush, added to the sense of uncertainty.

After the attacks of 9/11, it seemed that, in the face of the common threat of international terrorism and a united determination to eliminate it, the EU and the US had overcome the differences between their policies towards Russia. Russia's participation in the international coalition against terrorism suggested that US–Russian relations had become more cooperative. By the end of 2001, however, some of the issues that divided Russia and the US had reappeared. Given the solidarity that the war against terrorism appeared to demand, however, EU member states were less willing to oppose US policies, whether on behalf of Russia or because of their own convictions.

As the campaign against Iraq intensified in 2002, the harmony between EU and US foreign policy interests evaporated, and so did the improvement in US–Russian relations. A brief period of cooperation enabled the UN Security Council to adopt Resolution 1441 unanimously, declaring Iraq to be in material breach of previous UN resolutions and ordering it to allow UN inspectors immediate and complete access to the country to search for weapons of mass destruction. However, US and British attempts to forge a second Security Council resolution legitimising the use of force revealed deep fissures within the EU, and thoroughly undermined its Common Foreign and Security Policy (CFSP). Although Russia cooperated with France and Germany in opposing US policy, the EU as a whole was utterly divided in its response to the war. Adamant though Russia, France and Germany were in their opposition to the war, the primary concern of the EU soon turned to the need to re-establish internal cohesion and to preserve the transatlantic relationship, while the Russian government became preoccupied with saving the US–Russian partnership.

In order to examine this complex trilateral relationship, this chapter will begin with an overview of US and EU policy priorities in relation to Russia. The following section examines two issues that highlight the differences in US and EU policy towards Russia: the ESDP and Ballistic Missile Defence. The final section considers the impact of 9/11 and the war against Iraq, looking at Russia's role in the anti-terrorist coalition, the benefits that were expected in return for cooperation in the war against terrorism and the evidence that the US has reverted to its pre-9/11 policy with regard to Russia.

US and EU priorities

In central and eastern Europe, the 'new world order', the phrase coined by President Bush (Senior) in 1989 to characterise the system that would replace the Cold War, signified European unity. Americans and west Europeans, partly from guilt but also out of generosity, began to consider how best to assist the former socialist states of central and eastern Europe (CEE) in making the transition to liberal democracy and successful market economies. East Europeans were convinced that they would rapidly gain their rightful place within existing European institutions. No one gave much thought to the role that the Soviet Union would play in the new European order. When the USSR disintegrated and Russia and 14 other independent countries emerged from the ruins, the problem of incorporating the former Soviet Union into Europe's new security and economic systems was multiplied.

At first Moscow believed that the Warsaw Pact and NATO would be subsumed within a new European collective security system. To western leaders, however, there could be no European security without NATO. Moreover, most of the new CEE governments were convinced that NATO was the only reliable guarantee of their independence. In 1994, NATO launched its PfP, extending the invitation to Russia and the other former Soviet states as well as to the CEE. When Russia attacked Chechnya that year, the CEE governments became increasingly nervous about their future status and their determination to join NATO became even stronger. By now NATO had begun to reinvent itself for the post-Cold War world and enlargement eastwards fitted in with its new agenda.

The CEE governments believed that while their security required NATO membership, their future prosperity depended upon accession to the EU. The Union's member states agreed that membership was the best way to assist their economic and democratic transition, but they did not want to jeopardise their own recent political and economic achievements. They thus designed a 'pre-accession strategy' designed to facilitate the eventual incorporation into the EU of those CEE states that successfully made the transition to democracy and a market economy.

From 1994, therefore, both the EU and NATO became preoccupied with managing enlargement. However, an important subsidiary of the enlargement process in both cases was defining and establishing a new relationship with Russia – a relationship which, while not extending membership to either organisation, would ensure that Russia did not obstruct enlargement. EU member states also had active bilateral relationships with Russia, but the main focus here will be on the development of EU–Russian relations.[2] In the case of the US, both Russia's relationship with NATO and the bilateral relationship are considered because they were closely interconnected, both in Russian perceptions and in fact.[3]

Before looking at EU and US priorities with regard to Russia, it should be noted that their policies were based on a curious paradox. On the one hand, they shared the generally accepted premise that if Russia was integrated into the western-based international system, Russians would share the values, and, therefore, the interests, of other members of the system. In other words, areas of cooperation between the west and Russia would emerge naturally (Wallander 2000). This expectation derives from democratic peace theory, although in keeping with the prevailing economic ideology of the 1990s, it was thought that the market would produce both democracy and peace. In effect, this view was not very different from the idealistic views held by the Atlanticists or 'liberal westernisers' in Moscow, who also saw no reason for a divergence between Russian and western interests if they shared the same values (Malcolm *et al.* 1996). On the other hand, both the EU and the US embarked on policies that excluded Russia from full participation in the very institutions that they believed embodied the western values that they wanted Russians to acquire.

It should also be noted that both the Europeans and the Americans supported – in the name of reform and democracy – practices in Russia that diverged widely from the democratic norms that were accepted in the west. For example, although President Yeltsin's dissolution of the Russian parliament (the Supreme Soviet) in September/October 1993 was unconstitutional, the US administration and European governments explicitly supported his action.[4] Nor did they criticise him when he ordered the bombardment of the Supreme Soviet on 4 October 1993; on the contrary, President Clinton claimed that Yeltsin 'had no other alternative', while EU foreign ministers expressed their continued support for the Russian president and 'the process of reform'.[5] Knowledge about corruption, including the 'loans for shares' scheme in 1996 that funded President Yeltsin's re-election, was widespread. Yet western acclaim for Russian privatisation was unstinting and President Clinton called Yeltsin's re-election 'a triumph for democracy'.[6]

US–Russian relations

The economic reform undertaken by the young liberal economists in whose charge President Boris Yeltsin placed the Russian economy in 1992 was greatly influenced by US advisers. The reform concentrated on dealing with Russia's debt and its macro-economic problems, as well as on a programme of rapid privatisation at knock-down prices to a small number of favoured élites. The programme bred corruption and cost the Russian government popular support. US aid was focused on a narrow élite within the Russian government, which used support from the west to gain political influence. The US thus became implicated in causing the inequities that resulted from privatisation, the hardships produced by the implementation of International Monetary Fund programmes and the corruption that became endemic in Russia. Long before NATO expansion, therefore, anti-Americanism was rife in Russia (Wallander 2000). But so was US disillusion with the apparent failure of Russia's economic reform and its incomplete transition to democracy.

As far as NATO expansion was concerned, NATO members were anxious to reassure Russia that cooperation between Russia and the alliance would continue even if enlargement proceeded. They resolved to set up a separate permanent institution for relations with Russia. In May 1997 the Founding Act on Mutual Relations, Cooperation and Security between NATO and the Russian Federation established a NATO–Russia Permanent Joint Council 'to build increasing levels of trust, unity of purpose and habits of consultation and cooperation'. It would be 'the principal venue of consultation between NATO and Russia in times of crisis or for any other situation affecting peace and stability'.[7] It immediately became clear that Russian perceptions of the meaning of the Act differed widely from those of NATO members. While President Yeltsin maintained that the Act meant that NATO would have to consult the Russian government in the NATO–Russia Permanent Joint Council, President Clinton announced that Russia would have 'a voice in but not a veto over NATO's business'.[8]

The formal accession of Poland, Hungary and the Czech Republic to NATO was accompanied by the adoption of a new strategic doctrine, the announcement that the door to NATO membership remained open and the approval of a Membership Action Plan for aspirant members.[9] By then, however, the new strategic concept had already been put into practice in the air strikes against Serbia. Russian disapproval of NATO's action was vehement and it extended across the political spectrum (see Light *et al.* 2000). Most Russians, however, blamed the US, rather than NATO's European members; it was widely believed in Russia that NATO and the US were synonymous. On the other hand, Russian support for Milosevic and the 'dash to Pristina' – the unannounced and precipitous dispatch of Russian troops from Bosnia to 'capture' Pristina, the capital of Kosovo, before NATO ground troops could reach it – caused the Clinton administration to begin to question whether Russia was a reliable partner.

Well before the 2000 US election campaign, therefore, there was considerable mutual disillusion in Moscow and Washington about US–Russian relations. The US had a series of complaints about Russian policy. Russia's wars in Chechnya, its sale of nuclear technologies to Iran, its arms exports, the continual rhetoric against America's purported 'unipolarity', and Russia's adamant objections to ballistic missile defence (BMD) had become contentious issues in the bilateral relationship. Both President Clinton and Vice President Gore were determined to maintain positive engagement, however. Although they knew that Russia no longer had the political and economic power to influence western policy, they were aware of Russian sensibilities and careful not to deny frequent assertions that Russia was still a great power.

The foreign policy priorities of the incoming Bush administration did not differ substantively from those of its predecessor. According to George W. Bush's senior foreign policy adviser, Condoleezza Rice, 'George W. Bush believes that America has a special responsibility to keep the peace'. He was determined, she declared, to adopt a new nuclear strategy and to deploy effective missile defences at the earliest possible date.[10] However, Bush wanted to complete a strategic review before he discussed arms control and other substantive issues with the Russian leadership. In the first few months of the Bush presidency, therefore, neither he nor his advisers sought to reach a consensus with Russia about missile defence or anything else. There was, in effect, a long hiatus in the bilateral relationship. When Presidents Bush and Putin finally met in Ljubljana in June 2001, they quickly established a warm personal relationship. It was clear, however, that the same issues that had dominated US–Russian relations at the end of the Clinton presidency – the future of the Anti-Ballistic Missile (ABM) treaty, BMD, and the next round of NATO expansion – would continue to be major problems during the Bush presidency. In other words, the agenda that President Bush inherited consisted of all the intractable issues that President Clinton had failed to resolve in the bilateral relationship.

There was a great difference in style, however, between the Bush administration and its predecessor. There was no indication that President Bush wanted to reach a compromise on security issues. Although he continued to express his personal regard for President Putin, bilateral negotiations on arms control and on the ABM treaty were based on the implicit assumption that if Russia could not be persuaded to accept the US position on these issues, the Americans would proceed unilaterally.

The EU and Russia

The EU's policy towards Russia is set out in a number of agreements and documents. The basis of the relationship is the Partnership and Cooperation Agreement (PCA) which was concluded in June 1994. Its ratification was delayed as a protest against the first war in Chechnya and it came into force only on 1 December 1997, when a Cooperation Council and Cooperation Committee were established to monitor implementation. Less than the Europe Agreements that were designed to prepare aspirant states for EU membership, the PCA is, nevertheless, far more than an ordinary treaty on political and economic relations. Its aim is to develop closer political links, foster trade and investment, support the reform process in Russia and create the conditions necessary for the establishment of a future FTA between the EU and Russia.[11] EU aid to Russia is delivered via the Technical Assistance to Russia and the Commonwealth of Independent States (TACIS), established in 1991 and modelled on the Poland and Hungary: Aid for the Restructuring of Economies (PHARE) programme which had been set up to assist the east European former socialist countries. The main aim of EU aid to Russia is 'to support transition to a market economy and democracy'.[12] The third important document that sets out EU policy is the Common Strategy on Russia, adopted by EU member states in June 1999. A new instrument of the CFSP, the Common Strategy commits EU members to cooperate on policy towards Russia and, in particular, to assist in establishing a 'stable, open and pluralistic democracy in Russia'.[13]

A great deal of the discussion about EU–Russian relations centres on the progress – or lack of progress – in implementing these agreements. By the end of the twentieth century, the predominant tone on both sides was impatience. EU officials and politicians had begun to suffer from 'Russia fatigue'. They were, explicitly or implicitly, disappointed that progress had been so slow, and barely concealed their impatience with the tendency of Russians to indulge in special pleading. There was also considerable irritation at the constant reiteration of Russia's great power status. That claim may have been valid in the past, at least in terms of military power and political weight, but it manifestly did not correspond to the reality of the economic criteria that contribute to that status today. The war in Chechnya distressed EU politicians and also embarrassed them; when Russian officials disregarded their concerns about Chechnya, it suggested to European electorates that the EU's policy on human rights was selective. Russian politicians and officials, on the other hand, were equally distressed that the EU did not accept Russia's great power status and treated Russia as if it were any small state. They were offended by EU demands that related, in their view, to 'domestic' matters: in particular, they perceived EU statements – and sanctions – relating to Chechnya as improper and intolerable.

Despite the mutual disillusion, both sides were determined to persevere in developing their relationship. Apart from the 'low politics' of implementing the various EU–Russia agreements, a dense network of political consultations was established between the EU and Russia, including EU–Russia summits at regular six-monthly intervals and a steady flow of high level visits between Moscow and various European capitals. President Putin was committed to a closer relationship with 'Europe' and with the EU in particular, both because of a conviction that Russia is part of a 'greater Europe' and to offset the tensions in Russia's relations with the US. In his State of the Union address in April 2001, for example, Putin announced that integration with Europe was 'becoming one of the key areas of our foreign policy'.[14] As for the EU, according to the Europa website, the EU and Russia were bound to be politically close 'as the main players and immediate neighbours on the European continent'. Apart from necessity arising from proximity, there were extensive material links between the EU and Russia. Russia had become an increasingly important trading partner for the EU. Energy supplies represented 45 per cent of Russia's exports to the EU, which, in turn, accounted for 42 per cent of the EU's needs in imported natural gas (17 per cent of total gas consumption) and 17 per cent of oil imports.[15] In October 2000 the EU agreed an Energy Partnership with Russia, covering collaboration on a range of energy-related matters, including production sharing agreements and measures to ensure the safety and security of the energy transport infrastructure. Apart from mutual financial benefit (the EU is Russia's highest paying energy market while Russia is Europe's cheapest supplier), the EU hoped that 'a Russia that needs Europe as an energy customer is a Russia that might have a larger incentive to make the transition into a state with values more in tune with Western norms' (Jaffe and Manning 2001: 140).[16]

As the accession of the new CEE members drew closer, both sides were acutely aware of the importance of addressing a range of specific problems – regarding Kaliningrad (which will become an exclave in the EU), cross-border movement, and trade issues, amongst others – in a constructive manner. Even when there was conflict about the best way to resolve a problem (as there was, for example, about visa requirements for Kaliningraders who wished to travel to the rest of Russia) continual dialogue and negotiation was the hallmark of EU–Russian relations.

Issues that divide

ESDP

The Cologne European Council in June 1999 agreed to expand the EU's Foreign and Security Policy so that the EU would 'have the capacity for autonomous action, backed up by credible military forces, the means to decide to use them, and a readiness to do so, in order to respond to international crises without prejudice to actions by NATO'.[17] The problems in US–EU relations caused by ESDP are explored in Chapter 2 by Howorth in this volume, and it is clear that many of them relate to their bilateral relationship rather than to Russia. But Russia's response to ESDP casts an interesting light on the differences in Russian attitudes to the EU and to NATO, and on the problems this might cause for US–EU relations.

At first Russians did not perceive ESDP as a threat to Russian security. On the contrary, they appeared to welcome it. The tone and contents of the Medium-Term Strategy for the Development of Relations between the Russian Federation and the European Union (2000–10), the Russian government's response to the EU's Common Strategy on Russia, illustrate the point. The preamble comments positively on 'the creation of a defence identity and the consolidation of the CFSP of the EU'. One of the explicit aims of the Strategy is to create a reliable pan-European system of collective security and a united Europe 'without dividing lines'. The first section of the Strategy is titled 'Giving the Russia–EU partnership a strategic dimension'. It lists, as one step that could develop the Russia–EU partnership in the next decade, ensuring 'pan-European security by the Europeans themselves without either the isolation of the United States and NATO or their dominance on the continent'. Another step is 'promoting practical cooperation in the area of security (peacemaking, crisis management, various aspects of arms limitation and reduction, etc.) which could counterbalance, *inter alia*, the NATO-centrism in Europe'.[18] It seems that Russian policymakers thought at first that the ESDP would give them the opportunity to participate in European defence (see Danilov 2000). They also thought that it might be a means of driving a wedge between the EU members of NATO and the US.

There has never been any indication that the EU and its new defence plans were perceived as representing a threat to Russia. The EU was absent from the 'fundamental threats [to Russian security] in the international sphere' listed in Russia's National Security Blueprint, which was drafted and discussed in 1999 and adopted in January 2000. Nor was it mentioned in Russia's new military doctrine adopted in March 2000.[19]

Some Russian analysts perceived ESDP as a potential bridge rather than a wedge, believing that it offers a means by which Russia could continue cooperating with the west despite the difficulties that had arisen between Russia and NATO. Others argued that Russia's first priority ought to be re-engaging with NATO (Trenin 2000). They pointed out that international security was not a balance in which 'increasing the "European" weight would automatically weaken the American side of the balance'. On the contrary, it would only be possible to increase the European side of the balance if this did not undermine the transatlantic link (Danilov 1999). Although relations with NATO began grad ually to improve in May 2000, and ESDP developed more slowly than Russians expected, Moscow's support for ESDP has continued.

An economically and politically powerful EU with an independent military capacity fits well with Russia's vision of multipolarity as an alternative to the unipolar world that is commonly portrayed in Moscow as being the aim of the US. Moreover, ESDP appeared at first to offer a security system for Europe in which Russia might find a role. But when Javier Solana, EU High Representative for the Common Foreign and Security Policy, and Chris Patten, EU Commissioner for External Affairs, insisted that ESDP was intended to comple- ment, not to replace or substitute NATO, its potential for offering Russia a role became questionable.

Ironically, one reason why EU officials and various European political leaders began to insist that ESDP was intended to enhance and not undermine NATO was to allay US anxieties that Russia might use it to divide the European mem- bers of NATO from the US. EU assurances that the function of ESDP was to complement NATO were also addressed to those Eurosceptics who were appre- hensive that the US might use ESDP as an excuse to withdraw from NATO and Europe and retreat into isolation. An ESDP that complements NATO, however, exacerbates Russian perceptions that they are being excluded from Europe. Moreover, ESDP becomes a potential 'back door' to NATO membership for for- mer Soviet states like Ukraine (on the model of the way that the Federal Republic of Germany was integrated into NATO in 1955). The danger is that Russians will revert to the belief – prevalent during the Cold War – that the EU is simply NATO's economic arm. If this affects their attitude to the accession of former socialist states to the EU, EU–Russian relations will become more diffi- cult, adding to the problems ESDP represents to the US–EU relationship.

Ballistic missile defence

Well before the 2000 US presidential election campaign, ballistic missile defence had become a contentious issue in both US–Russian relations and US–European relations. EU and Russian concerns about missile defence were very similar. Ironically, however, fears that Russian pressure to oppose BMD was intended to drive a wedge between Europe and the US prevented the Europeans from coordi- nating their objections with Russia in an attempt to dissuade the US from pursuing the policy.

Missile defence had reappeared on the US domestic political agenda in the 1990s when the Republican Party began to accuse the Democrats of underestimat- ing the nuclear threat to the US homeland. A bipartisan Congressional Commission under the chairmanship of former Republican Secretary of Defence, Donald Rumsfeld, concluded in 1998 that there was a serious threat that rogue states like Iran, North Korea and Iraq could acquire the means (in part, from nuclear material and know-how that was believed to be leaking from the former Soviet Union) to strike the US within about five years. As a result of this assessment,

President Clinton allocated $7 billion over six years for the deployment of a limited BMD system in January 1999 and announced that his administration would examine the alterations that would be required to the Anti-Ballistic Missile Treaty to legitimise deployment. In July he signed the National Missile Defence Act, according to which the US would deploy an effective system against a limited ballistic missile attack as soon as it was technologically possible (Bowen 2001). Although he deferred a deployment decision to his successor in September 2000, it seemed that the question was 'not whether, but how' and what system would be deployed (Daalder *et al.* 2000). There was an immediate, negative reaction from Russia, China and EU member states. The Russians objected to any modification of the 1972 ABM treaty which was, they believed, as important to strategic stability in the post-Cold War world as it had been during the Cold War. They feared that even a limited ABM system would undermine their strategic nuclear deterrent. They argued that they – and other nuclear powers – would have to expand their nuclear arsenal and announced that if the US abrogated the treaty unilaterally, Russia would no longer be bound by its obligations, under the Strategic Arms Reductions Talks (START) II treaty, to reduce its offensive missiles (Trenin 2001). This would cause a new arms race entailing serious consequences for existing arms control agreements and making it impossible to negotiate further reductions in nuclear missiles.

President Clinton did not begin to consult his European allies about BMD until late 1999. His delay exacerbated their anxieties about the potential implications for the global strategic balance, as well as for multilateral disarmament and non-proliferation. Europeans were concerned that the US administration had presented them with a *fait accompli*, contributing to their perception of a growing unilateralism in US security policy. They cautioned against a unilateral withdrawal from the ABM treaty, arguing that it would send an implicit message to the world that the US did not consider itself bound by its international commitments.[20] They believed that BMD, a technological response to a political and diplomatic problem, was driven by pressure from the US defence industry and the desire to maintain a technological lead over the rest of the world (Cambone *et al.* 2000). While they shared the American concern about the danger of increasing missile proliferation, Europeans believed that the US paid too much attention to capability and not enough to intention. Above all, they were anxious about Russia's reaction to BMD and deployment, and feared that US deployment of ABM systems, particularly without prior Russian agreement to modify the ABM treaty, would lead to a new arms race (Gordon 2001).

Neither President Clinton's briefing meetings with his European allies in 1999–2000 nor the intensive consultation undertaken in 2001 by the Bush administration dispelled European anxieties about BMD. Although they were somewhat relieved that President Bush intended to deploy missile defences that were capable of defending not only the US, but also friends and allies and US forces overseas, they continued to put pressure on the US to pursue an agreement with Russia to amend ABM prior to deployment in an effort to legitimise missile defence and preserve the rationale of preventing an offensive–defensive arms race (Bowen 2001). It became clear, however, that while President Bush was prepared to inform them of his plans, he did not intend to modify them in the light of either European or Russian concerns. Bush did alter his stance on strategic missile reductions, signing a formal treaty with Russia in May 2002 in which each side undertook to reduce its nuclear arsenal from the 6,000 warheads permitted by START II to 1,700–2,200 warheads. Still, on 13 December 2001, Bush gave six months notice of his intention to abrogate the ABM treaty. On 13 June 2002, when US withdrawal became official, Russia made good on its threat to withdraw from the START II treaty. This means that although Russia will be limited to the 1,700–2,200 warheads specified by the new strategic missiles reductions treaty, it will no longer be banned from deploying land-based missiles with multiple warheads. The Soviet-era multiwarhead SS-18 and SS-19 missiles can remain at the core of its nuclear arsenal.[21]

After 11 September

Russians expressed immediate and very genuine sympathy for Americans after the events of 9/11. Ordinary people left bunches of flowers outside the American Embassy. The four national television channels replaced planned programmes and advertising with non-stop coverage of the situation in the US. President Putin decried the 'barbarous terrorist acts aimed against wholly innocent people' and expressed Russia's 'deepest sympathies to the relatives of the victims … and the entire suffering American people'.[22] Many Russians believed that Americans now understood what Russia had suffered from terrorism. The pictures of New York reminded Duma International Affairs Committee chairman, Dmitri Rogozin, of 'the images from Moscow in 1999'.[23] In fact, lower Manhattan looked much more like Grozny after Russia's aerial onslaughts, but this similarity did not strike any Russian government officials.

Putin promised Russian support to the US administration in the form of increasing the supply of weapons to the Northern Alliance fighting the Taliban government in Afghanistan, opening Russian airspace to US aeroplanes for humanitarian flights, and participating in 'search and rescue operations' once the attack against Afghanistan began. The Russian military objected to his policy and it took a great deal of effort to persuade them that active cooperation was necessary (Antonenko 2001: 54). As a realist and a pragmatist, Putin understood that Russia would become irrelevant if it did not cooperate. But he also believed that knowledge of the difficulties of fighting in Afghanistan, the intelligence that Russia had been gathering, and its relationship with the Northern Alliance were assets that would contribute to Russia's status and make Russia a valuable US ally.

Russian commentators and politicians, many of them sounding as if they had been well briefed, specified what benefits Russia should get in return for Russia's cooperation in the anti-terrorist coalition. First, western criticism of the war against Chechnya should cease. President Putin had always claimed to be fighting a war against international terrorism in Chechnya and he had long insisted that Osama Bin Laden was funding Chechen terrorists, many of whom had been trained by Al-Qaeda. In any case, while the US Air Force was pounding

Afghanistan, western leaders could not criticise Russia for doing the same thing in Chechnya. Commentators also hoped that western creditors would offer forgiveness or at least a re-scheduling of Russian debt. They also demanded more active assistance in attaining early membership of the WTO.

Above all, however, Putin hoped to be able to use the leverage of his support for the anti-terrorist coalition to obtain concessions on the security issues that divided Russia and the US. In particular, he expected that President Bush would soften his uncompromising stance on the ABM treaty and BMD and accept that a reduction in strategic missiles should be negotiated and enshrined in a formal treaty negotiated between the two sides rather than reached unilaterally on each side and sealed with a handshake. Last, he hoped that further NATO enlargement might be postponed or even abandoned. Overall, he expected that in return for Russia's cooperation, there would be general recognition of Russia's great power status and of its influence over the territory of the former Soviet Union, an area which Russia has always maintained is its 'near abroad' and within its own sphere of influence.

At first it seemed as if Russia would be rewarded. Western criticism of Russia's policy in Chechnya was muted. President Bush called on the Chechen leadership to sever its links with Arab and Islamic extremists, including Bin Laden, immediately and unconditionally. Chancellor Gerhard Schröder and Prime Minister Silvio Berlusconi went further, almost excusing Russia on Chechnya. The final EU–Russian summit statement in October 2001 did not mention Russia's human rights abuses in Chechnya. The common threat of international terrorism and a united determination to eliminate it appeared to put human rights issues and democratisation, previously very active ingredients of the foreign policies of both the US and the EU, on the back burner.

As we have seen, however, on the important strategic issues that had produced tensions in US–Russian relations, President Bush remained intractable. Far from abandoning BMD in response to the evidence that the US had more to fear from low tech threats than to weapons of mass destruction, he re-affirmed his determination to proceed. He rejected Putin's offer to amend the ABM treaty and, instead, gave notice that the US intended to abrogate it.[24] Although Bush softened his position on the issue of arms reductions, agreeing to negotiate a bilateral treaty rather than relying on unilateral reductions, he refused to destroy US warheads as part of the agreement. Instead they would be put into store in case of future need. NATO did not reconsider the question of a second round of enlargement. On the other hand, on 28 May 2002 a new NATO–Russia Council (NRC) was established in which Russia has an equal voice on certain 'soft' security issues such as peacekeeping, civil emergency planning, defence modernisation and the proliferation of WMD. The EU also intensified its cooperation with Russia. In October 2001 a Joint Declaration was adopted 'on stepping up dialogue and cooperation on political and security matters' such as 'increasing international security and crisis prevention and management in Europe, non-proliferation and disarmament, conventional weapons exports, the Organisation for Security and Cooperation in Europe (OSCE), the United Nations and combating international terrorism'. In addition to the existing regular consultations, one-off meetings would be organised between the EU's Political and Security Committee and Russia in response to events. Monthly meetings would be held between the EU Political and Security Committee Troika and Russia 'in order to take stock of consultations on crisis prevention and management'.[25]

The EU and NATO's European members probably retained their objections to the abrogation of the ABM treaty and the decision to develop and deploy BMD. In the wake of the events of 9/11, however, they gave no sign of it in public. In the light of President Bush's statement that those who were not with the US were against it, EU member states were reluctant to oppose US policy, whether on their own or on Russia's behalf.

President Bush's State of the Union address in January 2002, in particular his identification of an 'axis of evil', began to drive US–EU differences out into the open. It also created a coalition of shared interests between the EU and Russia. Both had strong reasons to oppose the extension of the war against terrorism to Iran, Iraq and North Korea. Moscow shared with European capitals considerable disquiet at signs that the US was abandoning coalition building and returning to unilateralism. It seemed possible that, in its next phase, the war against terrorism that initially drew the US, EU and Russia together, might drive Russia and the EU apart from the US. However, the longstanding fear that overt differences of opinion and policy would provide a wedge with which Russia could divide Europe from the US made it unlikely that the EU would collaborate with Russia to oppose US policies. As the campaign against Iraq intensified, and some EU member states – particularly Germany under Gerhard Schröder – began publicly to oppose a military attack, it seemed likely that the second phase of the war against terrorism would create fissures within the EU more than it would unite the EU and Russia.

When the attack on Iraq was launched, Germany, France and Russia resolutely opposed US and British policy. Even when the war was won, they insisted that the UN should be responsible for establishing the peace, organising the government and reconstructing Iraq. But far from providing the wedge with which Russia could divide Europe from the US, the primary concern within the EU soon became both the need to re-establish cohesion and 'to strengthen the transatlantic partnership, which remains a fundamental strategic priority for the European Union'.[26] Nor did the Russians attempt to use the war against Iraq as a wedge since, like the EU, they too were concerned with what they perceived to be a longer-term and more important foreign policy priority, that is the US–Russian partnership.

Conclusion

The differences in US and EU policies towards Russia at the beginning of the twenty-first century are not unlike the differences that existed during the Cold War. Now, as then, the US and the Europeans share a common perception about Russia, but they do not always agree on the best means of dealing with it. These transnational differences were carried over from the Cold War into the post-Cold War era, and from the Clinton to the Bush administrations. In essence they relate to differences in US and EU foreign policy in general.[27] Europeans believe that their interests are best served by developing rules in international organisations to govern international behaviour. The US is more ready to pursue its goals unilaterally. Europeans do not usually envisage themselves in combat with their potential adversaries, whereas Americans do. Europeans are used to, and are more prepared to live with, vulnerability than Americans are. They are also predisposed to 'soft' approaches to security, involving economic and diplomatic tools and policies. The US is more preoccupied with the 'hard' military and technological means of protecting its security.

These differences are reflected in EU and US relations with Russia. In EU–Russian relations, low politics predominates. The relationship is highly institutionalised, with a dense network of regular political consultations and economic negotiations which take place within a problem-solving framework. This is not to say that issues of high politics are never discussed, or that EU–Russia summits are devoid of the rituals of high politics. Nor is it to suggest that there are no intractable conflicts of interest between the EU and Russia. In general, however, the relationship is regularised, and there is constant contact at a variety of levels so that the relationship can never be purely confrontational. The US–Russian relationship, on the other hand, is far less institutionalised. High politics predominates, particularly under the Bush administration. The US sees no reason to compromise with Russia or to take its interests into account. As a result, the relationship is far more confrontational than the EU–Russian relationship. The difference, however, essentially concerns the best means of dealing with Russia. There is no discrepancy in their goals. Both want to ensure that although Russia is excluded from Euro-Atlantic institutions, it has a peaceful and cooperative relationship with them, and remains an ally rather than reverting to being an adversary.

Notes

1   The Gore–Chernomyrdin Commission was the name given to the US–Russian Joint Commission on Economic and Technological Cooperation.
2   The omission does not imply that bilateral relations were insignificant. On the contrary, they were important. However, space constraints prevent a detailed consideration. The EU Common Strategy adopted in 1999 was intended to provide a framework within which bilateral relations would take place.
3   According to Gordon and Steinberg (2001: 1), 'a revitalized NATO was an important tool for the maintenance of American engagement and leadership, and its expansion to the new democracies – especially given the delays in their efforts to join the European Union (EU) – was a key part of the strategy'.
4   Willy Claes, Belgian Foreign Minister speaking on behalf of the EU, conceded that Yeltsin had acted unconstitutionally, but expressed EU support for him. See Reddaway and Glinski 2001: 418–19.
5   Cited in ibid., p. 428, from the *New York Times*, 5 October 1993.
6   See Wedel (1998) for an account of western collusion in the corrupt privatisations. For President Clinton's remarks, see the *Washington Post*, 4 July 1996.
7   The text of the Founding Act can be found in the NATO Handbook, 1998 edition. NATO On-line Library. <http://www.nato.int/docu/handbook/1998/handbook.pdf> (accessed 11 November 2000).

8   President Yeltsin's remarks are quoted in *Krasnaya zvezda*, 28 May 1997; President Clinton's in <http://www.nato.int/usa/president/s19970514c.htm> (accessed 11 November 2002).

9   The new strategic concept and the Membership Action Plan are published in *The Reader's Guide to the NATO Summit in Washington, 23–25 April 1999* (NATO Office of Information and Press, Brussels, 1999).

10 Condoleezza Rice's speech to the Republican National Convention Tuesday, 1 August 2000. Transcription at <http://www.washingtonpost.com/wp-srv/onpolitics/elections/ricetext080100.htm> (accessed 11 November 2002). Formerly an academic specialist on Soviet strategy, Rice had published widely on Soviet and east European foreign and defence policy. She had been special assistant to President George Bush (Senior) for national security affairs and senior director for Soviet affairs at the National Security Council.

11 For the text of Russia's PCA agreement, see *Official Journal of the European Communities* (OJL) 327, 28 November 1997.

12 Apart from the programmes managed by TACIS, EU food aid flows through the European Agricultural Guidance and Guarantee Fund, while humanitarian aid is handled by the European Community Humanitarian Organisation (ECHO). See <http://europa.eu.int/comm/external_relations/ceeca/tacis/index.htm> (accessed 27 May 2001). See also Cox and Chapman (1999).

13 The Common Strategy towards Russia is published in *Official Journal of the European Communities* (OJL) (1999/414/CFSP), L157/1, 24 June 1999. The Russian government responded with its own Medium-term Strategy for relations with the EU, published in *Diplomaticheskii vestnik*, No. 11, 1999, pp. 20–8.

14 *Rossiiskaya gazeta*, 4 April 2001, p. 4

15 See <http://europa.eu.int/comm/external_relations/russia/intro/index.htm> (accessed 11 November 2002).

16 The EU–Russia Energy Partnership can be found at <http://www.europa.eu.int/comm/energy_transport/en/lpi_en_3.html#discussions> (accessed 11 November 2002).

17 Cologne European Council, Presidency Conclusions, Press Release: Cologne (4 June 1999) – No. 150/99.

18 *Strategiya razvitiya otnoshenii Rossiiskoi Federatsii s Evropeiskim Soyuzam na srednesrochnuyu perspektivu (2000–2010 gg)* (The Medium-Term Strategy for Relations of the Russian Federation with the European Union, 2000–10), *Diplomaticheskii Vestnik*, No. 11, 1999, 20–8.

19 'Kontseptsiya Natsional'noi Bezopasnosti Rossiiskoi Federatsii' (The Concept of National Security), *Nezavisimoye Voennoye Obozreniye*, 14 January 2000; 'Voennaya doktrina Rossiiskoi Federatsii' (The Military Doctrine of the Russian Federation), *Nezavisimaya gazeta*, 22 April 2000.

20 *EU/US news*, Volume II, No. 7, May 2001, pp. 8–9. <europa.eu.int/comm/external_relations/us/eu_us_news/7.pdf> (accessed 11 November 2002).

21 For the text of the Strategic Offensive Reductions Treaty see the White House website, at < http://www.whitehouse.gov/news/releases/2002/05/20020524-3.html> (accessed 11 November 2002). The Russian Foreign Minister's statement announcing the withdrawal can be found on the Ministry of Foreign Affairs website at <http://www.gov.ru/main/ministry/isp-vlast47.html> (accessed 11 November 2002).

22 Reuters, 11 September 2001.

23 He was referring to the destruction wrought by bombs to two apartment blocks. Interfax, 20 September 2002.

24 Remarks By the President on National Missile Defence, 13 December 2001, at <http://www.whitehouse.gov/news/releases/2001/12/20011213-4.html> (accessed 11 November 2002).

25   The EU's Political and Security Committee (created in 2000) consists of senior national and European Commission officials and is intended to link the ESDP to the CFSP. Its Troika consists of officials representing the rotating EU Council Presidency, plus (in the Prodi Commission) Solana and Patten. The Joint Declaration can be found as Annex 4 of the report on the EU–Russia Summit held in Brussels, 3 October 2000 at <http://europa.eu.int/comm/external_relations/russia/summit_10_01 /dc_en.htm>, accessed 13 September 2002.

26   European Council, Statement on Iraq, 20 March 2003, <http://europa.eu.int/comm /external-relations/iraq/intro/council200303.htm>, accessed 5 May 2003.

27   I draw here from Philip Gordon's (2001) explanation of the differences in US and EU approaches to BMD, which applies as much to foreign policy in general as to the issue of missile defence.

7 The US and Europe in the Balkans

John Peterson

America fights the wars, Europe does the dishes?[1]

(Hurd: 2001: 23)

The ballet between Americans and Europeans is interesting to observe: publicly they are all smiles; privately the Americans are scathing about European feebleness of will, while the Europeans fulminate against American arrogance. In practice, each side knows it can't do without the other.

(Ignatieff 2000: 23)

In spring 2001, two years after the outbreak of the war in Kosovo, the political balance in the Balkans[2] seemed to shift decisively. A pro-western, post-Tudjman[3] government was elected in Croatia. The downfall of Slobodan Milosevic – ultimately leading to his arrest and trial for war crimes – took place via democratic means and without bloodshed in Serbia. A fragile peace, at least, held in Bosnia.

Then, suddenly, the region appeared on the brink of yet another war. The failure of NATO peacekeeping forces to seal Kosovo's border with Macedonia allowed Kosovar Albanian rebels to mobilise arms and fighters to try to foment the discontent of Macedonia's large (and repressed) Albanian minority. In March 2001, Albanian rebels attacked the border town of Tetovo, defended by the poorly equipped and trained Macedonian army. Eventually, no fewer than 67,000 people, most of them Macedonian Slavs, became refugees, adding considerably to the enormous sum total of misery inflicted on ordinary citizens in the Balkans after the outbreak of the Yugoslav civil war in 1991.

The events in Macedonia prompted frantic diplomacy by the EU, while the new American administration of George W. Bush – still only a few months old – remained mostly in the background.[4] Within a month, EU foreign ministers were signing a new political and economic ('Stabilisation and Association') accord with Macedonia, which traded the promise of eventual EU membership for an end to discrimination against Macedonian Albanians. The political unity of the EU, and speed with which it had acted, led Srgjan Kerim, Macedonia's Foreign Minister, to claim, 'This is a Europe that speaks with one voice and that is efficient'.[5] For his part, Arben Xhaferi, a leading ethnic Albanian Macedonian, insisted that, 'Troops and weapons did not stop the violence. What did was the hope provided by the EU that it would intervene in starting political negotiations'.[6]

The period marked a decisive if little-noticed shift in the balance of power between the US and EU in the Balkans. Despite the fragility of the Macedonian settlement, and the role of NATO in preserving it, the actions, influence, and magnetism of the EU have made it the clear diplomatic leader of the west in the region. Carl Bildt, the EU's envoy to the region for most of the 1990s, goes as far as to claim that 'the new empire [in the Balkans] is the EU'.[7]

This chapter develops four central arguments. First, the EU was still a very young foreign policy player when the wars in ex-Yugoslavia first broke out, but it emerged after they ended with a mostly single and effective policy towards the region. Second, the experience of the Balkans suggests that an important but unappreciated force for European unity in foreign policy is American prodding. Third, the EU became accepted by the US as 'a diplomatic equal in the Balkans' (Gardner Feldman 2001: 10), and even a lead partner after the focus shifted from military action to reconstruction and democratisation. Finally, US–EU exchanges have begun to supplant NATO and state-to-state contacts as a conduit for transatlantic exchanges on foreign policy, not least because of the commitment of both sides to the 'logic of arguing' (Risse 2000), even if the US commitment to this logic became subject to fresh doubts under a post-9/11 Bush administration.

The mechanisms for US–EU cooperation

The pattern of American diplomacy towards Europe changed fundamentally in the 1990s, embracing a new, institutionalised dialogue with the EU, as opposed to its individual member states or 'NATO Europe'. First the Bush (Senior) administration, via the Transatlantic Declaration of 1990, and then Bill Clinton, via the 1995 New Transatlantic Agenda (NTA), made the EU itself a central focus of US diplomacy. In Clinton's case, concern about the severe transatlantic split over Bosnia combined with high level lobbying by the US ambassador to the EU, Stuart Eizenstat, produced a major upgrade on the Transatlantic Declaration in the form of the NTA. It locked both sides into a thick, multilayered set of exchanges between officials, representatives of civil society, and political leaders, with twice-annual high level summits at its apex (see Philippart and Winand 2001a, 2001b; Pollack and Shaffer 2001a).

The engine room of the process was meant to be a Senior Level Group (SLG) of US sub-cabinet officials, senior European Commission officials, and top officials of states holding the rotating EU presidency. Centrally placed in the US–EU political dialogue (see Figure 3), the SLG was to cover all transatlantic issues and work at the centre of a compartmentalised, 'hub and spokes' set of dialogues on trade, aid, environment, transborder crime and so on. In practice, however, the SLG became increasingly dominated by the US and European foreign policy communities, with exchanges focused on a relatively narrow agenda of 'straight' (that is, non-economic or environmental) foreign policy issues.[8]

Five years on, the European Commission (2001: 7) claimed that the NTA had produced 'many success stories, the most prominent being the effective co-

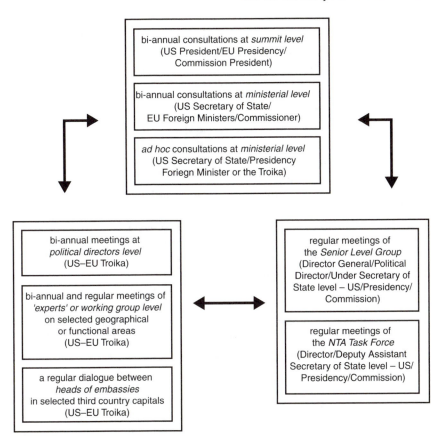

Figure 3 US–EU political dialogue
Source: Frellesen 2001: 322

ordination of policy and action in the Western Balkans'. Yet, results in other areas of policy were far less impressive. Both sides appeared to agree that the NTA process had become a 'vast bureaucratic symphony with few benefits' (European Commission 2001b: 16), which needed to become 'more action-oriented' (US State Department 2001: 1).[9]

One of the NTA's most vexing problems is that the urgent often drives out the important. Richard Holbrooke (1998: 67) mentions only one NTA summit in his Balkans diary and notes that it 'quickly turned into a Bosnia crisis session, and the rest of the agenda – including economic, trade, law enforcement, and environmental issues – was swept away'. Similarly, the 1998 London summit was dominated by a looming crisis over the Helms-Burton US trade law, leaving little time to discuss the deteriorating situation in Kosovo. Generally, however, the 'former Yugoslavia remained on top of the agenda of US–EU cooperation' throughout the 1990s (Frellesen 2001: 334).

Of course, the NTA framework was only one channel for transatlantic exchanges, and often not the most important one, especially when NATO intervened militarily in Bosnia in 1995 and Kosovo in 1999. The NATO operation in Bosnia was the first that it had ever undertaken in its history, and came at a time when its relevance was increasingly subject to question. NATO's bombing campaign in Kosovo began almost simultaneously with its 1999 Washington summit, which celebrated NATO's fiftieth anniversary and officially welcomed the Czech Republic, Hungary and Poland into its fold. However much NATO's interventions were driven by its perceived need to find a new, post-Cold War role,[10] the transatlantic exchanges that mattered most when the violence in the Balkans was at its worst took place within NATO.

Moreover, with the EU struggling to make its new CFSP work in 1994, both sides felt compelled to create the so-called Contact Group to coordinate western diplomacy towards Bosnia. The Contact Group brought together lead officials from the US and Russia along with Germany, France and the UK (and eventually Italy) in a cabal that left other EU states isolated. Its usefulness in keeping Russia on board and the US engaged could not be denied. The Contact Group – alongside the Group of Eight (G8) – facilitated the kind of agile, rapid decision making needed for crisis management, and also highlighted the EU's inability to provide it.

Meanwhile, bilateral (and multilateral) diplomacy between the US and the EU, and especially the European permanent members of the United Nations Security Council (France and the UK), shaped western policy after 1991 in important ways. Gradually, however, the UN was eased out of a front-line role in the Balkans. Especially after its humiliation in Bosnia, where UN-designated 'safe havens' were overrun with tragic humanitarian consequences, the UN was thoroughly marginalised by the time of Kosovo (see Travers 2001). In particular, the UN was forced to offer a humiliating apology after an internal investigation of its conduct in the days surrounding the fall of the safe haven of Srebrenica in July 1995, when approximately 7,000 Muslims were massacred (see Rohde 1997).[11]

The UN remained a player in the Balkans, not least because it administered post-war Kosovo alongside the EU and the OSCE. The International Criminal Tribunal for the former Yugoslavia in The Hague, to which the UN gave life, continued to pursue (with varying levels of assistance from NATO) and try war criminals, not least Slobodan Milosevic. But the widespread perception that the UN failed in Bosnia dealt a major blow to the organisation even before it failed to achieve consensus on what to do about Iraq in 2003.

In short, multiple institutions, above all NATO, were crucial channels of transatlantic exchange during and after the wars in the Balkans. However, after 1995 the transatlantic allies were locked by the NTA into meeting with each other biannually at the highest level, and at senior official levels another ten times per year (Philippart and Winand 2001b: 399).[12] The Balkans often dominated these exchanges, with policy effects that are examined below.

The record of US–EU cooperation

An evaluation of how much and how effectively the US and EU acted together in the Balkans after 1991 first requires analysis of each side's own policy actions towards the region.

The EU in the Balkans

The verdict on the EU's performance when hostilities in the Balkans initially erupted is quite clear: the Union failed miserably. In retrospect, the notion that the EU could somehow solve the problem by itself, brokering a peace settlement between Belgrade and the breakaway republics of Croatia and Slovenia, was naïve. The subsequent determination of Germany to recognise the independence of Croatia and Slovenia in 1991, although not without support from other EU member states, probably made the war in Bosnia inevitable.

The EU's performance during the Kosovo crisis is a matter of considerably more debate. One view holds that the EU was 'inconsequential' on Kosovo, and ended up either wielding old policy instruments that were inappropriate or supporting the initiatives of others, including NATO and the Americans (Ramirez and Szapiro 2001: 124). Advocates of this line tend to claim, along with the Greek Prime Minister Costas Simitis, that: 'The EU should have been bolder and developed an integrated strategy for the Balkans rather than intervening selectively and spasmodically'.[13]

Another view is that the EU came into its own as a foreign policy actor during and after Kosovo. The EU's aid effort to the Balkans – more than €5 billion from the Union alone (plus about the same from individual member states) in the 1990s – was massive. The EU's lead in applying economic sanctions and its 1999 Stability Pact for south eastern Europe, which included unilateral trade preferences, could fairly be described as 'the first EU preventative, strategic and pan-continental action' undertaken under the CFSP (Ramirez and Szapiro 2001: 130).

Furthermore, the EU emerged as a truly unitary foreign policy actor. The French President, Jacques Chirac, insisted that 'from Rambouillet through to the mission of the Finnish Presidency [of 1999], Europe showed a real solidarity and a real political dynamism'.[14] Once the NATO bombing over Kosovo began in late March 1999, the Union – especially Joshka Fischer, the German Foreign Minister, and Romano Prodi (at this point still Commission President-designate) – led efforts to find a diplomatic solution to the crisis. Fischer could rightly claim to be the father of the Stability Pact for south eastern Europe.[15] A German Green and former pacifist, Fischer commanded genuine respect in Washington (Gardner Feldman 2001: 19) – at least prior to the 2003 Iraqi war – and became a key ally of the US Secretary of State, Madeleine Albright, in pushing for a hard-line military response to Serb repression of Kosovar Albanians.[16] For his part, Prodi insisted, only days after the NATO bombing began, that the only solution for the Balkans was a 'new Southeastern Europe' closely associated to the EU. Within a few months after the bombing ended, the Union was co-chairing an international donor conference and then an international summit, which together channelled significant amounts of aid to Kosovo as well as Romania, Bulgaria, Macedonia, Albania and Bosnia.

Ultimately, the image of the EU as a key broker in the Kosovo conflict rests largely on the role played by Martti Ahtisaari, the Finnish President and the EU's envoy to the region. A fluent Russian speaker and experienced international diplomat, Ahtisaari (together with Victor Chernomyrdin, Russia's envoy) negoti-ated a ceasefire in early June 1999 that led to the withdrawal of Serbian forces from Kosovo. Having sealed the deal in Belgrade, Ahtisaari pointedly declined to hold a joint press conference with the US Deputy Secretary of State, Strobe Talbott, opting instead to report directly to the Cologne EU summit and appear at the EU's own press conference. Cologne saw European leaders adopt the Stability Pact for South Eastern Europe and, perhaps above all, anoint Javier Solana, NATO's Secretary-General and former Spanish Foreign Minister, as the EU's first High Representative for the CFSP.

This confluence of events and decisions, in some ways coincidental, made it easy to overplay the EU's new maturity as a foreign policy actor. NATO's role in ending the war was obviously crucial. Yet, the EU itself helped keep the European side of the alliance from collapsing despite the enormous domestic political diffi-culties of the Italian and Greek governments in supporting NATO bombing (see Deighton 2001). Moreover, Kosovo required a diplomatic solution of a kind that, arguably, could *only* have been brokered by the Union (together with Russia), with the Americans one step removed but clearly in the background. An arguably nec-essary, if insufficient, condition for European solidarity in Kosovo was the Clinton administration's stubborn insistence on it. In any event, the EU did enough in Kosovo to compel Ginsberg (2001: 357–8) to argue that:

> The EU did do what the EU traditionally does well: it contributed to the last minute diplomacy that led Milosevic to cease hostilities and it took interna-tional leadership of the stabilization of the countries of the western Balkans and of the reconstruction plan for Kosovo.

Later on, Solana emerged, alongside NATO's Secretary-General, Lord (George) Robertson, as the west's leading mediator in Macedonia. The pacification of the Macedonian conflict, which several times appeared ready to erupt during sum-mer 2001, suggested that the EU had learned to use the powerful symbolism of European unity as a diplomatic tool. In effect, the EU engineered a change of script: the discrediting of demands for ethnic separatism and the promulgation of values that could help the Balkans 'join Europe', including human rights, minority rights, and regional cooperation. As Albania's Foreign Minister put it:

> We want these borders to become less important. We are thinking of joining the EU so want this to be a region of cooperation. The philosophy of nation-alism, of extremism, goes against the principles of a united Europe. The nationalists and extremists want to close borders and create small nation-states. For us that would be counterproductive.[17]

The US and the Balkans

A close reading of the diplomatic history of the 1990s yields the verdict that US policy in the Balkans was truly decisive only twice.[18] The first time was after a (probably but not certainly) Serb mortar killed at least 37 people in a Sarajevo marketplace in February 1994, putting in motion a process ultimately leading to NATO action in Bosnia. The second time was when Serb forces and paramilitaries began systematic ethnic cleansing in Kosovo in spring 1999, again provoking a US-led military response. In between the Dayton summit on Bosnia (in 1995) and the Rambouillet conference on Kosovo (1999), the Balkans commanded little diplomatic attention in Washington. To illustrate the point, as late as February 1998 the US chief mediator in the Balkans described the Kosovo Liberation Army (KLA) as 'a small, irrelevant terrorist group'. Four months later, the KLA controlled about 40 per cent of Kosovar territory (Ramet 2001: 168).

Even when US policy was decisive, it was subject to powerful domestic constraints. The Dayton peace accord would have been undermined if Congress had not voted in favour of a large US contribution to the NATO peacekeeping force that was sent to enforce it, and Clinton had to lobby hard to get a positive vote. Just after NATO bombing began over Kosovo, no fewer than 41 US senators voted in favour of a motion that condemned the use of force against Yugoslavia.

The American aid effort to the Balkans never came close to matching the ambitions implied by Clinton's own injunction: 'if we can get peace, we should be prepared to put up a billion dollars' (quoted in Holbrooke 1998: 87). All US efforts to mediate in the Bosnian war relied heavily on what Richard Holbrooke (1998: 87) himself termed 'an obvious inconsistency': the promise of a 'comprehensive program for regional economic reconstruction', but very little US funding for it. By 2001 the American aid programme for the region, Support for East European Democracy (SEED), channelled about half of all of its funding – less than $400 million per year – to Bosnia. The entire SEED programme, with funding spread from the Balkans to the Baltics, was worth about same as EU aid to Kosovo alone.

The US paid in other ways: NATO spent nearly $6 billion on the military effort in Kosovo, and the Americans deployed 80 per cent of NATO aircraft and delivered 85 per cent of precision-guided munitions (UK House of Commons: 6). More than two thirds of troops in KFOR, the Kosovo peacekeeping force, were European. Yet, it was worth recalling that the original deadline for ending the US military presence in Bosnia was December 1996 (see David 2000). Nearly five years later, around 10,000 American troops were still on the ground in the Balkans when the Bush administration signalled that it wished to redeploy some or all to Afghanistan.

The toppling of hard-line nationalist governments via democratic elections in Serbia and Croatia in 2000 fed the view that the use of American military power brought peace to the Balkans, in much the same way as the Reaganite military build-up induced the collapse of the Soviet Union. Yet European complaints about the Clinton administration's lack of will to enforce the political side of the Dayton agreement in Bosnia were widely shared by American opinion leaders (see Lewis 1996: 6). In Kosovo, the Clinton administration badly miscalculated Milosevic's ability to hold out under fierce military attack. The weekend before a deal was struck to end the NATO bombing campaign, officials in the National Security Council admitted that the US stood on the brink of one its worst foreign policy disasters, and began seeking support for arming the KLA in lieu of bombing the Serbs, to the astonishment of European diplomats (see Peterson 2001: 181–2).

The Kosovo war ended because of deft diplomacy in which the EU was a major player. In retrospect, the outcome was difficult to celebrate as a triumph of either US foreign policy or NATO strategy (see Galen Carpenter 2000; Daalder and O'Hanlon 2000; Clark 2001). In Europe, at least, few quarrelled with the assessment of an Italian diplomat that the Balkans showed clearly how American foreign policy had become far 'more "issue-driven" than "vision-driven"' in the 1990s (Massari 2000: 104).

Transatlantic cooperation or conflict?

One way to gauge the importance of the NTA exchanges for western policy on the Balkans is to consider what transpired before and after the NTA was agreed in 1995. The four years after war broke out in 1991 were marked by plenty of transatlantic conflict or cases of solo diplomacy by the US, EU, or members of the latter. Germany shocked many of its EU partners, as well as the US, by unilaterally recognising Croatia and Slovenia in December 1991. The Clinton administration chose to ignore arms shipments from Iran to the Bosnian Muslims in 1994, when the US was meant to be helping to enforce an arms embargo. The Dayton accord was brokered by the US with EU diplomats literally locked out of the negotiating rooms.

By the time the NTA was agreed at the end of 1995, Croatia and Slovenia were internationally recognised states. The Dayton accord on Bosnia was in place. Kosovo was smouldering but subdued. Thus, the focus of the NTA was on 'peace and post-war reconstruction in the former Yugoslavia'. Specifically, the US and EU committed themselves to joint action to:

- restore respect for human rights in the Balkans;
- support the War Crimes Tribunal (WCT);
- establish democratic elections in Bosnia;
- demilitarise the region; and
- coordinate their aid efforts together with other international institutions.

(Gardner 1997: 123).

Scrutinising this list against eventual achievements, the record of post-NTA cooperation is mixed but not unimpressive.

Respect for human rights in ex-Yugoslavia was always going to be mainly a product of domestic political developments, as opposed to western policies. NATO's effort to ensure that war refugees had the right to return to their original homes achieved limited success at first (see Eldridge 2001: 46), but it was repeatedly endorsed by the

US and EU and eventually made considerable progress. As Paddy Ashdown, the EU's special representative (and international community's 'High Representative') in Bosnia put it, 'we've invented a new human right here, the right to return after a war' (International Crisis Group (ICG) 2002). More generally, western insistence that large aid infusions were conditional on human rights improvements gave a boost to the campaigns of reformist governments that were elected in Serbia and Croatia, as well as in the Muslim–Croat sector of Bosnia, in 2001.[19]

Both the US and EU gave considerable support to the WCT. The key to charging and apprehending suspected war criminals who remained at large was the US, as only it possessed the intelligence and military resources to get hold of suspects and then provide WCT prosecutors with the legal evidence needed to secure prosecutions. Nevertheless, following reports of suspected war criminals moving freely around the region, the 1997 election of the Blair government in the UK changed the equation considerably. Within months, British troops swooped on the Serbian enclave to seize a number of suspects, probably aided by American intelligence. By spring 2001, the biggest catch of all, Milosevic, was in a Serbian jail and then was shipped to The Hague after both the US and EU insisted that no new western aid would be available unless he faced trial there. The WCT had plenty of suspects in custody to keep it busy. An extraordinary experiment in the enforcement of 'moral univeralism' (Ignatieff 2000: 129), the WCT was an area where the US (at least under Clinton)[20] and the EU appeared to push each other to embrace something considerably higher than the lowest common denominator.

As for democratisation in the Balkans, US and EU efforts were mostly joint ones, and largely successful. In 1997, municipal elections in Bosnia and Assembly elections in Republika Srpska both took place peacefully. By 2001, the Muslim–Croat alliance in the Croat–Bosniak half of Bosnia was on the ropes, with Bosnian Croats pulling out of its joint federal executive. But both the US and EU moved quickly to condemn the move, and to encourage moderates and isolate extremists amongst the three ethnic groups in Bosnia. Transatlantic efforts to boost the Serbian opposition and map out a 'post-Milosevic scenario' were very closely coordinated and mostly led by the EU (see Gardner Feldman 2001: 9).

Demilitarisation in the region was mostly a NATO task, and one outside its traditional remit. The NATO force sent to Macedonia to supervise weapons collection from Albanian rebels ('Operation Essential Harvest') in August 2001 faced a daunting mission, with the Albanian–Kosovo border region awash with arms and criminal gangs trafficking them. Yet both Solana and Robertson, representing the EU and NATO, insisted that it must take place. Nearly half of the NATO force consisted of British troops, with the American contribution limited to helicopter lift support and medical facilities. In the event, Operation Essential Harvest went smoothly, despite doubts about how much it really accomplished (see ICG 2001b). At the very least, it showed the determination of the US and EU to try to pursue demilitarisation despite the difficulties of doing so in a region flooded with arms and inured to war.

The post-war aid effort saw the US and EU engage in far less coordination than was either desirable or even reasonable. The flamboyant UN 'governor' of

Kosovo, Bernard Kouchner, echoed American complaints about the lack of coor-dination between national European contributions, and between them and EU or US contributions, as well as delays in their delivery.[21] Meanwhile, US aid to the Balkans was miserly, with Congress capping the US contribution to Kosovo at 15 per cent of total western aid. Most American aid went to Bosnia and much of it was wasted due to rampant crime and corruption (see Eldridge 2001: 46–9). However, a number of attempts were made, at least, to coordinate US with European contributions and there is evidence that each side shamed the other on occasion into faster or more generous aid actions (see Frellesen 2001: 334–5; Gardner Feldman 2001: 7–8). Moreover, the Clinton administration lobbied Congress hard, alongside the EU, to defeat the Byrd-Warner Amendment (endorsed at the Senate committee stage on a vote of 23 to 3), which proposed to withhold American aid until Clinton certified that the EU had delivered on all of its commitments to Kosovo (Gardner Feldman 2001: 15–16).

In short, if the goals the US and EU set for themselves in the Balkans in 1995 are a true test of transatlantic cooperation, the two partners can be judged to have passed the test, although certainly not with anything close to a perfect score. By no means were all policy goals realised. Yet, the objectives set out in the NTA were defined and pursued, for the most part, in a truly joint way, and one which would have been far less easy to imagine in the absence of the NTA.

Bush and the Balkans

One week before Americans voted in November 2000, one US pundit bellowed: 'whoever wins the presidential election, Europeans can be sure that America's days as a well-bred doormat for EU political and military pretensions are coming to an end' (Bolton 2000). A few weeks later, the author of the diatribe was US Undersecretary of State for Arms Control. One journalist spoke for many in observing that the new Bush administration seemed 'philosophically further from European ideals and goals than perhaps any US administration in the last 50 years' (Baker 2001: 9).

Even in this new political context, there was evidence to suggest that some habits of transatlantic cooperation in the Balkans had become ingrained to the point where they would live through the change in the US administration. Before the terrorist attacks of 9/11, no other foreign policy problem of the post-Cold War era was more complicated or difficult to solve than the wars in the Balkans. It was not surprising that the transatlantic allies, each enchained by powerful domestic constraints, clashed bitterly on matters of strategy. Take, for example, enormous friction between the closest of bilateral allies – the US and UK – over the deployment of ground troops in Kosovo, with Albright essentially taking the UK side in arguing that ground forces could not be ruled out. Somehow, the transatlantic alliance lived through it.

One reason why is that the NTA process, while not eclipsing other channels of communication, gave the US and EU a conduit for dialogue that helped to smooth over disputes that flared *within* other channels, such as NATO or the UN.

For instance, the Chief Prosecutor of the ICT put the failure to apprehend suspected Bosnian war criminals down to a lack of cooperation between French and American units of the NATO-led multinational force.[22] Yet, considerable transatlantic solidarity was shown on the question of how to deal with the electoral defeat of Slobodan Milosevic in September 2000. Both the US and EU offered significant support, with aid and a promise to lift sanctions, to the Serbian opposition under Vojislav Kostunica.

Six months later, the western response to the outbreak of violence along the Kosovo–Macedonia border was single-minded and effective. It was EU-led but it featured vital US activism, including a visit by Bush's Secretary of State, Colin Powell, to Skopje.[23] It was also about what one would have expected under the Clinton administration.

Of course, it was possible to argue that the Balkans was a *sui generis* case, and the only region in the world where the US and EU operated something like a joint foreign policy. However, the NTA process also gave rise to transatlantic solidarity on other foreign policy issues where the EU was active and had real leverage: that is, in relations with the Union's 'near-abroad' (leaving aside the Middle East). By the end of the 1990s, the US and EU usually spoke with one voice and often combined resources on aid projects and support for democratisation in Turkey, Ukraine, Cyprus, the Caucasus, Russia, and central and eastern Europe (see Philippart and Winand 2001a).

Yet, in all of these places, as well as in the Balkans, it is now the EU that usually takes the policy lead on non-military questions and deploys real resources, especially aid or trade concessions. The Balkans is simply where the EU policy lead is most visible and expensive. To illustrate the point, the Union and its member states targeted more than €19 billion in aid to the Balkans for 2000–6, or in excess of seven times more than the US earmarked for 27 countries in Europe and 'Eurasia'.

Moreover, the EU has begun to lead even on 'hard' security in the Balkans by operationalising, for the first time, the capacity for crisis management built into its fledgling ESDP. In early 2003, the Union took over the UN-led police mission to Bosnia, and then NATO's 450-strong peacekeeping force in Macedonia. Far more ambitious was the Union's pledge to take on command of the 12,000-strong NATO peacekeeping operation in Bosnia by 2004, which was made possible after a landmark deal on EU–NATO relations at the 2002 Copenhagen EU summit.

In short, American political, economic and (particularly) military support are likely to remain essential to reconstruction in the Balkans for years to come. But the US is now effectively a junior partner to the EU in the Balkans, regardless of who is in the White House or what their attitude is to nation-building or multilateral cooperation.

Conclusion

The record of US–EU cooperation in the Balkans sheds light on the nature of the transatlantic relationship on matters of foreign policy more generally. First, policy cooperation in the Balkans has been considerably more intensive than cooperation on policy towards most other areas of the world, but also reflective of a fair amount of joint US–EU action in the regions to the Union's east and south. Second, the EU's policy leadership in the Balkans was unprecedented in a transatlantic context but also indicative of the Union's slow maturation as a unified foreign policy actor. By 2001 it was plausible to claim that 'today in the Balkans there is no distinctive British, German or French policy – as opposed to occasional jostlings for position' (Hurd 2001: 23).

After 1991, western policy in the Balkans was frequently subject to bitter Euro-American disputes. Ultimately, however, the alliance held. Why? At least part of the answer may be that both sides remained committed via the NTA process to joint action as a policy goal *per se* and, more broadly, to the 'logic of arguing'. This logic governs negotiations in which actors seek, above all, a 'reasoned consensus' on common goals, as opposed to a strict and complete fulfilment of their own fixed preferences (see Risse 2000).

A precondition for arguing (as opposed to bargaining) is that both sides come to the table prepared to change their preferences. Logical, well-structured arguments must have the potential to prevail over sheer, naked interests. Over the course of more than a decade of conflict in the Balkans, preferences were never fixed for long on either side of the Atlantic on much besides the general goal of 'peace'. Meanwhile, the NTA gave the US and EU institutions a set of forums that at least in theory accommodated this style of argumentation. The NTA's designation of the EU as a (even *the*) vital interlocuter of the US in transatlantic relations probably meant that the 'Europe' at the table was one that was more committed to the logic of arguing than was any other version (i.e. individual EU states or European NATO): whenever a lead external policy role is assigned to supra-national officials such as Javier Solana, or representatives of the EU's rotating presidency, for whom consensus-building *within* the EU is a constant preoccupation, 'Europe' becomes instinctively prone to the idea that reasoned consensus is a vital goal.

It may well be that US and EU interests simply converged or overlapped in the Balkans in the 1990s, and just enough to prevent outright rupture. It is also possible to argue that the US commitment to the logic of arguing disappeared along with the Clinton administration. Yet, George W. Bush was the third consecutive President – following Clinton and Bush Senior – to express America's aspiration for a Europe 'peaceful, undivided, and free' (all using these exact words) during his first visit to Europe (Gardner Feldman 2001: 2).

On the same trip, Bush also gave voice to the familiar litany that: 'When Europe grows in unity, Europe and American grow in security'.[24] In the Balkans, at least, one US policy aim has become well entrenched: to pressure, cajole or manoeuvre its European allies in the direction of unity, and in a way that chimes with wider US objectives. At every crucial juncture after 1991, a fundamental American objective was to encourage the EU to act as one; from the outbreak of the Yugoslav–Slovene conflict when US Secretary of State, James Baker (with DeFrank 1995: 483), judged it 'time to make the Europeans step up to the plate and show they could act as a unified power', to the outbreak of fighting in Macedonia. When the US disengaged, and thus did not press the objective as hard, the EU lapsed into internal

bickering and disunity, as it did over the recognition of Slovenia and Croa
However more mature the EU is now than it was in the early 1990s, it often s
needs the Americans to goad it to act as one. Regardless of transatlantic tensions
over Iraq in 2003, this role is emerging as perhaps the most important played by the
US as a 'European power'.

For its part, the EU will face enormous responsibilities in the Balkans far into
the future. Total annual EU aid to the region was still about €900 in 2003 but was
set to fall to about €500 per year by 2005. Reformist parties generally saw their
support decline in the Bosnian, Croatian, Kosovar, and Serbian elections in 2002
(amidst generally low turn-outs). Albania and Montenegro were far from 'solved'.
Bosnia's national wealth remained below half its pre-war levels. No country in the
region had attracted foreign investment of any appreciable magnitude. Alarm
bells went off in western capitals in late 2002 when reports surfaced of illegal
arms sales to Iraq by state-owned factories in the Serb region of Bosnia and
Serbia, and no less so than when earlier allegations were made (later denied by
NATO) that Al-Qaeda was operating in Bosnia, Kosovo and Albania
(Triantaphyllou 2001).

In the Balkans, as on most other foreign policy issues, the EU remained perfectly
capable of future disunity and hypocrisy. The George W. Bush administration
promised to be less tolerant of the EU's adolescent behaviour than its predecessor.
Yet, there was no doubt that the EU had succeeded in impressing upon political
leaders in the Balkans that they faced a 'fundamental choice ... between becoming
ever more Balkan, in the worst sense of the word, and becoming more European,
in the best sense of the word' (Bildt 2001: 158). The Union had succeeded in this
mission *only* because it had acted as one in the Balkans at crucial moments, usually
under American pressure and in close coordination with the US. But in the
Balkans, finally and really for the first time, it was the EU itself that took the lead
on a major foreign and security policy issue of transatlantic concern.

Notes

1 This question is posed by Hurd in a rhetorical sense. This chapter is an updated, con-
   densed, and considerably revised version of a Working Paper published by the
   European University Institute (see Peterson 2001).
2 For the purposes of this paper, 'the Balkans' refers to five states in the western part of
   the Balkan region: Albania, Bosnia, Croatia, Macedonia, and Yugoslavia (incorporating Serbia, Montenegro and Kosovo). Slovenia, which stood to join the EU in 2004, is
   mostly outside this paper's purview.
3 Franco Tudjman, a ruthless ultra-nationalist, was President of Croatia from 1991
   until his death in 1999.
4 No senior US official visited Macedonia in the six weeks after the outbreak of hostilities. The EU's High Representative, Javier Solana, made four visits and the German
   Foreign Minister, Joschka Fischer, made one.
5 Quoted in *Financial Times*, 10 April 2001.
6 Quoted in *European Voice*, 5–11 April 2001.
7 Quoted in *Financial Times*, 29 March 2000.
8 This point was confirmed in interviews with a variety of participants in the NTA
   process conducted in Washington, Brussels, London and Edinburgh in 2000–1.

9   Looking across the range of NTA activities, a rough estimate is that only about 5 per cent of the policy initiatives targeted in 1995 for US–EU exchanges have yielded some kind of actual joint action, while another 20 or 25 per cent have yielded some kind of cooperation, or adjustment of policy by one side taking account of the policy of the other (Philippart 2001). Overwhelmingly, the NTA simply involves the exchange of information.

10   Democrat Joseph Biden, the Chair of the US Senate's Foreign Relations Committee, claimed that 'A failure in Bosnia would signal the beginning of the end for NATO' (quoted in David 2000: 6). Some believed Kosovo actually did send this signal; the exposure of NATO Europe's military weakness and US frustration with 'excessive European meddling' in the planning and operation of the NATO campaign in Kosovo helps explain why the US (mostly) refused European offers to contribute militarily to the war in Afghanistan in 2001 (Gordon 2001/02).

11   The UN was far from alone in shouldering the blame for Srebrenica. An investigative report in 2002 uncovered a long series of avoidable errors by Dutch political leaders and army commanders (working under a UN mandate) that were crucial to the massacre (see Netherlands Institute of War 2002).

12   The frequency of meetings obviously cannot be taken as an indication of the importance of the exchanges. The point was reinforced in 2001 when both sides agreed that US–EU summits should be scaled back to one per year (instead of two) in future (see Commission 2001; US State Department 2001).

13   Quoted in *Financial Times*, 28 July 1999.

14   Quoted in *Financial Times*, 7 June 1999. Many would dispute the claim about the Rambouillet process, launched by the Contact Group and chaired by the Americans to try to achieve a political settlement on Kosovo during the winter of 1998–9 (see Rubin 2000a, 2000b).

15   The Stability Pact for south eastern Europe was launched in June 1999 under the auspices of the OSCE, but as an EU initiative which wove together the efforts of the Union, NATO, G8, and international financial institutions to promote reform in the Balkans. However, the EU's own Stabilisation and Association Agreements (SAA), eventually offered to Albania, Macedonia, Bosnia, Croatia and Yugoslavia, were viewed as far more important in the region because they offered the prospect of eventual EU membership (see UK House of Commons 2000), even if only two had been signed (with Croatia and Macedonia) and only Croatia's was in the process of implementation by early 2003.

16   According to Rubin (2000b: IX), Fischer stunned fellow ministers during a conference call by blurting out, 'Refugees being herded into boxcars, the killing of intellectuals, there hasn't been anything like this since the Nazis'.

17   Paskal Milo, quoted in Judah 2001: 37.

18   Arguably, a third case was the US diplomacy leading to a peace deal between Greece and Macedonia in September 1995, which defused very powerful tensions and led to the lifting of a Greek economic blockade of the former Yugoslav republic.

19   Western efforts to promote reform in the Republika Srpska half of Bosnia were largely fruitless and it remained mostly 'unreformed and true to its wartime self' (ICG 2001c: 1).

20   Things changed under the Bush administration: Washington suspended aid to Belgrade in early 2002 over non-cooperation on war criminals, but the EU refused to follow suit (Abramowitz and Hurlburt 2002).

21   See Kouchner's comments quoted in *Financial Times*, 17 December 1999.

22   Quoted in *Financial Times*, 22 August 2000.

23   The perception in the region that the US tacitly favoured the ethnic Albanians in the conflict was illustrated by an attack on the US Embassy in Skopje by Macedonian Slavs in July 2001. As such, the claim that the crisis in Macedonia was averted through the use of 'Colin Powell's fax machine' is a gross oversimplification (see Judt 2002: 17).

24   Quoted in 'Bush's Berlin speech extracts', available at <http://news.bbc.co.uk/1/hi/world/europe/2004982.stm> (accessed 21 January 2003).

8   The Middle East

Focus of discord?

Costanza Musu and William Wallace

The terrorist attacks of 9/11 arose from deep antagonism between the US and Muslim radicals within the Arab world – and further deepened that antagonism on both sides. In contrast, European governments were neither the target of Al-Qaeda nor central players in the western response. No European government had significant influence in Saudi Arabia; only the UK had close relations with any governments in the Gulf. Individually and collectively, European governments had failed to wield any influence over the Arab–Israeli conflict, as the increasingly close relationship between Israeli governments and US administrations shut European allies out.

Once the intervention in Afghanistan had successfully dislodged the Taliban regime, western strategy towards the Muslim world became a central – and highly contentious – issue in transatlantic relations. It exposed very different styles of foreign policy – between 'civilian power' Europe and military power US, as well as between European governments collectively operating as regional powers and the US operating a global strategy. It brought out different assumptions about relations between 'civilisations' – between the 'Judaeo-Christian' western world and the Muslim world. Accusations of 'appeasement' and 'anti-semitism' on one side, and undertones of anti-Americanism on the other, have added a bitterness to the public debate echoing that of the 1973–4 European–American dispute – which had also focused on Israel and the Arab oil-producing world. It was primarily over policy towards the Middle East region, both towards the Arab–Israeli conflict and the 'axis of evil' states of Iraq and Iran, that US–European relations deteriorated after the surge of transatlantic sympathy and solidarity that followed 9/11. Considerable mutual distrust characterised the relationship one year later.

Transatlantic discord partly reflected the gross imbalance of military power deployable across the Middle East region. The US, with the ability to deploy extensive air, naval and ground forces across the region, was able to pursue its own grand strategy, if necessary without reference to its European allies. European governments, without the option of resorting to military force except under American leadership, necessarily preferred multilateral diplomacy and negotiated compromise. But the roots of discord also reflected different historical experiences. Britain and France, which had had strategic approaches to the Middle East, now lacked the military or political weight to act alone, but the EU's cumbersome procedures for common foreign policy had not yet agreed any European strategy, beyond declarations of principles and diplomatic exchanges. Different domestic assumptions about western interests in the region also pulled transatlantic governments apart. American strategy, potentially unilateral, met European aspirations for influence, unavoidably multilateral, producing contradictory pressures for convergent and divergent approaches.

Allies of a kind: the roots of discord

American and European approaches to the Middle East have reversed in the 45 years since the Anglo-French attempt (in collaboration with Israel) to force regime change in Egypt. In 1956 Great Britain was the dominant external power in the Middle East, and France the colonial power in North Africa. Both saw Gamel Abdul Nasser as the personification of Arab radicalism, and his displacement as the key to its defeat. The Eisenhower administration however insisted that there were broader western interests at stake in relations with the independent Arab oil-producing states, and brokered a withdrawal that left the Suez Canal in Egyptian hands and the Nasser regime still in power. The reversal in American and European positions began with the 1967 Middle East war, as the French government moved from a pro-Israeli to a pro-Arab stance and as the US moved to become the major source of political, financial and military support for Israel. The 1973 Middle East war took this development further, with the US providing crucial support and re-supply for Israel, and the member governments of the European Community responding by launching a 'Euro-Arab Dialogue', despite the active disapproval of the US administration.

Over nearly three decades since then, differences of approach to the Middle East have lain behind many of the most delicate transatlantic differences on the terms of the political and security partnership.[1] With Britain's announcement in 1967 of the withdrawal of its remaining forces from the Arabian/Persian Gulf, the US emerged in its turn as the dominant external power in the region, with fleets in both the eastern Mediterranean and the Indian Ocean, and bases from which to project air power. The US worked with and through a succession of strategic partners within the Middle East: first Iran, until the overthrow of the Shah, then Saudi Arabia, and increasingly also Israel – and Turkey. European governments pursued active trade policies towards the oil-producing states of the Gulf, in particular, seeking to offset their oil-dependence through exports of manufactures, technology and services. But successive US administrations made it clear that it was for Washington to define western security and political priorities towards the region, and for its European partners to provide support, and if necessary financial assistance.

Consultations among west European governments about autonomous initiatives towards the Middle East, within the framework of European Political Cooperation, were actively discouraged, both from American missions in Europe and directly from Washington. Discussions within NATO about 'out of area' security threats were implicitly about deployment of forces to North Africa and the Middle East, under American leadership and following American priorities. Under US leadership, NATO launched its own Mediterranean Dialogue, in competition with successive EU initiatives towards its dependent south. Divergent approaches to the Israel–Palestine conflict have often been at the core of US–European differences; but different assumptions about regimes in Iran, Iraq, Syria and Libya have also divided transatlantic allies. The European approach has rested on 'civilian power' instruments: diplomacy, trade, financial assistance. The American approach has rested on all these *and* the ability to project credible military power.

Divergence in political approaches to the region has reflected divergent domestic contexts for policy since the 1970s, as well as divergent geopolitical interpretations of the region. The political organisations of America's six million Jews have gradually become more conservative in orientation, and more supportive of the settlement policies of Likud governments. American Christian fundamentalists have also taken up the cause of Israel, interpreting the Bible in support of its contemporary claims, with demonstrable effect on George W. Bush's foreign policy. Meanwhile Islam in America, was, until recently, most visibly the religion of black power. It is now difficult to think of a single Islamic figure who could claim to be a 'leader' of American Muslims, and who could act as an effective voice for their interests in the corridors of American power.

In many European countries, by contrast, substantial Muslim migration has accustomed rising generations to its diverse culture. Political dialogue, social interaction, and economic and financial interdependence have built links between élites. Some 12 million Muslims were living in the EU in the 1990s, a substantial majority of them born within the EU and citizens of member states. The long-established Jewish communities in Britain (300,000) and France (600,000), as well as the small remnant in Italy (30,000) have remained close to Labour politics – and politicians – in Israel, and grown less supportive of the hard-line positions adopted by Likud.

For European governments, the Mediterranean is the near south, the Middle East an extension of the EU's 'Mediterranean' partnership policies. 'EuroMed' extends as far as Jordan and Syria, incorporating the complex politics of the Arab–Israeli conflict within a 'partnership' primarily designated as economic. In the 1970s the pursuit of Mediterranean partnership overlapped with a Euro-Arab Dialogue that included all the Arab League countries from Morocco to Oman (but not Iran); in the 1980s there was a separate 'dialogue' with the Gulf states. Thus, Europe could be accused of policy incoherence in the face of the complex politics of the region. A more charitable view would be that the international politics of the Gulf are only partly linked to the Arab–Israeli tension of the western Middle East, and that the issues that drive (say) Algerian domestic politics and foreign policy are rather different from those that drive the politics and foreign policy of Yemen.

For the US, the Mediterranean has been the southern flank of NATO, and the essential west–east corridor through which to project power across the Middle

East and Central Asia. Since the end of the Cold War American strategists have expanded their definition of the region, as 'the greater Middle East', to include not only Turkey but also the Turkic-speaking countries of central Asia, promoting pipelines from the Caspian across the Caucasus through Turkey that will deliver oil to the west without passing through Iran or the Gulf, thus weakening the hold of the Gulf states on global oil markets. The first Bush administration's concept of 'rogue states' also redefined its strategic approach: Iraq, Iran and Libya were central to this concept, Syria a further 'state of concern', with only North Korea lying far beyond the imagined limits of the greater Middle East. Iraq's occupation of Kuwait, in August 1990, was a direct challenge to global order and global energy security, to which European states responded under American leadership. But the predominant pattern of European policies was of differentiated relations with particular states and groups of states. American policymakers, in contrast, have designed strategic concepts for the entire region – though finding it difficult to reconcile policies towards Israel with policy towards the region as a whole, in particular their partnership with Saudi Arabia.

The depth of radical Muslim antagonism to the US revealed by the 9/11 attacks thus burst upon governments and publics on opposite sides of the Atlantic with significantly differing perceptions of the Middle East, of the Israel–Palestine conflict, and of the Arab and the Muslim world. The immense political and psychological impact on the US of this direct attack unavoidably widened the gap. European observers sympathised with the suffering and felt the outrage. But they placed this new scale of transnational terrorism within the context of the lower level of transnational terrorism their countries had suffered over the previous generation – which had included Arab terrorist attacks against American (and Israeli) targets on European soil. As observers, too, of American strategy towards the region over previous years, largely without influence over that strategy and often critical of its sweep, there was an unavoidable undercurrent of differentiation: a feeling that the US and the Muslim world were locked into a confrontation that both jeopardised European security and ignored European views.

The rest of this chapter explores the development of this differentiation since the end of the 1960s, the interaction of European and American approaches to the region, and their policies towards the oil-producing states, the Israel–Palestine conflict, and Arab and Muslim regimes. It thus attempts to place the Middle East policy of the George W. Bush administration, and transatlantic responses to the devastating attack by Al-Qaeda terrorists from Saudi Arabia, Egypt and Yemen, in a historical context.

America in Britain's place: regional hegemony 1970–90

To see the US Sixth Fleet at anchor in Crete's Souda Bay, where in previous centuries British, Venetian and Ottoman fleets had sheltered, is to capture an image of the US as regional hegemon, projecting power across the eastern Mediterranean and the near East. American displacement of the British and French as external forces in a weakly-integrated region of insecure regimes had begun with the 1954 overthrow of the Mossadeq government in Iran, in an American-inspired coup that gave the US a close relationship with a state previously within Britain's imperial zone of influence. The failure of the Franco-British intervention in Egypt in 1956, followed by changes of regime in 1958 in Iraq, French withdrawal from Algeria in 1961, the Baath takeover in Syria in 1966 and the collapse of the monarchy in Libya in 1969, marked staging posts in the decline of British and French influence. This decline culminated in Britain's withdrawal of troops from Aden, and its announcement in 1967 that it would withdraw its remaining forces from 'East of Suez', leaving only a limited engagement in Oman and training agreements with the Gulf sheikdoms and with Saudi Arabia.

The American partnership with Saudi Arabia dated from World War II, and was built upon mutual interests in oil and security. The post-1954 'strategic partnership' with Iran had extended from Pakistan across Iraq to Turkey in the anti-Soviet Central Treaty Organisation (CENTO), although it was broken by the revolution in Baghdad in 1958. The 1973 Arab–Israeli war deepened American engagement, both to Israel and to Israel's hostile neighbours. American efforts to persuade Egypt to pursue more constructive relations with Israel led to a new political partnership from 1979 post-Camp David. American troops were committed to Lebanon (where US marines had already briefly landed in 1958) in 1982, and remained until terrorist attacks on US barracks as well as French troops forced withdrawal. From 1973 onwards, American diplomats were actively engaged in attempts to mediate between the Israeli government and its Arab neighbours. From 1977, the shift in the governing coalition in Israel from Labour to Likud also cooled Israeli relations with western Europe, and warmed relations with the US. The personal hostility that Prime Minister Begin expressed towards European political leaders strengthened the impression that only American policymakers had influence and standing in Israel.

The unexpected collapse of the Shah's regime in Iran in 1979, transformed America's position in the Gulf region. The humiliation of the occupation of the US Embassy in Teheran, with American diplomats taken hostage, was deepened by the failure of the US military operation to rescue them. American support flowed to Iraq in its ten-year war with Iran, with the tacit approval of Saudi Arabia, the Gulf states and Kuwait (although there were clandestine exchanges with Iraq's enemy in the 'Iran-Contra affair'). American ships patrolled the Gulf throughout the 1980s, protecting Kuwaiti and other oil tankers. Missiles from an American ship shot down an Iranian airliner, mistaken for a military aircraft, in 1988. Partnership with Saudi Arabia had now expanded into a substantial military build-up, as Washington looked to Riyadh to replace Teheran as the bastion of western-sponsored stability in the Gulf area.

European political influence, in contrast, had shrunk with the withdrawal of European forces. West European governments had hoped in the 1960s to shift from a coal-based energy economy to nuclear power. But the rising costs and uncertainties of nuclear energy, and the ready availability of cheap oil from North Africa and the Middle East, had led instead to dependence on imported oil. The impact of the 1967 Arab–Israeli war, and of the Israeli occupation of the West Bank that followed, also led to a gradual shift in attitudes towards the conflict, most of all on the political left and in the younger generation, who no longer saw Israel as a progressive democracy establishing a European-style state, and increasingly saw Palestinians as suffering under colonial occupation in an anti-colonial age. But most governments maintained established positions. The most detailed exchange of views at the first meeting of European Community (EC) foreign ministers in the context of political cooperation in November 1970 had been on the situation in the Middle East, with the French government failing to persuade its five partners to adopt a more critical approach to Israel (Wallace and Allen 1977).

The success of the Organisation of Petroleum Exporting Countries (OPEC) in rapidly raising oil prices, between 1970 and 1973, inflicted a sharp shock on west European economies. The OPEC oil embargo that followed the 1973 Arab–Israeli war, and was targeted most sharply at the pro-Israeli Dutch government, was a greater shock. Against the background of shifting public opinion, European governments now acceded to French proposals for a change of policy, agreeing with a delegation of Arab ministers at the Copenhagen European summit to launch a 'Euro-Arab Dialogue' between the EC and the Arab League. The American response was furious, with relations between Henry Kissinger and Michel Jobert, the French Foreign Minister, descending to personal invective. The US was attempting to broker 'small steps' away from confrontation between the Arab coalition and Israel, while bringing together western oil-consuming states under its leadership in a new International Energy Agency. Meanwhile, French-led European initiatives threatened to undercut Washington's diplomacy. The Gymnich and Ottawa agreements, in the summer of 1974, which resolved this transatlantic dispute, included American acceptance that European Political Cooperation might develop alongside the NATO framework, in return for a 'gentlemen's agreement' that the then-nine EC countries would not pass any definitive resolutions which might adversely affect US interests, above all in the Middle East.

The Euro-Arab Dialogue therefore developed in some ways as a charade, with European governments determined to avoid discussing the political issue that most concerned their Arab partners. Working groups proliferated on economic and technical cooperation, while European banks competed to attract investment from revenue-rich oil producers, and European companies (and their governments) similarly competed to capture their markets. By the time that the Dialogue collapsed, with the expulsion of Egypt from the Arab League after the Camp David Agreement with Israel in 1979, very little of substance had been achieved, though some of those involved on both sides claimed it had played a significant role in mutual education and familiarisation.

In the aftermath of the Iranian revolution and the Soviet invasion of Afghanistan, west European disquiet with the quality of US foreign policy leadership provoked one further attempt at collective diplomacy towards the Middle East, culminating in the Venice Declaration agreed by the nine EC foreign ministers in June 1980. Cutting across the continuing Camp David process, and setting out a more generous approach to Palestinian rights, it was welcomed by Arab states but strongly resisted by the Carter administration. Even though the Declaration had been toned down under US pressure, Israeli Prime Minister Begin called its proposals on Jerusalem and the removal of 'illegal' settlements 'a Munich surrender' (Greilsammer and Weiler 1987: 144; see also Allen and Pijpers 1984). The Palestinian Liberation Organisation, still unreconciled to the idea of two states on Palestinian soil, declared in its turn that the Declaration was the product of American blackmail. The Reagan administration, on entering office, made its opposition to autonomous European diplomacy in the Middle East even clearer, leaving successive foreign ministers in the rotating EC Council presidency to conduct fact-finding tours of the region without attempting more.

European relations with the Arab world therefore continued to be conducted primarily through trade policy: managed by the European Commission, rather than by national governments. Almost all the states around the Mediterranean – including Israel – were economically dependent on access to EC markets, and anxious for European investment. The Italian government had proposed a 'global' strategy towards cooperation with Mediterranean states as early as 1964. Preferential trade agreements had been signed with the three Mahgreb states in 1969, with Egypt in 1972, with Israel (under politically sensitive circumstances) in 1975, and with Jordan, Lebanon and Syria in 1977. Through the 1980s, therefore, multilateral conversations through what had become the Global Mediterranean Partnership served a similar purpose to those within the Euro-Arab Dialogue before: to maintain diplomatic contacts and focus on economic issues, while skirting round the central political questions. Greek, Spanish and Portuguese accession to the EC, however, made it more difficult for European negotiators to satisfy demands for concessions on agriculture or textiles, in spite of widening trade deficits in the EC's favour. Even in this field, the EC had little to offer its Middle Eastern partners.

The pattern of western relations with the Middle East that we observe today had thus already been set before the end of the Cold War. The US defined political and security policy, backed up by military forces and active diplomacy. European governments attempted to use economic relations as an indirect route to political partnership. But they stumbled over the conflicting interests of the EU's southern member states and their trans-Mediterranean competitors, over attempts to introduce political conditions into economic agreements, and over the inclusion of Israel in their 'global' approach. American leadership was even more dominant in the Gulf, in spite of European hesitations over the degree of US hostility to Iran's post-revolution regime. By the end of the 1980s, minesweepers and frigates from several European navies were assisting the US in keeping the Gulf open to shipping. Palestinian terrorism against American and Israeli targets erupted across western Europe, but it was the US that responded to evidence of Libyan sponsorship, bombing Tripoli and Benghazi in 1986. With different degrees of quiet dissent or open criticism, European governments disagreed with the American bias towards Israel, and its anti-Iranian engagement in the Gulf. American policymakers in their turn criticised the pro-Arab bias of European governments, and their dependence on American power to maintain the flow of oil through the Gulf.

Rogue states, peace processes and foreign policy 1991–2000

The collapse of the Soviet Union transformed the geopolitics of the Middle East. Radical regimes such as Syria lost their external support. Neither Iraq nor Iran could hope to play one superpower off against the other. Israel could no longer claim to be a western bastion against Soviet expansion. The US was left as the unchallenged regional hegemon, balancing between Saudi Arabia and Israel as its strategic partners.

Reformulation of western policies was, however, disrupted by the unanticipated Iraqi invasion of Kuwait in August 1990. The Bush (Senior) administration responded rapidly and firmly, assembling a coalition under UN auspices in support of US military forces, which successfully drove Iraqi forces out. After a brief French attempt to mediate, west European governments showed solid support for this coalition. Britain contributed an effective division to allied ground forces, as well as aircraft. France provided a smaller land force, and Germany offered a substantial financial contribution to the costs of US operations. British and Dutch forces also led the post-war operation to protect and feed Kurdish northern Iraq, once it became clear that Saddam Hussein's regime in Baghdad had succeeded in surviving the defeat. Post-intervention western strategy towards the Gulf oil producers was, nevertheless, shaped by Washington alone. A major US base in eastern Saudi Arabia was developed to contain Iraq, with further air and naval facilities along the Gulf. The Pentagon developed the concept of 'rogue states' which linked Iraq with Iran, Syria and Libya, as threats to regional order, supporters of terrorist groups, and investors in weapons of mass destruction.[2] The incoming Clinton administration, in May 1993, articulated the doctrine of 'dual containment', thus justifying its deeper engagement with Saudi Arabia in countering threats from both Iraq and Iran.

Iraqi missile attacks on Israel, as well as Saddam Hussein's pan-Arab rhetoric, had made clear the impossibility of separating the politics of the Gulf states from the Israel–Palestine conflict. Iranian rhetoric, and continuing support for Hezbollah in the Lebanon, made this even clearer. The Bush (Senior) administration therefore followed up its victory in Kuwait by convening a conference on the Middle East in Madrid in August 1991. EU governments claimed 13 seats round the table, one for each member state and another as a collective entity, symbolising for American negotiators their illusory unity. But it was secret diplomacy under a Norwegian umbrella, rather than the public efforts of American or EU governments, which created the 'Oslo Process' in 1993 – followed through to public agreement under American auspices, with the Agreement signed on the White House lawn before President Clinton. The EU attempted to wield its more limited diplomatic instruments to reward the Rabin government with a more generous trade agreement. But the complexities of detailed negotiations and the lobbying efforts of vested interests within both the EU and Israel blunted its political impetus. Its completion coincided with Benjamin Netanyahu's victory in the 1996 Israel election.

The CFSP that the EU had agreed in the 1992 Treaty of European Union, as well as the EU's external economic diplomacy, had understandably been focused in the early 1990s on central and eastern Europe. The southern member states which held the rotating presidency in 1994–5 were keen to redress the balance. The Spanish presidency in November 1995 thus launched the ambitious 'Barcelona Process', redefining and expanding previous Mediterranean policies into a 'Partnership' which promised sharp increases in financial assistance and moves towards a Mediterranean FTA over 15 years.

In some ways the Barcelona Process complemented the Madrid and Oslo processes. The EU had been given the chair of the Regional Economic Development Working Group, one of the five groups set up after the Madrid conference. This move reflected not only the EU's dominant role in regional trade, but also Washington's expectation that the EU would provide the largest share of financial assistance. Relaxation of tensions between Israel and its Arab neighbours was a precondition for the EU's Barcelona initiative; as the Oslo Process ran into the sand in the following years, so too did the EU's Mediterranean Partnership. There remained, however, much suspicion in Washington about European diplomatic activity in this region. Under US leadership, NATO had launched a parallel Mediterranean initiative in 1994, with an overlapping agenda that extended to good governance and administrative reform. The priority that the US gave to security concerns and instruments did not fit easily with western European economic instruments. Accusations from Washington that the European allies were trading with the enemy while America kept the peace were recurrent.

UN sanctions on Iraq, after the 1991 Gulf war, were largely respected by European governments and companies. The trickle of embarrassing revelations about German, French, and British evasions of earlier restrictions on transfers of nuclear-related technology strengthened their commitment. However, the unilateral attempt by the Republican-controlled US Congress, under the 1996 Iran/Libya Sanctions Act, to extend sanctions to other states met with vigorous resistance. European governments did not share Washington's analysis of the nature of the Iranian regime. Nor did it seem to them wise to drive Iran back into isolation when Iraq was hostile and Afghanistan unstable. President Clinton suspended enforcement of the Act throughout his term of office. But the threat, and the intent behind it, remained as irritants to transatlantic relations (Haass 1999; see also Blackwill and Sturmer 1997; Gordon 1998).

Similar irritants and misunderstandings recurred in approaches to oil. Americans saw themselves as defending energy security for western Europe and Japan. For their parts, European governments saw the US as attempting to impose its strategic priorities on oil markets, even as they blocked investment by European oil companies in Iran. American dependence on OPEC oil in the mid-1990s, indeed, was far higher than British or German (for which North Sea oil provided secure supply), though considerably lower than for France or Italy.

Overall American oil consumption and imports, furthermore, rose steadily throughout the 1990s, while higher taxation and energy conservation in Europe held oil consumption and dependence levels stable.

The Clinton administration was active in Middle East diplomacy from its inauguration until its final hours of office. The President himself invested time and prestige in Arab–Israeli negotiations, at Camp David, at Wye Plantation, even visiting Israel, Palestine, Egypt, Syria, Jordan, Kuwait and Saudi Arabia in attempts to promote agreement. Secretaries of state and special negotiators shuttled endlessly back and forth. In the Gulf region, in contrast, the emphasis was on containment. The US and Britain continued to enforce the 'No Fly Zones' over Iraq, although France gradually withdrew its support from the end of 1996. Forward positioning of equipment and bases in the Gulf region increased America's ability to project decisive military power. A terrorist attack on an American barracks in Saudi Arabia in 1996, and another on an American ship in Aden harbour in 2000, signalled the rise of a network of opposition to US domination of the region. But these were seen as containable incidents, strengthening the case for cooperation with friendly regimes.

The period of the Netanyahu government in Israel, from 1996–9, was particularly difficult for the Clinton administration. The Oslo process faltered, while Israeli settlements in the occupied territories continued to grow. Benjamin Netanyahu proved adept at exploiting American domestic politics, building alliances with evangelical Christian conservatives, who now argued that God had given the whole of the land of Israel to the Jews. His replacement by Ehud Barak in May 1999 reopened the prospect of a negotiated settlement. Mistrust and division on both sides, however, made for slow progress, leaving President Clinton to host more talks at Camp David in the middle of the campaign to elect his successor, in July 2000, with a final – and unsuccessful – effort to strike a deal under American sponsorship just before President George W. Bush's inauguration in January 2001.

There was little that European governments could do to influence such delicate negotiations. All sides accepted that only the US had the leverage to persuade both sides to compromise. Nevertheless, from the Barcelona Conference on, the EU collectively attempted to play a modest political role. A Spanish diplomat, Ambassador Miguel Moratinos, was appointed the EU's 'special envoy' for the Arab–Israeli peace process, shuttling between the various capitals, reporting back to EU foreign ministers, and coordinating as far as possible with his American opposite number. European officials monitored elections in the Palestinian territories and advised the Palestinian Authority on security and policing.

By and large, however, there was a double division of labour. The US controlled the political negotiations, while the Europeans promoted economic relations; the US provided financial support to Israel, European governments to Palestine. European financial assistance to the Palestinian Authority accounted for 54 per cent of all aid funding over the years 1994–8, for a total of around $1.5 billion, against $280 million from the US. Both the US and EU governments provided substantial aid to Egypt, with the US also rewarding Turkey and Jordan for their support of its Middle East strategy. The disadvantage of this financial division of labour was that it sharpened the perception of the pro-Israeli lobby in Washington that European governments were biased in favour of the Palestinians. Later, in 2001–2, there was bitterness also on the European side as American-supplied Israeli aircraft demolished much of the Palestinian infrastructure for which EU external assistance had paid.

The Bush administration's agenda

All new administrations in Washington enter office determined to differentiate themselves from their predecessors in foreign policy. The Bush administration felt particularly strongly about differentiation on the Middle East, where – from their perspective – Clinton's overactive diplomacy had demeaned the presidency without achieving a settlement. They were committed to a much more 'selective engagement' in global diplomacy, to what Richard Haass, the new head of policy planning in the State Department, called 'a la carte multilateralism'.

This was, furthermore, a Republican administration, bringing into office particular memories and myths, and particular domestic links and interests. The Reagan administration had strongly opposed revolutionary Iran. The first Bush administration had gone to war against Iraq, but – to the regret of many of its partisans – not carried through to the removal of Saddam Hussein. It had been Republican senators and congressmen who had wanted to impose unilateral sanctions on Iran. Likud politicians in Israel had actively cultivated close links with the Christian conservatives who were now a powerful force within the Republican party coalition. Republican strategists, in turn, had been cultivating Jewish organisations and voters in such crucial states as Florida, aiming to win them away from their traditional Democratic loyalties. On the other hand, both the new president's father and Vice-President Cheney had long-established relations with the Saudi royal family. The new president had appealed directly to Arab-Americans during his election campaign, and had won a clear majority of their votes (Pollack 2002). The George W. Bush administration thus had conflicting priorities: supportive of Israel, but also strongly committed to strategic partnership with Saudi Arabia and to vigorous maintenance of dual containment of Iraq and Iran.

There was, therefore, little interest in Washington in taking up again the thankless task of mediation, as the second *Intifada* followed the breakdown of the Barak–Arafat negotiations and the replacement of Barak as Israeli prime minister by Ariel Sharon. The sympathies of the new administration were with the Israeli government. The breakdown of the negotiations was widely understood within the US as the responsibility of Palestinian intransigence, in the face of the most generous peace offer any Israeli government had put forward. Here was another source of transatlantic divergence: presentation of developments in Arab–Israeli relations in the American and European media had diverged further and further over the previous decade, to a point where politicians and publics on opposite sides of the Atlantic 'saw' the conflict very differently. American reporting had stressed Palestinian terrorism and Israeli insecurity. The European media generally stressed the growth of Israeli settlements and the constraints of occupation.

The narrow Republican victory in the presidential election brought a diverse – and divided – coalition into office. The ideological Right, well entrenched in Washington think-tanks and journals over the previous decade and with considerable influence over leading Republicans in the Senate and the House, promoted an 'America first' foreign policy, as against the multilateral internationalism for which they blamed the Bush (Senior) administration. Their unilateralist rhetoric carried anti-European undertones. NATO, with its consultative procedures, was widely seen as an obstacle to the effective projection of power on American terms. Jewish neo-Conservatives did not shrink from labelling European societies as structurally anti-semitic for their criticism of the Israeli government's behaviour in the occupied territories. Right-wing promotion of ballistic missile defence also focused attention on WMD in 'rogue states'. Conservatives and Christian fundamentalists accepted Samuel Huntington's post-Cold War concept of a 'clash of civilisations', with its anti-Muslim undertones. Donald Rumsfeld as Secretary of Defence, a veteran of the Reagan and Ford administrations, was (with Vice-President Cheney) the most sympathetic to these views. Colin Powell as Secretary of State was attacked from the right as a promoter of multilateral cooperation and compromise. The attacks of 9/11 thus struck a divided administration, which had not yet begun to define a coherent strategy towards the Middle East.

After 9/11: divergence or convergence?

The immediate American response to 9/11 focused on Afghanistan. But the discovery that the suicide hijackers, and the Al-Qaeda network as a whole, were recruited from Arab countries focused the widely-posed question, 'Why do they hate us?', on the wider Muslim world. Pursuit of the funds that had underwritten the assault put the spotlight on Muslim charities, including some with close links to the Saudi élite. The declaration of a 'war on terrorism' swept together anti-American and anti-Israeli terrorist groups across the region, allowing the Sharon government to claim that it was again the bastion of western civilisation in its confrontation with Muslim fundamentalism. For American national security conservatives, it also provided a rationale for pre-emptive action against Iraq. On 13 September 2000, Secretary of State Rumsfeld raised potential action against Iraq during their daily briefing. The following day his deputy, Paul Wolfowitz, argued explicitly that the US should now commit itself to 'ending states who sponsor terrorism', to the discomfort of Colin Powell and top US military commanders (Woodward 2002: 60–1).

The immediate European response was one of solidarity and sympathy with the US. Article 5 of the NATO Treaty was invoked, for the first time in the Alliance's 52-year history, and the European allies offered to share in the expulsion of Al-Qaeda and its supporters from Afghanistan. Yet, unavoidably, European perceptions differed from American. European societies had experienced transnational terrorist attacks over the previous 30 years, including several attacks on US (and Israeli) targets on European soil. Some 3,000 people had been killed in the UK during the Irish Republican Army campaign, a comparable number to those killed in the World Trade Centre. For European élites who had criticised the approach of successive US administrations to the Arab–Israeli conflict, the preoccupation with 'rogue states', and the 'clash of civilisations' concept, there was a sense of being caught in a confrontation between the US and the Muslim world – in which vital European interests were at stake, but over which European policymakers had little or no influence.

Throughout the previous decade, successive US administrations had called for NATO to transform itself into an alliance to meet threats from 'out of area'. Now that an immediate threat had emerged, however, the Bush administration deflected its allies' proposals for an alliance framework for forces against the Taliban regime, fearing another Kosovo-style multilateral negotiation – and opted for a 'coalition of the willing' instead, drawing only selectively even on British troops already in the region for 'exercises' in Oman.

Nevertheless, British, French, German and Danish special forces played supporting roles in the ground campaign. Once the regime had collapsed, the overwhelmingly European ISAF was established in Kabul, under British command and UN authorisation. By the end of 2001 the Taliban regime had been defeated and Al-Qaeda dispersed, and attention both within Europe and the US had turned to the wider political and cultural context within which Al-Qaeda had attracted activists and funds.

To the extent that there was a coherent and concerted response from European governments to the wider problems of the Middle East region at the end of 2001, it remained consistent with the evolution of European approaches over previous years. Al-Qaeda had grown over a long period, as European experts perceived it, exploiting resentment of American hegemony across the region, in particular of American support for authoritarian regimes and its bias towards Israel. The threat to the US that sprouted in the Middle East was also a product of American neglect of the consequences of their proxy victory over the Soviet Union in Afghanistan, and of the future employment of the Muslim fighters they had trained. What was needed was a broad diplomatic approach to the region, including an active and concerted attempt to bring the Israel–Palestine conflict back to the negotiating table. Moreover, a dialogue with 'friendly' Arab authoritarian regimes, that took the UN Development Programme's *Arab Human Development Report* as its frame of reference, was clearly needed.[3]

Continued containment of Iraq was accepted as necessary. In approaching the competing factions that governed Iran, however, European priorities differed sharply from those of the US, preferring engagement with domestic groups promoting democratisation to confrontation. European economic interests in the region, governments noted, were much larger than American. Flows of refugees from the region – most significantly Iraqi Kurds and Afghans in 2001–2 – fed into western Europe far more than into North America. In terms of power projection and political influence, however, European governments were acutely conscious of their limited capabilities in the face of American regional hegemony.[4]

The predominant American approach to the region was set out by President Bush in his 'axis of evil' speech in January 2002, which linked the efforts of Iraq and Iran (and North Korea) to acquire WMD with their sponsorship of terrorism. Though there was no evidence linking any of these states directly to Al-Qaeda, this conceptual framework transmuted the war on terrorism into the pre-existing framework of rogue states and WMD, and thus into a potential war on Iraq. Iranian and Iraqi support for terrorist groups attacking Israel was an important part of their inclusion in this category, indicating how closely the Arab–Israeli conflict and the war on terrorism were linked in American minds. The priority for western Middle East policy, in this formulation, was regime change in Iraq, combined with continued containment of Iran. The removal of a regime that encouraged Palestinian intransigence would in itself ease the Arab–Israeli conflict. The European allies would be invited to play supporting roles in the 'coalition of the willing' assembled to enforce disarmament – and/or regime change – on Iraq, and to pay for subsequent social and economic reconstruction.

In parallel with this unilateral redefinition, however, the US State Department pursued a multilateral approach, with cooperation with European governments a key factor. On 10 April 2002 Colin Powell announced the formation of a Madrid 'Quartet', taking up again the agenda of the 1991 Madrid conference with the more manageable foursome of the UN Secretary-General, the EU High Representative for Common Foreign and Security Policy (Javier Solana), and the Russian Foreign Minister (Igor Ivanov). The focus of this approach was on pursuing a two-state solution to the Israel–Palestine conflict, with the active engagement of outside actors, and without waiting for the outcome of confrontation with Iraq. Good personal relations between Powell and Solana were a significant feature of this common approach – even though the cumbersome structures of EU diplomacy also squeezed the Commissioner for External Relations (Chris Patten) and the foreign minister of the member state holding the Council presidency into the 'single' EU seat. Formally, at least, EU and US approaches had converged on this aspect of Middle East policy. However, it remained unclear whether the US administration beyond the State Department was seriously committed to this exercise, and whether national governments within the EU were fully behind their collective representatives.

Iraq and after

Over the summer of 2002, hard-liners in Washington, led by Vice-President Cheney, had attempted to commit the administration to war on Iraq, leaving it to other states to decide whether to follow a firm American lead. But in September, partly in response to pressure from Tony Blair, whose public support for American actions since 9/11 had won goodwill and critical influence in Washington, President Bush took the case for enforcement of WMD disarmament against Iraq to the multilateral forum of the United Nations. In a victory for Powell, the result was a unanimous endorsement (even by states such as Syria) of a UN resolution – itself a compromise Euro-American text – by its Security Council.

It briefly appeared that private British influence within Washington, and public criticism and hard negotiation by the French government, had combined to divert American policy from pre-emptive military action to multilateral inspection, backed by the threat of force. As the US military build-up in the Gulf continued, however, and the returning UN inspectors took up their thankless task of searching for WMD, the determination of many within Washington to overthrow the Iraqi regime – whether WMD were found or not – again became clear. Having taken their case to the Security Council, the US administration nevertheless refused to be constrained by the UN. Explicit refusal by the German government to accept any use of force against Iraq, and active French opposition to a second Security Council resolution which would have set a short deadline before military intervention would take over from inspection, sparked as bitter a divide between Washington and Paris (and now also Berlin) as occurred in 1973–4. French alignment with Russia, in threatening to veto a US-sponsored resolution before the Security Council, deepened the rift; French obstruction of an American request that NATO provide additional defence support to Turkey in the event of a military conflict with Iraq deepened it still further. A Franco-German attempt to define the common European position as opposition to US intervention provoked first a joint counter-statement from eight EU member governments, led by Spain, the UK and Italy, and then (with active American encouragement) a similar statement from ten EU applicant states. Thus, in March 2003, the US led into Iraq a coalition of the willing, with the UK as its most important military partner, and smaller contingents from Poland and other applicant states, against the embittered opposition of the French and German governments, with anti-American demonstrations erupting across Europe.

France's intransigence rested on its insistence that the US must accept the multilateral constraints of UN approval, and pay as much attention to the Israel–Palestine conflict as to the threat of rogue states. Blair was pursuing essentially similar objectives, despite the UK's active participation in the Iraqi war. After the remarkably short and successful military campaign of March–April, President Bush symbolically flew to Belfast to promise that the Quartet's 'road map' towards an Israel–Palestine settlement would now be published; that he would devote 'as much time' to the Middle East peace process as Tony Blair had to the peace process in Northern Ireland; and that the UN would have a 'vital role' in the reconstruction of Iraq.

There was thus some common ground on which to re-establish European consensus and transatlantic understanding. But Pentagon conservatives, with aggressive rhetoric, were simultaneously calling for the US to 'punish' Germany and France and to increase political and military pressures on Syria and Iran, while suggesting that this triumphal projection of American power would demonstrate the irrelevance of 'old Europe' – and of NATO – to American strategy. French political leaders, in turn, showed little sign of accepting that this was now America's moment in the Middle East, to which others must necessarily defer. French political efforts, at home and abroad, were directed to establishing closer relations with the Muslim world, implicitly suggesting that the US was pursuing a 'clash of civilisations'. With a deeply divided group of European governments facing an internally-divided Washington, much would depend on the American effort to rebuild Iraq's economy and society, as well as on whether the search for weapons of mass destruction would provide retrospective justification for a war most Europeans had opposed. Divergent assumptions and interests – about the severity of the threat posed by Saddam Hussein's regime, about the link between the struggle against Islamic terrorism and the Israel–Palestine conflict, about western policy towards the Arab and Muslim worlds as a whole – had led to the worst crisis in transatlantic relations in at least 30 years. The Middle East was, again, the focus for transatlantic discord.

Notes

1   The Atlantic Council (2002: 1) puts this more strongly: 'The affairs of the Middle East have been uniquely contentious between the principal European countries and the United States for over 50 years'.

2   The role played by Colin Powell as Chief of Staff in developing the post-Cold War concept of 'rogue states' is explored by Klare (1995).

3   This report, written by a group of Arab economists and social scientists, was published by the UN Development Programme on 13 September 2001. Unsurprisingly, it attracted little attention at the time, but was widely quoted during 2002 by writers arguing the case for social and political transformation of authoritarian Arab regimes.

4   Atlantic Council (2002) sets out the consensus of European views on the basis of interviews in London, Paris, Berlin and Brussels in July 2002. On the broader European response to US policy after 9/11, see Wallace (2002a, 2002b).

9 Unilateral America, multilateral Europe?

Mark A. Pollack[1]

> A common thread is that we Europeans are instinctive multilateralists and want the US to be more committed to multilateral solutions.
>
> (Solana 2002: 15)

> Multilateral agreements and institutions should not be ends in themselves.
>
> (Condoleeza Rice, quoted in Wolf 2002: 23)

Both before and especially since the inauguration of George W. Bush as President of the US, policymakers and commentators on both sides of the Atlantic have presented a stark contrast between a multilateralist EU and a unilateralist America. EU officials including Javier Solana have presented Europe as inherently multilateralist, arguing that the Union's unique experiment in multilateral integration has predisposed it to seek multilateral solutions to global as well as regional problems. By contrast, Bush's America has been perceived by European policymakers and analysts as being profoundly unilateralist in orientation, walking away from a number of multilateral treaties such as the Kyoto Protocol on climate change and the International Criminal Court, and more generally refusing to be bound in its pursuit of the US national interest by multilateral rules and institutions.

In this chapter, I suggest that there is an element of truth to these claims – specifically, the contemporary EU and the US *do* differ significantly in their support for multilateral rules and institutions, with the Bush administration far more sceptical than the collective EU position about the utility of multilateral agreements across a range of issue-areas. Nevertheless, the common depiction of a multilateralist Europe contrasting with a unilateralist America is misleading, since it ignores both historical and contemporary variation in EU and US support for multilateral rules and institutions. Specifically, the chapter makes two interrelated arguments about the sources and the nature of US and EU support for multilateralism. First, both US and EU support for multilateralism is – and has always been – selective, reflecting the international power position and the domestic political interests of states on each side of the Atlantic. Indeed, as we shall see, the EU's 'instinctive' multilateralism is a legitimising myth for European countries that have always been, and remain, selective in their support for multilateral cooperation both among themselves and with third countries. Similarly, the US has historically supported the creation of the world's most important multilateral institutions, and remains supportive of and engaged with at least a sub-set of those institutions insofar as the Bush administration considers them to serve the US national interest.

Second, the respective multilateral preferences of US and the EU have changed substantially over the past two and a half decades, with the US becoming increasingly suspicious of the multilateral institutions it helped to establish during its period of post-war hegemony, while the EU has increasingly overcome its ambivalence about multilateralism, seeking to export its 'domestic' model and policies to wider multilateral forums (see Keohane 2002; Nicolaïdis and Howse 2002). To borrow David Vogel's (2001) expression, the US and the EU orientation towards multilateral rules and institutions can be described as 'ships passing in the night', with the EU increasingly (but not invariably) inclined to support multilateral rules and institutions and the US increasingly (but not invariably) sceptical of both new and existing multilateral agreements. Understanding the trajectory of these two ships, and the reasons for their passing, represents the primary ambition of the chapter.

What is multilateralism, and why do states support it?

Multilateralism is an abstract concept, more easily defined by what it is *not* – namely, it is not purely unilateral or bilateral – than by what it *is*. In an influential discussion of the term, John Gerard Ruggie (1993) and his colleagues have suggested that multilateralism, as an organising principle, is characterised by three properties: indivisibility (roughly, the scope of international cooperation); generalised principles of conduct (general rather than particularistic or case-by-case rules for relating to other states); and diffuse reciprocity (in which state gains and losses from cooperation are calculated over the long term rather than for each specific agreement) (Caporaso 1993: 54–5). The relative importance of these three concepts may be debated, but the central point of this literature is that multilateralism as an organising principle constitutes 'a belief that activities ought to be organized on a universal basis at least for a "relevant" group (for example, democracies)' (Caporaso 1993: 55). As such, multilateralism as a general principle is broader than support for any given multilateral institution. Furthermore,

> [M]ultilateralism is a demanding organizational form. It requires its participants to renounce temporary advantages and the temptation to define their interests narrowly in terms of national interests, and it also requires them to forgo ad hoc coalitions and to avoid policies based on situational exigencies and momentary constellations of interests.
>
> (Caporaso 1993: 56)

Defining multilateralism in this way raises the question why any state – or a bloc of states like the EU – would agree to limit their options in this way, rather than leaving themselves free to pursue other unilateral or bilateral options.

In most international relations theory, state preferences about the form and the substantive rules of international institutions are considered to be *derived* preferences; that is to say, states do not prefer unilateral, bilateral or multilateral institutions for their own sake, but these institutional preferences are derived from states' *substantive* preferences for, say, access to world markets for given commodities, or security guarantees against a menacing neighbour, or collective action to address problems such as climate change. Put simply, states prefer multilateral institutions to unilateral action insofar as those institutional choices contribute to the realisation of substantive preferences like wealth, power, and quality of life (Martin 1993; Jupille 2000; Fioretos 2001).

This notion of institutional choice as a derived preference has three important implications for the study of multilateralism generally, and for our understanding of US and EU foreign policy positions specifically. First, if and insofar as states have different substantive preferences about issues like international security, world trade and global warming, we should expect these differences to manifest themselves as differences among states about the form of institutions designed to address those problems. For this reason, we should expect that states – even democratic states with honest leaders – will not necessarily agree on the form of international institutions if their substantive preferences are dissimilar.

Second, we should not expect the institutional preferences of individual states to be monolithic in favour of, or in opposition to, multilateral rules and institutions across all issue-areas. Instead, we should expect to see states supporting multilateral rules and institutions selectively across issue-areas, favouring binding rules and strong institutions in some issue-areas but opposing them in others, as a reflection of their issue-specific preferences about economics, security, the environment, and so on.

Third and finally, a state's support for multilateralism – like the substantive preferences that underlie that support – should reflect both a state's position in the international system, and the nature of its domestic political system. Let us consider each of these factors, international and domestic, in turn.

Power, weakness, and multilateralism

Few students of international politics would disagree with the notion that a state's preference for multilateral or other types of institutions is related in some way to its power and position in the international system. Yet from this common position, views diverge about the relationship between state power and state preferences for multilateralism.

Since the 1970s, a number of 'hegemonic stability theorists' have argued that hegemonic powers are most likely to favour the establishment and maintenance of multilateral institutions, from which they benefit disproportionately. After World War II, for example, the US emerged not only as one of two superpowers and the dominant global actor in the west, but also as the primary architect of, and dominant player in, a raft of multilateral institutions including the UN and its specialised agencies, the Bretton Woods institutions (the World Bank and the International Monetary Fund), the General Agreement on Trade and Tariffs (GATT), the NATO alliance, and other multilateral organisations. In this view, the making of today's multilateral world was essentially the hegemonic project of a dominant US, although such institutions, once established, could and did persist after the relative decline of the US as a hegemonic power (Keohane 1984).

A starkly contrasting view, however, has been offered by Robert Kagan (2002; 2003), whose influential essay 'Power and Weakness' posits that support for multi- lateral rules and institutions is inversely (not directly) proportional to state power. In Kagan's view, great powers – like the countries of eighteenth-century Europe, or contemporary America – 'often fear rules that may constrain them more than they fear the anarchy in which their power brings security and prosperity'. For this reason, Kagan argues, great powers tend to favour the use of military force and to shun multilateral institutions that might limit their ability to employ power to achieve their ends in the international system. By contrast, Kagan continues, mil- itarily weak countries – like eighteenth-century America or contemporary Europe – have fewer unilateral or military options, and therefore favour multilateral insti- tutions and restraints on the use of military force in international politics.

There is surely an element of truth in Kagan's account, in which George Bush's America is simply unwilling to accept significant multilateral constraints in a war on terrorism that it can wage, at least in part, through its own military and other resources. Yet, as we shall see presently, Kagan's account provides a highly selective reading of international history, accepting too uncritically the EU's benign self-portrait as inherently multilateralist, and ignoring completely the United States' formative role in the creation, during the early post-war era, of the most important multilateral institutions in the contemporary world. Indeed, the US case presents a major puzzle for purely systemic accounts, which cannot explain why a hegemonic US fostered the growth of multilateral institutions in the 1940s, while resisting many of those same institutions today. To understand the ebb and flow of US and EU support for multilateral rules and institutions, there- fore, we need to look at domestic politics as well.

Domestic politics and multilateral preferences

One of the most striking aspects of international relations theory over the past decade has been the move by theorists to incorporate domestic politics and domestic preference formation into the explanation of foreign policy behaviour (Moravcsik 1997). Simplifying considerably, liberal theories of national preference formation posit that foreign policy preferences emerge out of a principal-agent interaction between national electorates and interest groups on the one hand, and the governmental actors who represent them on the other. In the language of Robert Putnam's 'two-level games', each country is represented at the interna- tional level (Level 1) by a 'chief of government' (or COG), who interacts diplomatically with other governments and strikes agreements on the basis of her substantive preferences; at the domestic level (Level 2), however, each COG must

secure ratification for the agreement with her own domestic constituencies, plac
ing limits on the ability of COGs (especially those in democratic countries) to
engage in (or depart from) multilateral agreements without the agreement of
national electorates, interest groups, and legislatures.

In this liberal view, a given government's support for multilateral rules and
institutions is determined not (only) by state power and weakness in the international system, but also by the substantive preferences of both COGs and
their constituents for goods such as power, wealth, and environmental protection. In the case of the US, therefore, we should expect to see support for
multilateralism vary primarily as a function of the preferences of the president,
but the president will also be constrained by the preferences of the electorate
and the Congress – particularly the Senate, whose approval is required for the
ratification of international treaties. In the more complicated EU case, we
need to consider not only the relationship of national electorates and interests
to their respective legislatures and governments, but also the varying role of
supranational actors like the European Commission, which is empowered as
the sole representative of EU member states in international trade and plays
(alongside the Council Presidency and Secretary-General) a coordinating function in other issue-areas vis-à-vis third countries.

Given the obvious complexities of both state and EU preference formation, I
make no attempt here to develop or test a complete theory of domestic preference
formation, which is beyond the scope of the current chapter. However, if we
undertake a theoretically informed survey of US domestic politics over the past
five decades, we find a story of gradually waning support for multilateral rules
and institutions among US lawmakers and (to a varying extent) presidents. On the
European side, by contrast, the EU's traditionally defensive posture in its core
competence of trade policy has been replaced by a more open, but still selective,
support for multilateral trading rules as a result of the Union's internal programme of single-market liberalisation. Let us consider each case, briefly, in turn.

The US: multilateral architect to aggressive unilateralist

The post-war history of US foreign policy presents a puzzle for students of multilateralism: why a powerful US supported multilateral institutions during the 1940s
and 1950s, while increasingly regarding them as hindrances at the turn of the
twenty-first century. Contrary to Kagan's equation of multilateralism with weakness, it was a hegemonic US that, in the immediate aftermath of World War II,
fostered the development of multilateral rules and institutions, including the UN
and its specialised agencies, the Bretton Woods institutions, the GATT, and a multilateral NATO alliance based on the principle of collective security. To be sure,
the US was not indiscriminate in its advocacy of multilateralism; the US
Congress, for example, failed in 1948 to ratify the International Trade
Organisation agreement, while the Roosevelt administration itself insisted on a
great-power veto in the UN Security Council, an important exception to the general principle of multilateralism in the UN and its agencies. Nevertheless, as John

Ikenberry (2000, 2001) points out, successive US administrations calculated that the economic and security benefits of a multilateral order outweighed the loss of US autonomy within multilateral rules and institutions:

> In effect, the US spun a web of institutions that connected other states to an emerging American-dominated economic and security order. But in doing so, these institutions also bound the US to other states and reduced—at least to some extent—Washington's ability to engage in the arbitrary and indiscriminate exercise of power. Call it an institutional bargain. The price for the US was a reduction in Washington's policy autonomy, in that institutional rules and joint decision-making reduced US unilateralist capacities. But what Washington got in return was worth the price. America's partners also had their autonomy constrained, but in return were able to operate in a world where US power was more restrained and reliable.
>
> (Ikenberry 2001: 18)

Within two decades, however, the US had begun to show signs of a waning commitment to multilateral rules and institutions. Contrary to Kagan's 'power and weakness' argument, but consistent with hegemonic stability theory, American reticence about multilateral rules and organisations came into the open during the 1970s, a period of relative US decline resulting from superior economic growth rates in Japan and western Europe, the acquisition of a substantial nuclear deterrent by the Soviet Union, increasing US dependence on foreign oil supplies, and the international and domestic trauma of the Vietnam war.

Perhaps the earliest sign of declining US support for multilateral institutions came in the late 1960s and early 1970s, when the dollar – the lynchpin of the international monetary system – came under increasing pressure as private investors (as well as the French government of President Charles de Gaulle) sought to exchange their dollar reserves for gold. In 1971, President Nixon unilaterally announced the end of the dollar's convertibility into gold, effectively jettisoning the Bretton Woods monetary system. Two years later, Nixon first devalued the dollar by 10 per cent, and later announced that the dollar would be allowed to float on international currency markets, ushering in the contemporary floating exchange-rate system.

At the same time that the Bretton Woods institutions were coming under stress from declining US economic hegemony, the US found that many of the UN's core institutions – including the General Assembly as well as various specialised agencies and multilateral negotiations – had become forums for an increasingly assertive Group of 77 (G77) less developed countries (LDCs) with an agenda of radical political and economic reform. The challenge from the G77 arose in part from the effects of decolonisation, which increased the numbers of LDCs and hence voting majorities in many international institutions, and in part from the principle of sovereign equality, which gave these states formally equal voting power with much larger powers such as the US within multilateral institutions such as the UN General Assembly and specialised agencies such as UNCTAD and UNESCO.[2] Within these institutions, G77 countries openly challenged the liberal economic order established by the US, calling instead for a New International Economic Order in areas as diverse as trade, aid, debt, outer space, and the oceans, and using their voting power within multilateral forums to achieve their aims (Krasner 1985).

Faced with these challenges, the initial US response during the Nixon, Ford, and Carter years was to remain engaged in the UN and other international institutions, even as its ability to influence outcomes in those institutions declined (Krasner 1985: 11). By the late 1970s, however, even the liberal internationalist Carter administration had grown wary of the majoritarian institutions of the UN, most vividly depicted by then-US Ambassador Daniel Patrick Moynihan's memoir, *A Dangerous Place* (1978).

US estrangement from multilateral rules and institutions continued and intensified during the presidency of Ronald Reagan. The continuing challenge from majoritarian UN institutions clashed repeatedly with the priorities of a Reagan administration that combined a domestic programme inspired by social and economic conservatives with a foreign policy dominated by renewed resistance to the Soviet Union. In 1982, for example, the US announced that it would not ratify the UN Convention on the Law of the Sea, which had been negotiated for over a decade within a universal and majoritarian (one-state, one-vote) forum, objecting to G77-inspired provisions that would have designated deep-seabed resources as the 'common heritage of mankind'. Later that year, the administration announced its withdrawal from UNESCO, which it claimed was mismanaged and politicised; and in 1984 it withdrew funding from the UN Fund for Population Activities (UNFPA), claiming that the organisation had provided funding for population-control programmes featuring forced sterilisation and abortions. The administration's rocky relationship with the UN was further poisoned when the US refused to accept a critical 1985 decision of the International Court of Justice in a case concerning the US mining of Nicaraguan harbours. Even in areas such as international trade, where Reagan pressed repeatedly and ultimately successfully for the opening of the Uruguay Round of GATT, the administration angered its trading partners with the use of Congressionally mandated 'Super 301' and 'Special 301' measures designed to open foreign markets to US exports through the use of unilateral trade sanctions (Bhagwati 1990).

The administrations of George Bush (Senior) and Bill Clinton witnessed (respectively) the collapse of the Soviet Union and the emergence of the US as the world's only superpower. Yet, contrary to Kagan's claim that great powers abjure multilateral commitments, both administrations sought to improve US relations with the UN and other multilateral institutions. The Bush Senior administration, most notably, placed the UN – albeit its 'minilateral' Security Council rather than the genuinely multilateral General Assembly – at the centre of its vision of a New World Order, and obtained UN support for both the 1991 Gulf War and its December 1992 decision to commit US troops to a humanitarian intervention in Somalia.

The Clinton administration came to office with a similar commitment to what Secretary of State Madeleine Albright would later call 'assertive multilateralism'. This commitment would bear fruit in the successful ratification of the treaty creating the World Trade Organization as well as in the US decision to commit to military activities under NATO command in Bosnia after 1994 and in Kosovo in 1999. Nevertheless, despite its professed multilateral intentions, the Clinton administration faced significant domestic as well as international obstacles that limited the US commitment to multilateral rules and institutions in practice. As Stanley Hoffmann (2001) points out, these obstacles included periodic opposition from a Pentagon that resisted both multilateral pressures to act (most notably in cases of humanitarian intervention) as well as multilateral restraints on US military action (as in the case of the 1996 treaty banning anti-personnel land mines and the selection of targets in the Kosovo campaign), as well as sustained opposition from an increasingly hostile Republican Congress. During the course of Clinton's presidency, the Republican membership of Congress witnessed a shift from a previously dominant tradition of internationalism to a new focus amongst newer members on domestic affairs accompanied by deep suspicion of the UN and other multilateral institutions (Spiro 2000). Personified by Jesse Helms in his role as Chairman of the Senate Foreign Relations Committee, these Congressional constraints – together with Clinton's political weakness following his impeachment in 1998 – limited the administration's ability to pursue a strongly multilateral foreign policy. Examples of such constraints included the US decision not to sign the 1996 Land Mines Treaty, the decision not to send the 1997 Kyoto Protocol to a hostile Senate, the defeat of Clinton's efforts to ratify the Comprehensive Test Ban Treaty in the Senate, the inability of the administration to persuade Congress to release US back dues to the UN, and Clinton's last-minute signature in late 2000 of the treaty establishing the International Criminal Court.

Put simply, US scepticism of multilateral rules and institutions had grown significantly over several decades before the inauguration of George W. Bush in January 2001, reflecting both domestic and international developments. It therefore seems likely that even a Gore administration would have encountered difficulty pursuing a strongly multilateral foreign policy. Nevertheless, the Bush administration did mark a significant change in tone from the Clinton years, giving Congressional unilateralists a number of allies in the White House and the Pentagon. Despite Secretary of State Colin Powell's professed commitment to multilateralism, Bush and many of his advisers remained strongly averse to multilateral constraints on US action. During his first months in office Bush angered US allies by withdrawing from multilateral negotiations in areas such as biological weapons and the rights of children, withdrawing the United States' signature from the International Criminal Court and seeking to exempt US forces from its reach, and above all pronouncing the Kyoto Protocol dead despite strong support for the agreement in Europe. By the summer of 2001, European analysts had good reason to fear that US detachment from multilateral institutions, already significant under Clinton, had become the primary thrust of US foreign policy under Bush.

In this context, the attacks of 9/11 appeared, at least initially, to have altered drastically both the context and the priorities of the Bush administration's foreign policy. While existing goals, such as the expansion of NATO and missile defence, would remain, the war against terrorism had become the Bush administration's highest priority – and one that could only be pursued, or so it was argued, through the maintenance of a large international coalition. And indeed, within days of the 9/11 attacks, the administration began to assemble a wide-ranging coalition against terrorism, including Russia, Pakistan, Saudi Arabia, and a NATO alliance which for the first time invoked Article 5 of the NATO Treaty. At the same time, the administration moved quickly to mend US relations with the UN, including the rapid payment of back dues and the confirmation of John Negroponte, whose appointment as US Ambassador to the UN had languished as a relatively low priority in the Senate. The following year, seeking support for a potential US war against Iraq, Bush announced that the US would return to UNESCO following a 20-year absence.

Yet, the imperatives of the war against terrorism did not lead, in either the short or the long term, to a fundamental reshaping of the Bush administration's positions on a number of multilateral issues. Writing in late 2001, Steven E. Miller (2002: 21) summarised the limited nature of the Bush administration's conversion to multilateralism: 'Although the United States will want and need international help and support in its war against terrorism ... assuming that the demands of coalition-building will inevitably compel Washington to alter course dramatically, to reverse unpopular lines of policy, or to abandon past priorities is a mistake'.

Indeed, the administration's foreign policy over the next year combined a selective embrace of some multinational initiatives – most notably the explicit support of the UN Security Council for the war in Afghanistan, as well as the successful launch of a new WTO negotiating round at Doha, Qatar, in November 2001 – with the continuation of strongly unilateral policies in others. The war in Afghanistan, for example, included no formal role for the NATO alliance or for NATO members other than the UK. The Bush administration also returned to previous positions in areas such as ballistic missile defence, climate change, and the International Criminal Court. Bush's selective embrace of multilateralism could also be seen in his policy towards Iraq. In late 2002, the administration sought and obtained a UN Security Council resolution calling for the return of international weapons inspectors and threatening unspecified consequences in the event of Iraqi non-compliance. Faced with implacable French and Russian opposition to a second Security Council resolution authorising the use of force, however, Bush proved willing to strike Iraq with a selective 'coalition of the willing', and without multilateral approval from either the United Nations or NATO.

In sum, the Bush administration's foreign policy, both before and after 9/11, represents a continuation and intensification of a long-term trend in which successive US administrations have been increasingly reticent to accept the constraints of multilateral rules and institutions. Under Bush, the US remains selectively engaged with some multilateral institutions – most notably the WTO and the UN Security Council – but the administration's willingness to act unilaterally, or on the basis of *ad hoc* 'coalitions of the willing' rather than existing multilateral institutions, remains troubling to America's European partners.

Europe: the road to (selective) multilateralism

The notion of the EU as an inherently multilateral actor in global politics is a powerful one, perpetuated not only by European public officials and analysts, but also by American scholars like Kagan (2002: 1,11), who contrasts American views of power with those of the EU in the broadest possible terms:

> Europe is turning away from power, or to put it a little differently, it is moving beyond power into a self-contained world of laws and rules and transnational negotiation and cooperation. It is entering a post-historical paradise of peace and relative prosperity, the realization of Kant's 'Perpetual Peace' … The means by which this miracle has been achieved have understandably acquired something of a sacred mystique for Europeans, especially since the end of the Cold War. Diplomacy, negotiations, patience, the forging of economic ties, political engagement, the use of inducements rather than sanctions, the taking of small steps and tempering ambitions for success— these were the tools of Franco-German rapprochement and hence the tools that made European integration possible.

Furthermore, Kagan argues, having subjected their own interstate relations to the rule of law, 'Europe's experience of successful multilateral governance has in turn produced an ambition to convert the world'. Indeed, Kagan (2002: 12) goes so far as to identify US unilateralism as the primary threat to Europe's multilateralising mission.

Once again, there is a strong element of truth to Kagan's portrait – and European officials' self-portrait – of the EU as the primary defender of multilateral rules and institutions. However, the EU's commitment to multilateralism – both within the Union and in its relations with the wider world – is more recent, and more selective, than either the Union or its critics (or supporters) generally acknowledge. In a recent article, for example, Orfeo Fioretos (2001: 215) suggests that EU member states support specific forms of multilateral cooperation if and insofar as such cooperation allows them to sustain their comparative economic advantage. State preferences for 'integration' among member states are not monolithic, with some states favouring and others rejecting European integration across the board. Instead, according to Fioretos, states are selective in their support for specific multilateral rules and institutional forms, favouring those that are likely to produce favourable 'policy streams' over time in a given issue-area. The UK, for example, is widely considered to be an opponent of deeper multilateral cooperation, yet in areas such as financial services (where the UK possesses a longstanding comparative advantage thanks to the City of London) the UK has been a leader in pressing for ambitious and legally binding EU rules to liberalise trade. Similarly, 'integrationist' countries such as Germany and Italy may favour multilateral cooperation generally, but oppose binding multilateral rules or institutional reforms that might threaten valued domestic policies (for instance, German opposition to the proposed EU Directive on corporate takeovers, and Italian concerns over the extent of the EU's common arrest warrant).

The selective and contested nature of EU multilateralism is reflected as well in the long and tortuous development of its CFSP. There can be little doubt that the Union has made great strides in the coordination of national foreign policy positions through the increasingly elaborate network of coordinating committees that now regularly meet to hammer out, and represent to the world, common EU positions in a broad range of issue-areas (Forster and Wallace 2000). In recent years, moreover, EU cooperation has extended increasingly to the realm of defence. Nevertheless, as Jolyon Howorth points out in this volume, significant obstacles remain to a genuinely common foreign and defence policy for the Union, most notably in the unwillingness of EU members to authorise qualified majority voting on foreign and defence policy issues. Indeed, even within areas that are the subject of CFSP deliberations, unilateral initiatives by the Union's larger states have been common, ranging from the unilateral German decision to recognise Croatia and Slovenia in 1991 to the British decision to side with the US on Iraq in 2003. In the CFSP as in other areas, EU member states have carefully balanced the benefits of common policy positions with their continuing desire for flexibility in the making of important foreign policy decisions, resulting in a CFSP that combines the aspiration of a genuinely multilateral foreign policy with the continuing latitude for individual states to adopt independent stances on specific issues.

The selective nature of the EU's multilateralism is perhaps best illustrated, however, in the case of external trade policy – the oldest and most extensive external competence of the Union, and hence where we might expect the Union's internal multilateralism to manifest itself as support for the principles of multilateralism at the global level. Here we find that, despite the strength of the EU's trade mandate, the Union's trade policy, and its attitude toward multilateral GATT rules, were largely defensive through the mid-1980s, with the EU attempting to defend the CAP, European audiovisual subsidies and quotas, and other domestic policies from repeated challenges under GATT law. Indeed, as recently as 1982, the EU opposed the Reagan administration's demands for the opening of a new trade round, fearing the imposition of new and unwelcome rules on agriculture and audiovisuals.

After the mid-1980s, EU policy toward the GATT took on a more constructive tone, with the Union making difficult concessions to help complete the Uruguay Round in 1994, and later making extensive use of WTO dispute settlement procedures to challenge the unfair trading practices of its partners, including the US. Again contrary to Kagan's 'power and weakness' argument, however, the EU's increasing engagement with the multilateral trading system reflected not weakness, but the revitalisation of the internal market programme in the 1980s and the increasing acceptance of neoliberal trade policies among the Union's member governments (Woolcock 2000). Indeed, the contemporary EU has been a strong supporter of the Doha Development Agenda, pressing for a wide-ranging negotiation covering trade, environment, and competition issues. The Union has also become a leading promoter of harmonised international regulatory standards, seeking to export its common European standards to the rest of the world.

Nevertheless, in trade as in other areas, the Union's support for strong multilateral rules and institutions remains selective, reflecting the substantive concerns of its member governments and especially their collective desire to preserve both national and EU-level policies from attack in the WTO. Despite its wide-ranging agenda for the WTO round, for example, the Union demonstrated a strong preference to limit its commitment to agricultural trade liberalisation, while at the same time seeking to keep audiovisual services off the WTO agenda through the retention of the 'cultural exception' first enunciated in the Uruguay Round.

This tension between multilateral norms and valued domestic policies is most evident in the area of food safety, where the Union has sought to defend domestic regulations from legal attack within the multilateral WTO dispute resolution mechanism. In 1999, for example, the WTO Appellate Body ruled with the US that the Union's ban on hormone-treated beef, undertaken in response to strong consumer preferences, was inconsistent with EU obligations under the Sanitary and Phytosanitary Agreement of the WTO, and ordered the Union to bring its domestic legislation into line or face US retaliation. Yet, facing opposition from European public opinion and hopeful of producing scientific findings that would eventually justify the ban, the EU failed to comply with the Appellate Body's decision. The result was the imposition by the US of punitive tariffs of $116.8 million against EU agricultural products such as *foie gras*, Roquefort cheese, and Dijon mustard. The EU and the US continued to consult regularly about the case, but the Union remained firm in its refusal to alter its domestic law, and the US persisted in the application of retaliatory sanctions (Pollack and Shaffer 2001).

The Union's staunch defence of its domestic food safety regulations against WTO legal disciplines, moreover, extends beyond the beef-hormones dispute to other areas, most notably the regulation of GM foods. As in the beef-hormones case, the US Food and Drug Administration has ruled that most GM foods are not substantially different from conventional foods, and therefore require no special procedures for approval or marketing, and on that basis US farmers and seed producers have quickly embraced GM foods and crops. By contrast, the EU, having experienced a series of food-safety scares over the past decade, has taken a more cautious approach, citing the 'precautionary principle' allowing regulation of risks even in the absence of clear scientific evidence. Specifically, the EU has adopted a series of Regulations and Directives laying down specific approval procedures for GM crops as well as requiring the labelling of foods from genetically modified varieties, while the Council of Ministers has maintained a *de facto* moratorium on the approval of new GM varieties even as the EU's scientific committees have continued formally to approve a number of varieties as posing no health risks to consumers. In response, the US challenged the EU moratorium before the WTO, while EU representatives insisted that 'in a democracy you have to take into account fears of the people, and the people in many European countries are concerned about genetically modified food'.[3]

The fundamental point here is that, like the US, the EU has sought to secure the adoption and implementation of multilateral rules that will support its domestic goals and priorities, while simultaneously protecting valued domestic legislation in areas like agriculture, audiovisual services, and food safety from attack within multilateral forums, even at the cost of defying WTO legal rulings. The EU remains, on the whole, a strong supporter of multilateral rules and institutions. Such support, however, reflects not an ideological or instinctive respect for multilateralism *per se*, but a sophisticated and instrumental calculation by EU member governments regarding the types of multilateral rules and institutions most conducive to the satisfaction of the Union's domestic and international preferences.

Conclusion

Both before and after 9/11, the contrast between the Bush administration's weak support for multilateral institutions and European enthusiasm for such institutions was unprecedentedly stark – so much so as to invite generalisations about the knee-jerk unilateralism of the US and the inherent multilateralism of the EU. As satisfying as such a depiction may be – particularly to the Bush administration's critics – there is little to be gained analytically from such an oversimplification, and much to be gained from a more subtle understanding of the selective nature of European as well as American support for multilateralism. As we have seen, both the US and the EU selectively support multilateral rules and institutions, as a function of their respective international positions as well as the domestic preferences of their governments and political constituencies. In this regard, the most thoughtful critiques of US foreign policy, such as that recently offered by Joseph Nye (2002), understand the long-term domestic and international sources of American opposition to multilateralism in making their case for a stronger US engagement with multilateral institutions, demonstrating that the Bush administration's aversion to multilateral commitments is – at least in some cases – myopic and ultimately self-defeating for a US that seeks to exercise global leadership. Such a case can and should be made, but broad caricatures of the US and the EU as Platonic ideal types of unilateralism and multilateralism do not help us make it.

Notes

1 I am grateful to Helen Wallace and William Wallace for challenging discussions on the subject of US and EU support for multilateralism, and to John Peterson for extensive comments on earlier drafts of this paper.
2 These are, respectively, the UN Conference on Trade and Development and the UN Educational, Scientific and Cultural Organisation. In other international institutions, such as the UN Security Council and the Bretton Woods Institutions, power differentials were explicitly acknowledged through weighted voting schemes that allowed the US and other great powers to retain greater influence over institutional outcomes.
3 Tony Van der Haegen, the EU Expert for Food Safety in Washington, DC, quoted in Becker 2003.

10 Conclusion

The end of transatlantic partnership?

John Peterson and Mark A. Pollack

The relationship between Europe and America evolves constantly, in response to both international developments and political changes on each side of the Atlantic. It resists simple characterisations. Even the considerably narrower liaison between the US and EU, which has mostly preoccupied our authors, has changed beyond recognition in the past 15 years and shows few signs of standing still. However, despite all the complexity surrounding the central subject of this book, it can be argued that we are left with a final, surprisingly simple set of questions: is the transatlantic relationship a durable alliance, with the potential to evolve into a 'strategic partnership', even in the face of the triple shocks of the George W. Bush administration, the war against terrorism and the war with Iraq? Is the relationship reinforced by forces of habit and history – even if 'Europe' is more often the EU than ever before? Is the transatlantic alliance buttressed, perhaps above all, by shared interests in global security and stability, and especially by very powerful functional pressures for cooperation in the war against terrorism?

To pose the question in another (in some ways opposite) way, if there ever *was* scope for a transatlantic 'strategic partnership', has that scope narrowed or widened as a result of recent developments? After all, we find an administration in the White House that seems far less concerned about Europe than the previous two, and far less multilateral in terms of its instincts and behaviour more generally. These traits were visible in bold relief when the US went to war with Iraq, in defiance of much of Europe and majorities of world opinion, in early 2003. Meanwhile, American society becomes ethnically less 'European', and incidentally more Asian and Latin American, every day.[1] Very serious trade wars over steel and US tax treatment of exports, inflamed by the rampant legalisation of the global trading system, show that diplomacy is being squeezed out of economic relations. They also make a mockery of the idea that intense transatlantic economic interdependence encourages 'partnership'.

Moreover, the transatlantic security alliance appears to be disintegrating; the Americans are far ahead in the so-called Revolution in Military Affairs (that is, broadly, the application of new technologies to weaponry and war-fighting), and will only increase their lead over Europe in the foreseeable future, to the point where there will be very little that Europe and the US can do together militarily. At an even more basic level, there remains the fundamental question of whether

US and European security interests have diverged in the absence of a Sov: threat. One view holds that 'the Soviet Union united the West, the Middle E: divides it' (Garton Ash 2003: 34). Almost no one believes that the tacit division of labour that has emerged – the US fights, the UN feeds, the EU funds – is the basis for a healthy security partnership.

A rather different, but still primordial question that lurks behind the basic 'durability' question is whether American support for European integration, which has remained strong and consistent throughout the post-war period (Lundestad 1997; Bossuat and Vaicbourdt 2001), is coming to an end. Paradoxically, just as the EU is doing what the Americans have most wanted it to do since the Cold War ended – enlarge to take in the countries of central and eastern Europe – is the EU about to become a far less effective, decisive, and action-oriented institution? Many in Washington think it is quite ineffective and indecisive already. An EU of 25 member states (and growing) could easily become a very different kind of international organisation; a *framework* institution like the OSCE, where governments can discuss their problems but rarely solve them, as opposed to the action-oriented institution the EU has become, or at least aspired to be, in recent years. The effect would be to exacerbate American frustration with the EU, which appears to have accumulated in recent years, and increase American indifference towards Europe.

Here, we make a final effort to confront these questions by culling evidence from the preceding chapters. First, we examine the evidence about the actual impact of the election of George W. Bush on transatlantic relations in terms of tangible interests and policies, as opposed to rhetoric and mood. Second, we revisit the questions of whether and how much 9/11 transformed transatlantic relations. Third, we consider the recent evolution of the US–EU relationship and particularly the transatlantic split over the 2003 war in Iraq. We conclude with some final reflections about the prospects for a strategic US–EU partnership evolving from the starting point of an international world that is widely viewed as 'unipolar'.

The election of George W. Bush

Throughout this volume, most of our contributors have visibly struggled to come to clear, clean, simple judgements on precisely what about transatlantic relations changed, and by how much, as a direct consequence of the election of George W. Bush in 2000. Quite frequently, our authors have described a particular policy act or gesture by the Bush administration – in Macedonia, in the steel dispute, on money laundering – as 'just about what the Clinton administration would have done'. It would be surprising if there were fewer such cases, as foreign policies typically change far less and less dramatically when governments change than is the case in most areas of public policy. Paradoxically, most governments come to power determined to develop a foreign policy that is clearly distinct from that of their predecessors, and the Bush administration was no exception (see Legro and Moravcsik 2001). Yet, to take one policy example, even an administration that seemed ideologically – even *theologically* – opposed to nation-building has found itself having to contribute to an international (and, incidentally, Europe-led) effort to reconstruct post-war Afghanistan, and considering how to mount a similar effort in post-Saddam Iraq.

In all of the issue-areas surveyed in this volume, there is evidence of considerable continuity as well as change in the transition from Clinton to Bush. In foreign and defence policy, Jolyon Howorth (Chapter 2) clearly distinguishes between three categories of problem that preoccupied the US and Europe as Clinton gave way to Bush. The first, extending to the Balkans and ESDP, saw very little change in US policy despite initial European concerns. The second, incorporating missile defence and US military doctrine, found the Bush administration taking forward policies – such as the commitment to implementing a working missile defence system, and thus withdrawing from the 1972 ABM Treaty in order to do so – that had been actively considered by the Clinton administration but not adopted largely out of concern for allied sensibilities. Similarly, while the treatment of 'rogue states' had long been a primary source of transatlantic contention under Clinton, the Bush administration's post-9/11 declaration of an 'axis of evil', and its determination to secure Iraqi disarmament through pre-emptive attack if necessary, substantially increased the gulf separating the US from most European governments (see p.134 onwards below). The third category – US attitudes towards international treaties and conventions – obviously witnessed substantial change.

By contrast, Baldwin *et al.* (Chapter 3) find it virtually impossible to ascribe any significant change in the transatlantic economic relationship to the election of George W. Bush, even if electoral considerations may have shaped the steel dispute and 2002 US Farm Bill in ways that were specific to the calculations of an incumbent Republican administration.[2] Similarly, there is little in Wyn Rees' chapter (4) to suggest that cooperation on justice and internal security policy is any more or less a 'fragile flower' under Bush than it was under Clinton. In fact, a major source of tension post-9/11 in this sector turned out to be the Clinton-era 'Antiterrorism and Effective Death Penalty Act'.

There is perhaps more evidence of change in the transition from Clinton to Bush in Daniel Bodansky's treatment of environmental diplomacy (Chapter 5) and the analysis of the Middle East offered by Costanza Musu and William Wallace (Chapter 8). Bodansky notes that transatlantic splits on bio-engineering, chemicals, trade, and climate change were already apparent under Clinton, not least because of his need to work with a Republican Senate. Nevertheless, Bodansky concludes that the election of George W. Bush 'changed the equation dramatically', and made transatlantic agreement on major environmental issues such as climate change – never consummated but always achievable under Clinton – impossible.

In the Middle East, the Clinton administration expended considerable diplomatic effort, up until the very last days of its time in office, to find a settlement in the Israel–Palestine dispute. George W. Bush came to office determined not to have his office 'demeaned' by a fruitless quest for agreement between parties whose positions had become intractable. The domestic political equation clearly matters here, with the Republican right giving sustenance to the 'Likudisation' of US policy under Bush, a development that would have been unlikely under Clinton (or Gore). Yet, following an initial pre-9/11 period of disengagement by the Bush team, there seems little change in the US attitude toward EU involvement in the Middle East, with the Union's participation in the Colin Powell-backed 'quartet' allowing broadly the sort of involvement that the Union had under Clinton.

In the Balkans and Russia, there is little evidence that Bush's election induced major changes. Peterson's analysis (Chapter 7) implies that the EU would have emerged as the policy leader in the Balkans, with considerable American encouragement, even if Gore had beaten Bush in 2000. Similarly, Margot Light (Chapter 6) finds that the Bush administration inherited an agenda of 'intractable issues' that had not been resolved under Clinton. Meanwhile, basic differences in US and EU approaches to Moscow – America's based on hard power and high politics, the EU's focused on soft power and low politics – were unlikely to be altered very much by a change in the US administration.

Finally, in terms of support for multilateral rules and institutions, Mark Pollack (Chapter 9) suggests that declining US support for multilateralism has been a decades-long secular trend, reflecting both international developments and domestic restraints imposed by a Republican-controlled Congress. As we have seen, the Clinton administration's ostensible commitment to multilateralism co-existed with numerous acts that could only be described as 'unilateral', including its decision not to sign the 1996 treaty on anti-personnel land mines. Nevertheless, the Bush administration's abrupt dismissal of the Kyoto Protocol, its unprecedented removal of the US signature from the treaty establishing the International Criminal Court, and its more general willingness to abandon multilateral negotiations in favour of unilateral actions and 'coalitions of the willing' represent a significant intensification of US unilateralism.

In all of these areas, two factors make judging the impact of Bush's election on US–EU relations difficult. One is that many analysts (see Mearsheimer 1990; Walt 1998/99; Rodman 1999) detected drift or division in the transatlantic relationship as a 'secular' trend before Bush's election. Gauging whether the Bush administration accelerated that trend by comparison with a potential Gore administration takes us into the difficult realm of counter-factual reasoning. The second is, of course, the difficulty of disentangling the impact of the Bush administration from that of 9/11 on US foreign policy and transatlantic relations.

All of that said, it is difficult to find any analyst – in this volume or elsewhere – who would argue that the transatlantic relationship was stronger by the middle of George W. Bush's first term than it was when Bush was elected. There is no doubt that predictions or warnings of a transatlantic divorce became considerably more frequent and prominent after Bush's election than before it (see Daalder 2001; Matthews 2001; Moïsi 2001; Kagan 2002). And no one suggested that transatlantic relations were stronger because Bush was President.

The impact of 9/11

Intially, at least, most students of transatlantic relations felt a strong sense that 'everything changed' after 9/11. In their immediate aftermath, the attacks of

9/11 seemed to unite the US with its European and NATO allies in the face of a new and common adversary. Within months, however, it became clear that the US would not turn to NATO to fight the war in Afghanistan, and other transatlantic differences – over the treatment of prisoners at Guantanamo Bay, the 'axis of evil,' and Iraq – suggested that the ongoing war against terrorism could corrode the transatlantic alliance.

So, did 9/11 transform US–EU relations? The evidence uncovered by our authors suggests: yes, in some ways, but less so than is commonly assumed. In the foreign and security policy arena, Howorth finds an increasing will among Europeans to cooperate with the US on foreign and security policy, but also increasing tension between the two sides over the unilateral conduct of the US war in Afghanistan, over Iraq, and over the future of the Atlantic alliance. At first glance, then, 9/11 seems to have had on balance a damaging effect on the transatlantic partnership. It is important to note, however, that many of these tensions – including the overwhelming military dominance of the US, American impatience with the pace of European defence spending, the question of missile defence, and differences about the proper way to engage with Iraq and other rogue states – were palpable during the Clinton years. In this context, 9/11 and the subsequent war on terrorism acted primarily as catalysts, posing more sharply questions that had been at least already latent in the relationship.

In other issue-areas as well, we find greater than expected continuity in transatlantic relations before and after 9/11. In economic relations, Baldwin *et al.* are cagey about the notion that the launch of the Doha Development Agenda (whatever its eventual fate) less than two months after 9/11 was a product of joint US–EU leadership to achieve global solidarity in the face of a common terrorist threat (Chapter 3). As we have seen, transatlantic cooperation on justice and home affairs *was* given a boost, mostly because the EU was pushed to come to internal agreements that it could not agree pre-9/11. But as Rees makes clear, by no means did the troubles in this area of US–EU relations disappear (Chapter 4). And 9/11's main impact on environmental diplomacy was, in Bodansky's view, to confirm the Bush administration's belief that the Kyoto Protocol and other environmental agreements were 'second-tier' issues (Chapter 5).

It is perhaps in relations with Russia and western policy in the Balkans that change, clearly attributable to 9/11, is most perceptible. As Margot Light points out in Chapter 6, the US relationship with Russia seemed to be headed for difficult times at the start of the Bush administration, whose enthusiasm for missile defence and NATO enlargement, coupled with its disdain for arms control treaties, put the administration on a collision course with both Russian and European views. Following 9/11, however, Russian President Vladimir Putin cast his lot clearly with the US in the war on terrorism, calculating that Russian support would translate into dividends elsewhere in the relationship, including by muteing western criticism of the ongoing war in Chechnya. US use of military bases in former Soviet states in southern Asia during the Afghani campaign was the first manifestation of this change. Perhaps the most durable was

NATO's enlargement in late 2002 to take in seven new central and eastern European states, including three Baltic states which were formerly part of the Soviet Union, with barely a whisper of dissent from Moscow. The groundwork had been laid earlier in 2002, when a new set of NATO–Russia exchanges were agreed that all but made Russia a member itself of the Alliance. As Gordon (2001–2: 89) had expected, 9/11 had the effect of 'reminding Russia of its common interests with the West ... help[ing] to transform long-hostile NATO–Russia relations' and, perhaps ultimately, 'promot[ing] peace across the continent'.

As for the effort to rehabilitate the Balkans, 9/11 mostly reinforced the Bush administration's determination to reduce or end the US military presence, and the EU's determination to use the region as a staging post for the first actual use of the ESDP. But allegations of Serbian arms sales to Iraq and claims that Al-Qaeda operated in the Balkans reminded both the US and EU that today's failed states could easily become tomorrow's rogue states. Again, even the staunchest ideologues in the Bush administration could not deny that nation-building had moved up several notches in the hierarchy of western policy objectives after 9/11.

In the Middle East, finally, 9/11 left undiminished the longstanding US–European disagreements about the Arab–Israeli conflict and the treatment of rogue states such as Iraq and Iran. As Musu and Wallace imply (Chapter 8), the Middle East is perhaps *the* single foreign policy issue on which US–EU differences (as opposed to 'US–European') are the most longstanding and deeply rooted. After all, the first truly substantive and effectual EU foreign policy, agreed under the old European Political Cooperation mechanism, was the 1980 Venice Declaration recognising the right of the Palestinians to an independent homeland.

Similarly, regarding Iraq, the European contribution to the US-led coalition in the 1991 Gulf War left an impression of solidarity that obscured solo acts of French diplomacy before the war and German haggling afterwards over the cash price it had to pay to support an allied effort to which it did not contribute militarily (Peterson 1996: 71–2). Few foreign policy issues divided the US and Europe during the Clinton years – or, for that matter, European states (France and the UK particularly) – more than UN sanctions against Iraq. Saddam Hussein's continued rule was a standing agenda item for hawks in the George W. Bush administration, many of whom believed that Europeans were being duped by Saddam's propaganda, especially about the effect of sanctions on Iraq's weakest citizens. But transatlantic divisions on Iraq were deep partly because they were longstanding.

What *was* surprising after 9/11 was how often the US and Europe appeared to disagree despite the potential, at least, for the war on terrorism to galvanise the transatlantic alliance and induce collective action as the Cold War had done. Of course, divergence was far clearer in terms of policy form, style and presentation than in policy substance in most areas. In important respects, 9/11 *did* induce impressive, unprecedented collective action. Take, as one example, the EU's move (based in large part on American intelligence) to freeze the assets of 11 international terrorist organisations and seven individuals in May 2002. It marked the first time that the EU had ever taken such action against non-European organisations.

The move was 'wholeheartedly welcome[d]' by senior US officials.[3] Yet here, as is so often the case, EU policy was not identical to US policy and not by coincidence. The Union froze the assets of individuals linked to Hezbollah, the Lebanese militant group, and Hamas, the Palestinian group, but not the organisations themselves (both branded as terrorist groups by the US). The intent was to make a distinction – an important one to many European governments – between terrorists and legitimate political groups. The full extent of US–European divisions over the Middle East and rogue states, however, would be revealed only a year after 9/11, with the start of the debate over the war in Iraq.

Beyond Afghanistan: US national strategy and Iraq

Thus far, we have considered the effects of the election of George W. Bush and that of 9/11 and the war on terrorism separately, in order to parse out the respective impact of each on the transatlantic partnership. In the longer term, however, the real importance of these two events may lie not in their independent effects but in how they eventually interacted with one another. The Bush administration was populated by a diverse collection of foreign policy specialists, ranging from traditional realists such as Powell and Rice, who favoured a selective embrace of multilateral institutions and conceived the US national interest modestly, to neoconservatives including Rumsfeld and Wolfowitz, who shared a broader and more ambitious agenda for US foreign policy and a generalised disdain for multilateral institutions. As such, the most significant effect of 9/11 may have been indirect and internal to the Bush administration: it tipped the balance towards the neoconservatives, whose subsequent policy imprint was indelible on the new American doctrine of pre-emptive war, the naming of the so-called 'axis of evil', and the conduct of the war with Iraq (Purdum 2003). The Iraqi war, in turn, created new and arguably unprecedented tensions in the transatlantic relationship, while at the same time putting the EU's Common Foreign and Security Policy (CFSP) under severe strain.

The question of what to do about Iraq had arisen in the immediate aftermath of 9/11, when Wolfowitz in particular had pressed forcefully for a strike on Iraq as a response to the terrorist attacks on the US. The initial responses of principal foreign policy figures within the administration ranged from mild surprise to shock. At the time, Bush sided with Powell and others in the administration who preferred to focus on Afghanistan and Al-Qaeda, and to avoid jeopardising the multilateral coalition the administration sought to build in the war on terrorism (Woodward 2003).

By the beginning of 2002, however, the fighting was largely over in Afghanistan. Attention thus shifted to continuing US concerns about the development of weapons of mass destruction by rogue states. These concerns were first articulated in Bush's January 2002 State of the Union address, in which Iraq was mentioned, along with Iran and North Korea, as part of the 'axis of evil'.

By September 2002, the administration had released a revised *National Security Strategy* that, amongst other innovations, provided explicit arguments for the pre-emptive use of US force against rogue states developing weapons of mass destruction. Defying the view that even a nuclear-armed Iraq could be success-fully contained and deterred, the US administration argued that 'deterrence based only upon the threat of retaliation is less likely to work against leaders of rogue states more willing to take risks, gambling with the lives of their people, and the wealth of their nation'.[4] In light of this purported failure of deterrence and containment, and 'to forestall or prevent such hostile acts by our adversaries, the United States will, if necessary, act pre-emptively' (White House 2002).

By autumn 2002, it was clear that Bush had sided decisively with Wolfowitz and other officials determined to use military force, if necessary, to disarm Saddam Hussein and achieve 'regime change' in Iraq. At the urging of its European allies and the State Department, however, the administration initially sought international support and legitimacy for its policy through the United Nations Security Council. Addressing the UN General Assembly in September 2002, Bush challenged the UN to demonstrate its relevance by countering the 'grave and gathering danger' of Iraq. Bush stressed that Iraq had flouted no fewer than a dozen previous Security Council Resolutions requiring its disarmament and suspended cooperation with UN weapons inspectors, who had been expelled from Iraq in 1998. The US therefore proposed a new Security Council Resolution ordering Iraq to comply with UN resolutions or face the threat of military force.

The Bush administration's assertive policy towards Iraq was not *only* a source of disaffection within the transatlantic alliance; it also exposed fault lines among European governments, and between European élites and public opinion. Among EU governments, the US hard line towards Iraq was supported most strongly by British Prime Minister Tony Blair, who staked his leadership on the question of Iraq despite the strong opposition of most of the British public and much of his own party. But it was also supported by other (mostly centre-right) governments in Spain, Italy, Denmark, Portugal and the Netherlands. Moreover, the US line was embraced by most governments in the EU candidate countries of central and eastern Europe, which remained grateful for US support during the Cold War and continued to look to Washington, rather than to the EU, to guarantee their security.

By contrast, the prospect of military action in Iraq was vigorously opposed by the German government of Chancellor Gerhard Schröder, who had campaigned successfully for a second term as Chancellor on a strongly anti-war platform. Meanwhile, the French government of President Jacques Chirac, practising a tra-ditional Gaullist policy of seeking to maximise French and European influence and restrain the US, lined up with their post-war German allies[5], with Belgium and Luxembourg usually in tow. While supporting the goal of Iraqi disarmament, both Schröder and Chirac – along with Russia's Vladimir Putin, with whom they frequently conferred – consistently opposed pre-emptive military action against Iraq. In this sense, US Defence Secretary Donald Rumsfeld's characterisation of France and Germany as 'old Europe', although crude, *did* capture a sharp cleav-age within the EU: between France and Germany on one hand and other current and candidate members on the other.

This cleavage reappeared with remarkable consistency within the UN Security Council, in NATO, and within the EU's Common Foreign and Security Policy (CFSP). During the initial UN Security Council debate on the proposed US resolution, the US and UK sought the adoption of a single, toughly worded resolution that would authorise the automatic use of military force in the event of Iraqi non-compliance. France and Russia (as permanent members) and Germany (as a rotating non-permanent member) resisted any 'automaticity' in the resolution, insisting that, in the event of a 'material breach', the US would have to return to the Security Council for a second resolution explicitly authorising the use of force against Iraq. On 8 November 2002, after weeks of laborious negotiations, the Security Council unanimously approved a compromise in Resolution 1441, which outlined an enhanced inspections regime and threatened unspecified 'serious consequences' in the event of Iraq's failure to comply. Even Syria voted in favour of Resolution 1441.

Its adoption, however, only papered over sharp differences between the two sides. As the US became increasingly insistent on labelling Iraq as being in material breach, Powell appeared before the Security Council on 5 February 2003 and presented US evidence of Iraqi non-compliance. Iraq's behaviour, Powell argued, constituted a clear pattern of deception, and the US began to press for a second UN resolution authorising the use of force. Many remained unconvinced by Powell's presentation. Subsequently, the French Foreign Minister, Dominique de Villepin, and his German counterpart, Joschka Fischer, issued a joint proposal on 9 February calling for an intensified weapons-inspection regime, including a tripling of the number of inspectors and the addition of surveillance flights over Iraq. The Franco-German proposal was rejected out of hand by the US.[6] The Security Council remained stalemated throughout February and early March, with the permanent members split between an Anglo-American faction (supported by non-permanent members Spain and Bulgaria) in favour of military force, and a French and Russian alliance (supported by China as well as Germany) arguing that inspections be allowed to continue.

In mid-February, the debate spilled over from the United Nations into NATO. The Bush administration sought to convince Turkey to allow US troops access to Turkish military bases from which a possible attack on northern Iraq could be launched. Thus, it proposed that NATO agree to transfer Patriot missile systems, AWACs reconnaissance planes and other assets to defend Turkey in the event of a possible attack from Iraq. Once again, France and Germany (supported by Belgium) blocked the proposed action, on the grounds that it prejudged the inevitability of war with Iraq. Under pressure from the US and other NATO allies, and after days of bitter negotiations, Germany and Belgium eventually agreed to the proposed measures, which were adopted within the NATO Defence Planning Council, of which France is not a member (Bernstein and Weisman 2003). Despite this minor victory, however, the Bush administration discovered once again on 1 March that it could not count on the unanimous support of NATO, when the Turkish Parliament rejected a proposal to allow US troops to use Turkish territory as a staging area for war against Iraq.

Within the EU, the Iraqi question threatened to undermine years of progress in the creation of the CFSP, as well as to poison relationships between existing EU member states and the candidate countries of central and eastern Europe. The EU of 15 essentially papered over their differences, issuing *communiqués* on Iraq that focused on areas of agreement, such as the importance of a UN role in post-war Iraq, aiming higher than the lowest common denominator but also downplaying deep substantive differences.[7] Tensions between current and future EU members burst into the open in February 2003, after most central and east European governments publicly stated their support for the US position on Iraq. Speaking after a European summit in Brussels, Chirac stated bluntly that the candidate countries had missed 'an opportunity to keep quiet' about Iraq, and even suggested that countries such as Romania and Bulgaria had endangered their chances of joining the EU (Smith 2003). Chirac's comments predictably stoked a backlash among central and east European leaders, and deepened the schism between 'old' and 'new' Europe.

The final rupture came in early March, when the foreign ministers of France, Russia and Germany repeated their fundamental opposition to war and to any second UN resolution.[8] Soon afterwards, Chirac went as far as to say that he was prepared to veto 'under any circumstances'. Faced with the prospect of French and Russian vetoes, the US and its allies in the Security Council introduced a draft second resolution giving Iraq a final deadline of 17 March to disarm, hoping to secure the support of at least a majority of the (15) members of the Security Council, thereby isolating France and Russia. After a week of intense diplomacy, however, the resolution's sponsors were able to count on support only from the US, UK, Spain and Bulgaria. The text was thus withdrawn and final preparations for war, without a UN mandate, were begun.

The war in Iraq ended more quickly, and with fewer Iraqi and coalition casualties, than any but the most optimistic Pentagon supporters had forecast, even if US war planners seemed ill-prepared for dealing with the post-war challenges of restoring order and building democracy in Iraq. In any event, the brevity and apparent success of the US-led war effort arguably limited the damage to the transatlantic alliance, and allowed Europe and America to concentrate on healing the rifts that opened up during the prelude to the war. The importance of doing so was underlined most clearly by Blair, who sought desperately both during and after the war to find elements of unity between the US and EU.

The months immediately following the war saw the Bush administration and the EU seeking, with varying degrees of success, to minimise their differences over issues such as the administration of post-war Iraq and the Arab–Israeli conflict, while preventing the spread of tensions from the security sphere to the economic relationship. The Bush administration indicated its willingness to allow the UN to play a 'vital' (albeit secondary) role in post-war Iraq. The French government – on the defensive following the brief and successful US-led war – signalled that it would agree to drop UN sanctions against Iraq as favoured by the US. Moreover, a Bush administration that had largely withdrawn from the Arab–Israeli conflict finally published a 'road map' for peace that had been drawn up by the Quartet (the US, EU, Russia and the UN), and Powell followed up with his first visit to the region in nearly a year. Within NATO, the bitter disputes over Turkey lingered, prompting wider US doubts about the alliance as a war-fighting organisation.[9] Still, the alliance agreed to take on post-war peacekeeping roles in Afghanistan and Iraq. On the economic front, US officials, including Trade Representative Robert Zoellick, indicated that the US would not attempt to 'punish' France or other EU countries for their position on Iraq, and promised to engage the EU in moves to kick-start the slow-moving talks on the Doha Development Agenda.

Nevertheless, substantial tensions remained on both the security and economic sides of the relationship. Although the US and the EU agreed in principle to a UN role in Iraq and the removal of sanctions, the precise arrangements remained in flux and the lines of dispute were nearly identical to those of the pre-war UN debate. In the Middle East, the Bush administration joined the EU in pressing for a settlement of the Arab–Israeli conflict. But it remained unclear whether the Bush administration, facing an election in 2004, would press the Sharon government to compromise over delicate issues such as Israeli settlements in the West Bank. Despite official statements to the contrary, the end of the war in Iraq threatened actually to worsen US–EU trade relations, with the US freed (at least temporarily) from the demands of coalition-building and able to press its trade interests vigorously, as it did in May 2003 when it tabled a WTO legal case against the EU over genetically modified foods (Becker 2003).

Perhaps most disturbingly in terms of the long-term prospects for the relationship, the Bush administration indicated that it would begin to try to play European national capitals against each other, rather than dealing with the Union as a whole, on a range of security and other issues.[10] Such an approach was not, of course, entirely new, as evidenced by the Clinton administration's negotiation of individual Open Skies agreements (on airline services) with European governments over the strenuous objections of the Commission. Nevertheless, the Bush administration's apparent disposition to reward and punish individual European states for their differing positions on Iraq points our attention again to the crucial importance of European unity, not simply for Europe but also for the nature and the health of the transatlantic partnership.

The EU: what kind of partner?

An undercurrent of this volume, informing every chapter implicitly or explicitly, has been the maturation of the EU. After (and even before) the Cold War ended, it emerged as both the main European interlocutor to the US in transatlantic relations and an increasingly global power. The Euro, the ESDP, and the EU's contribution to the war on terrorism all testify to the Union's ambitions and increased importance in international politics.

Even before Iraq, however, the EU was never short of critics. Outside of its core economic competences, the EU's international achievements have always seemed very modest, even empty, when considered alongside its ambitions. A prime example is the ESDP. A lack of tangible progress or any strategic concept to guide it has prompted a raft of stinging accusations that the Union is merely 'playing at greatness' (Lindley-French 2002a), as opposed actually to achieving great power status.

The EU still often runs into trouble trying to sell the US on new policy cooperation via the ESDP or the Common Foreign and Security Policy (CFSP) or its mechanisms for common internal security policies. The trouble arises because all continue to feature fundamental European divisions. Such divisions, already visible during the early 1990s in the Balkans, were painfully manifest once again over Iraq in 2002–3, when the EU lapsed into its habitual practice of issuing carefully scripted communiqués that mostly focused on issues – however secondary in importance – on which agreement could be reached.[11]

In fairness, the EU shows considerably more solidarity on crucial foreign policy issues – including Iraq and the Middle East as well as North Korea, Zimbabwe, and others – than it is given credit for in the media. Arguably, the Union has used the enlargement process as its most effective tool of *foreign* policy, coaxing revolutionary economic and political reforms out of its neighbours to the east and south. It is easily forgotten that the EU responded to 9/11, at least indirectly, by embracing a bold, 'big bang' enlargement of ten or more new states to stabilise its immediate neighbourhood – when the smart money prior to 9/11 was on an enlargement of around four or so (Missiroli 2002). Few in Washington seemed to remember that there was no other issue of European integration that successive post-Cold War administrations, along with most members of Congress, cared about more deeply than enlargement.

Furthermore, it would be risky to bet *against* a major overhaul of the CFSP – or, for that matter, the Justice and Home Affairs pillar – in the EU Treaty reforms set to take place by 2004. One of the mostly widely-shared views within the Convention on the Future of Europe, charged with preparing a draft 'constitutional treaty' for consideration by EU governments, was that making the Union a more effective global actor was a burning, urgent priority.

Yet it is also reasonable to think that no revolution is on the horizon. As long as the EU retains its awkward, delay-prone and quite strictly intergovernmental system for determining foreign policy, the CFSP will invite the ire of critics who dismiss it as 'little more than a good old-fashioned alliance' (Lindley-French 2002a: 799), and not even a terribly effective one: 'the political deficiencies and debilities of even this united Europe make it unlikely that a European vision of international order will provide a serious alternative to that of the United States in the foreseeable future' (Rieff 1999–2000: 8).

A central problem is that the CFSP remains a political tool designed mostly to advance the development of the EU as a system of political union. It remains as much – perhaps more – an internal EU policy than a tool for projecting Europe's power abroad or defending EU citizens. The most important goal of most internal EU negotiations related to the CFSP remains simply *agreeing*, as opposed to solving foreign policy problems. The effect has been to detach the EU 'from the strategic environment in which it resides, with the result that strategy and policy come to be driven by internal political factors rather than external realities' (Lindley-French 2002a: 809). Thus, for example, the Petersberg tasks – humanitarian and rescue missions, peacekeeping, etc. – become a substitute for military doctrine because they happen to reflect what could be classified as 'shared European values'.

Under the CFSP, the Union is considerably better at saying things – and saying them with something like one voice – than it was under the old European Political Cooperation mechanism. But it is only marginally better at *doing* things in foreign policy. In the eyes of Washington, 'ironically, while European nations criticise America for isolationism, they have become entirely absorbed in their own affairs over the past decade ... [Europe's] disarray and resentment ... not US unilateralism [is] the greatest threat to the Atlantic Alliance today' (Zakaria 2001: 31).

In a contest to determine the 'biggest threat' to the transatlantic relationship, American unilateralism and European disarray would probably finish tied in a dead heat. However, the transatlantic 'values gap' that was often alleged to have surfaced after Bush's election – over the death penalty, the environment, abortion, religion and gun control – would appear only much further down the list of threats. Whatever their quarrels, it remains clear that norms, values and culture bind the EU and the US together far more strongly that either party is 'bound' to any other part of the world.[12]

That said, it is difficult to deny a fundamental and perhaps growing asymmetry between American and European power and perceptions on the most urgent questions of international politics. In particular, the military gap between the US and Europe, a consequence of America's Revolution in Military Affairs coupled with Europe's ostensible disarmament after 1990 (Lindley-French 2002a: 810), has become a yawning gulf. Perhaps even more ominously, there are signs that US and European perceptions of their respective strategic interests may be diverging, with the US increasingly determined to counter threats from terrorist groups and rogue states around the world, if necessary through the unilateral use of military force, while European countries increasingly seek security through engagement with problem states and multilateral institutions. Against this broader backdrop, it is easy to see why the EU's ambitions in defence policy are seen as trivial by American policymakers and commentators.

In the early twenty-first century, the EU – either as an institution or collection of individual states or some combination thereof – remained quite some distance from being capable of strategic partnership with the US. There was no doubt that the Union, considering where it was starting from, had taken huge steps forward towards developing that capability. And George W. Bush would not be president forever. But whether the EU would, one day, be capable of assuming or even demanding reciprocity from the Americans, remained an open question. It is a question this book simply cannot answer.

Notes

1   To illustrate the point, by the early twenty-first century the number of US students in secondary education who were studying Spanish was considerably higher than the combined total of students learning French, German, or Italian (Vaicbourdt 2001).

2   Even saying this much is subject to dispute, as the 2000 presidential race was so close – including in several farming and steel states – that a Gore administration may well have adopted very similar policies.

3   Quoted in *Financial Times*, 3 May 2002, p.4.

4   As usual, Bush himself stated the point even more bluntly, noting that, 'After September 11th, the doctrine of containment just doesn't hold any water, as far as I'm concerned' (quoted in Stevenson and Preston 2003). For good presentations of the viability of containment vis-à-vis Iraq, see Kenneth Pollack (2002) and Mearsheimer and Walt (2002).

5   In early 2003, while celebrating the 40th anniversary of the Elysée Treaty (which symbolised Franco-German post-war reconciliation and mandated close policy coop-eration), Germany and France pledged to 'coordinat[e] their positions closely to give peace every possible chance'. Rumsfeld's response to journalists' questions about European opposition to a war with Iraq was: 'You're thinking of Europe as Germany and France. I don't. I think that's old Europe ... vast numbers of other countries in Europe [are] not with France and Germany on this. They're with the United States'. See 'EU allies unite against Iraq war', available at: <http://news.bbc.co.uk/1/hi/world/europe/2683409.stm> (accessed 22 January 2003) and 'US Set to Demand That Allies Agree Iraq is Defying UN', New York Times, available at <http://www.nytimes.com/2003/01/23/international/middleeast/23IRAQ.html?todaysheadlines> (accessed 24 January 2003).

6   Powell's own response to the initiative was scathing: 'What France has to do and what I think Germany has to do ... is read 1441 again ... I don't think the next step should be "Let's send in more inspectors to be stiffed" [deceived]. Tripling the number of inspectors doesn't deal with the issue. This idea of more inspectors, or no-fly zones, or whatever else may be in the proposal that is being developed is a diversion, not a solution' (quoted in Black *et al.* 2003).

7   To illustrate, an extraordinary EU summit on 17 February insisted that 'War is not inevitable. Force should be used only as a last resort ... [but] Baghdad should have no illusions: it must disarm and cooperate immediately and fully. Iraq has a final opportunity to resolve the crisis peacefully. The Iraqi regime alone will be responsible for the consequences if it continues to flout the will of the international community and does not take this last chance'. See Council of the European Union, Presidency Conclusions, Extraordinary European Council, Brussels, 17 February 2003, 6466/03, POLGEN 7 (available at <http://ue.eu.int/en/Info/eurocouncil/index.htm>; accessed 18 May 2003).

8   'We will not allow the passage of a planned resolution that would authorise the use of force', said de Villepin. 'Russia and France, as permanent Security Council members, will fully assume all their responsibilities on this point' (quoted in Henley *et al.* 2003).

9   In particular, amidst signals (even from Powell) that the Bush administration would seek to 'punish' France for its opposition to the Iraqi war, Wolfowitz told the Senate Armed Services Committee that a reconsideration of NATO decision-making rules would be considered: 'I think we need to look very carefully at where France is bene-fiting from a one-way street, where they benefit and don't contribute' (quoted in McCartney 2003).

10 For example, a group of EU officials visiting the White House in spring 2003 were told by a senior Bush administration official that America's new policy towards Europe was one of 'disaggregation' (quoted in *The Economist*, 26 April 2003, p.40).

11 Take, as an example, the communiqué issued on behalf of the member states following the 16 April European Council meeting in Athens, where the members
emphasised their agreement on the importance of a UN role in Iraq and of finding a
solution to the Israel–Palestine problem, while side-stepping other issues that continued to divide the Union. See 'Presidency's Statement on Iraq, Athens 16/4/2003',
accessed on 6 May 2003 at <http://www.eu2003.gr/en/articles/2003/4/172534/
print.asp>

12 Possibly with Canada, Australia, and New Zealand excepted. We are grateful to
Jolyon Howorth for sharing his thoughts on this point and more generally for stimu-
lating our thinking about a wide range of issues with which we grapple in this chapter.

Bibliography

Abramowitz, M. and Hurlburt, H. (2002) 'Can the EU hack the Balkans?', *Foreign Affairs* 81 (5): 2–7.

Agence Europe (2002) 'Adoption of mandate for negotiating legal extradition cooperation agreement with USA', no. 8201, 27 April: 10.

Albright, M. K. (1998) 'The right balance will secure NATO's future', *Financial Times* 7 December: 16.

Aldrich, R. J. (2001) *The Hidden Hand: Britain, America and Cold War Secret Intelligence* (London: John Murray).

Allen, D. J. (2002) 'A Competitive Relationship: the Maturing of the EU–US Relationship, 1980–2000' in Ramet, S. P. and Ingebritsen, C. (eds) *Coming in From the Cold War: Changes in US–European Interactions since 1980* (Boulder and Oxford: Rowman and Littlefield).

Allen, D. and Pijpers, A. (1984) (eds) *European Foreign Policy-making and the Arab–Israeli Conflict* (The Hague: Kluwer Academic Publishers).

Allen, D. and Smith, M. (2002) 'External policy developments' in Edwards, G. and Wiessala, G. (eds) *The European Union: Annual Review of the EU 2001/2002* (Oxford and Malden MA: Blackwell): 97–115.

Andréani, G., Bertram, C. and Grant, C. (2001) *Europe's Military Revolution* (London: Centre for European Reform).

Antonenko, O. (2001) 'Putin's gamble', *Survival* 43 (4): 49–59.

Atlantic Council (2001) *Changing Terms of Trade: Managing the Transatlantic Economy* (Washington DC: Atlantic Council of the United States), April (available at <http://www.acus.org>, accessed 12 November 2002).

Atlantic Council (2002) *Elusive Partnership: US and European Policies in the Near East and the Gulf* (Washington DC: Atlantic Council of the United States), September (available at <http://www.acus.org/Publications/Default.htm>, accessed 11 November 2002).

Baker, G. (2001) 'Bush heralds era of US self-interest', *Financial Times* 24 April: 9.

Baker, J. A. III with DeFrank, T. M. (1995) *The Politics of Diplomacy* (New York: G. P. Putnam's Sons).

Bannerman, E., Everts, S., Grabbe, H., Grant, C. and Murray, A. (2001) *Europe after September 11th* (London: Centre for European Reform).

Becker, E. (2003) 'US takes food dispute to the WTO', *International Herald Tribune*, 14 May: 1, 4.

Beise, M. (2002) ' "Doha" and beyond', *Internationale Politik* 3 (Fall): 47–50.

Benedick, R. E. (1998) *Ozone Diplomacy: New Directions in Safeguarding the Planet* (Cambridge MA: Harvard University Press).

Bennett, C. (2001–02) 'Aiding America', *NATO Review* 49, Winter (available at <http://www.nato.int/docu/review/2001/0104-01.htm>, accessed 26 January 2003).

Bernstein, R. and Weisman, S. R. (2003) 'NATO settles rift over aid to Turks in case of war', *New York Times*, 17 February: 1, 17.

Bildt, C. (1998) *Peace Journey* (London: Weidenfeld and Nicolson).

Bildt, C. (2000) 'Winning the broader peace in Kosovo', *Financial Times* 19 January: 23.

Bildt, C. (2001) 'A second chance in the Balkans', *Foreign Policy* 80 (1) January–February: 148–58.

Black, I., Norton-Taylor, R. and Borger, J. (2003) 'US fury at European peace plan', *The Guardian*, 6 March (available at <http://www.guardian.co.uk/iraq/story 10,2763,892464,00.html> accessed 18 May 2003).

Blackwill, R. and Sturmer, M. (1997) (eds) *Allies Divided: Transatlantic Policies for the Greater Middle East* (Cambridge MA: The MIT Press).

Blinken, A. J. (2001) 'The false crisis over the Atlantic', *Foreign Affairs* 80 (3): 35–48.

Bodansky, D. (1994) 'Prologue to the Climate Change Convention' in Mintzer, I. M. and Amber Leonard, J. (eds) *Negotiating Climate Change: The Inside Story of the Rio Convention* (Cambridge: Cambridge University Press).

Bolton, J. (2000) 'The European threat to NATO's future', *Financial Times* 2 November: 25.

Boniface, P. (2001) 'The spectre of unilateralism', *Washington Quarterly* 24 (3): 139–47.

Bossuat, G. and Vaicbourdt, N. (2001) (eds) *États-Unis, Europe et Union Européenne: Histoire et Avenir d'un Paternariat Difficile (1945–99)* (Brussels and New York: PIE-Peter Lang).

Bowen, W. Q. (2001). 'Missile defence and the transatlantic security relationship', *International Affairs* 77 (3): 485–507.

Cambone, S., Daalder, I., Hadley, S. J. and Makins, C. J. (2000) *European Views of National Missile Defence* (Washington DC: Atlantic Council of the United States) Policy Paper, September.

Caporaso, J. (1993) 'International relations theory and multilateralism: the search for foundations' in Ruggie, J. G. (ed.) *Multilateralism Matters: the Theory and Praxis of an Institutional Form* (New York: Columbia University Press): 51–90.

Charnovitz, S. (2001) 'Rethinking WTO trade sanctions', *American Journal of International Law* 95 (4): 792–832.

Clark, W. K. (2001) *Waging Modern War: Bosnia, Kosovo, and the Future of Combat* (New York: Public Affairs).

Clarke, M. and Cornish, P. (2002) 'The European defence project and the Prague Summit', *International Affairs* 78 (4): 5–43.

Cooper, R. (2002) 'The new Liberal imperialism', *Observer* (London), 7 April (available at: <http://www.observer.co.uk/worldview/story/0,11581,680117,00.html>, accessed 27 January 2003).

Council of the European Union (2002) 'Highlights in EU–US cooperation, July 2001–June 2002', 10487/02, 28 June, Brussels.

Cox, A. and Chapman, J. (1999) *European Union External Cooperation Programmes* (London: Overseas Development Institute).

Daalder, I. H. (2000) 'Europe: rebalancing the US–European relationship', *Brookings Review* 18, Fall 2000: 22–5.

Daalder, I. H. (2001) 'Are the United States and Europe heading for divorce?', *International Affairs* 77 (3): 553–67.

Daalder, I. H., Goldgeier, J. M. and Lindsay, J. M. (2000) 'Deploying NMD: not whether, but how', *Survival* 42 (1): 6–28.

Daalder, I. H. and O'Hanlon, M. E. (2000) *Winning Ugly: NATO's War to Save Kosovo* (Washington DC: Brookings Institution).

Danilov, D. (1999) 'Potentsial'nyi soyuznik Moskvy' (Moscow's potential ally), *Nezavisimoye Voennoye Obozreniye*: 47.

Danilov, D. (2000). 'Rossiya v bolshoi Evrope: strategiya bezopasnosti' (Russia in a larger Europe: security strategy), *Sovremennaya Evropa* (Contemporary Europe), 2: 50–61.

Dannheisser, R. (2001) 'Senate joins House in approving anti-terrorism bill', *Washington File* 25 October (available at <http://www. usembassy.org.uk/terror247.htm>, accessed 6 June 2002).

Dassù, M. and Whyte, N. (2001–02) 'America's Balkan disengagement?', *Survival* 43 (4): 123–36.

David, C.-P. (2000) '"At Least 2001": US security policy and exit strategy in Bosnia', *European Security* 9 (1): 1–21.

de Durand, E. (2001) *The United States and the Alliance* (Paris: IFRI).

Deighton, A. (2001) 'The European Union and NATO's war over Kosovo' in Martin, P. and Brawley, M. R. (eds) *Allied Forces or Forced Allies? Kosovo and NATO's War* (New York: St Martin's Press).

Delpech, T. (2002) 'Four views of 9/11', *Internationale Politik* 3 (Fall): 3–8.

Department of State (2001) *Patterns of Global Terrorism* (Washington DC: US Government Printing Office), April.

Dockrill, S. (2002) 'Does a superpower need an alliance?', *Internationale Politik* 3 (Fall): 9–12.

Duke, S. (2002) 'CESDP and the EU response to 11 September: identifying the weakest link', *European Foreign Affairs Review* 7 (2): 155–75.

EABC (2002) *The United States and Europe: Jobs, Investment and Trade* (Washington DC: European–American Business Council) 8th edition, Spring.

Economist (2000) 'Colombia: send in the cows', 25 November: 92.

Eisenhower, S. (2002) *NATO at Fifty: Perspectives on the Future of the Atlantic Alliance* (Washington DC: Eisenhower Institute).

Eldridge, J. L. C. (2001) 'Kosovo: land of uncertainty', *European Security* 10 (2): 34–66.

European Commission (2001a) 'EU response to 11th September – European Commission Action', Memo/01/375, Brussels, 16 November 2001, (available at <http://europa.eu.int/geninfo/keyissues/110901>, accessed 11 June 2002).

European Commission (2001b) 'Reinforcing the transatlantic relationship: focusing on strategy and delivering results', Communication from the Commission to the Council, COM (2001) 154 final, 20 March.

European Commission (2002), 'EU response to 11 September – latest update on European Commission action', briefing on 12 March 2002 (available at <http://europa.eu.int/news/110901/index.htm>, accessed 10 June 2002).

European University Institute (2002) *The Political Economy of the Transatlantic Partnership* (San Domenico di Fiesole, Italy: Robert Schuman Centre for Advanced Studies) 15 March.

Everts, S. (2001a) *Unilateral America, Lightweight Europe? Managing Divergence in Transatlantic Foreign Policy* (London: Centre For European Reform).

Everts, S. (2001b) 'A new phase in US–European relations' in Bannerman, E., Everts, S., Grabbe, H., Grant, C. and Murray, A. (2001) *Europe after September 11th* (London: Centre for European Reform).

Everts, S. (2002) *Shaping a Credible EU Foreign Policy* (London: Centre for European Reform).

Featherstone, K. and Ginsberg, R. (1996) *The European Community and the United States in the 1990s: Partners in Transition* (London and New York: Macmillan and St Martin's Press) 2nd edition.

Fioretos, O. (2001) 'The domestic sources of multilateral preferences: varieties of capitalism in the European Community' in Hall, P. A. and Soskice, D. (eds) *Varieties of Capitalism: The Institutional Foundations of Comparative Advantage* (New York: Oxford University Press): 213–44.

Forster, A. and William W. (2001–02) 'What is NATO for?', *Survival* 43 (4): 107–22.

Freedman, L. (1982) 'The Atlantic crisis', *International Affairs* 58 (3): 381–99.

Freedman, L. (2002) (ed.) *Superterrorism: Policy Responses* (Oxford: Blackwell).

Frellesen, T. (2001) 'Processes and procedures in EU–US foreign policy cooperation: from the Transatlantic Declaration to the New Transatlantic Agenda' in Philippart, E. and Winand, P. (eds) *Ever Closer Partnership: Policy-Making in US–EU Relations* (Brussels: PIE-Peter Lang).

Frost, E. (1997) *Transatlantic Trade: a Strategic Agenda* (Washington DC: Institute for International Economics).

Frum, D. (2003) *The Right Man: the Surprise Presidency of George W. Bush* (New York: Random House).

Galen Carpenter, T. (2000) *NATO's Empty Victory: a Postmortem on the Balkan War* (Washington DC: CATO Institute).

Gardner, A. L. (1997) *A New Era in US–EU Relations? The Clinton Administration and the New Transatlantic Agenda* (Aldershot and Brookfield VT: Ashgate).

Gardner Feldman, L. (2001) 'Comparative differences in US and EU Balkans policies: an American perspective on the political dimension', *AICGS German Issues* 26: 1–29.

Garthoff, R. (1985) *Détente and Confrontation: Soviet–American Relations from Nixon to Reagan* (Washington DC: Brookings Institution).

Garthoff, R. (1994) *The Great Transition: American–Soviet Relations and the End of the Cold War* (Washington DC: Brookings Institution).

Garton Ash, T. (2003) 'Anti-Europeanism in America', *New York Review of Books* 13 February: 32–4.

Gedman, J. (2002) 'Transatlantic ties after 9/11: an American view', *Internationale Politik* 3 (Fall): 13–18.

Ginsberg, R. H. (2001) 'EU–US relations after Amsterdam: "Finishing Europe"' in Philippart, E. and Winand, P. (eds) *Ever Closer Partnership: Policy-Making in US–EU Relations* (Brussels: PIE-Peter Lang).

Ginsberg, R. H. (2002) 'United States–European Union political relations in the Bush administration', Paper presented to the Sixth Biennial Congress of the European Community Studies Association, Brussels, December.

Global Leaders of Tomorrow Environment Task Force (2002) *2002 Environmental Sustainability Index* (available at <http://www.ciesin.columbia.edu/indicators/ESI/>, accessed 24 January 2003).

Gnesotto, N. (2001) 'Terrorism and European integration', *Western European Union Institute for Security Studies Newsletter*: 1.

Gnesotto, N. (2002) 'Demilitarization in Europe, depoliticisation in the US', *Internationale Politik* 3 (Fall): 25–8.

Gompert, D. and Larrabee, F. S. (1998) *America and Europe: a Partnership for a New Era* (Cambridge: Cambridge University Press).

Gordon, Michael R. (2000) 'Bush would stop US peace-keeping in Balkan fights', *New York Times* 21 October.

Gordon, P. H. (1998) *The Transatlantic Allies and the Changing Middle East*, Adelphi Paper 322, International Institute for Strategic Studies (Oxford: Oxford University Press).

Gordon, P. H. (2001) 'Bush, missile defence and the Atlantic Alliance', *Survival* 43 (1): 17–36.

Gordon, P. H. (2001–02) 'NATO after 11 September', *Survival* 43 (4): 89–106.

Gordon, P. H. and Steinberg, J. B. (2001) *NATO Enlargement: Moving Forward*, Brookings Policy Briefs, 90: 1.

Gori, F. and Pons, S. (1996) (eds) *The Soviet Union and Europe in the Cold War, 1943–53* (Basingstoke and New York: Macmillan).

Grant, C. (2000) *Memorandum to the US President: a European Perspective on Global Alliances* (London: Centre For European Reform), internal document.

Grant, C. (2002) 'The eleventh of September and beyond: the impact on the European Union' in Freedman, L. (ed.) *Superterrorism: Policy Responses* (Oxford and Malden MA: Blackwell).

Greilsammer, I. and Weiler, J. H. H. (1987) *Europe's Middle East Dilemma: the Quest for a Unified Stance* (Boulder: Westview Press).

Guerrieri, P. (2002) 'The shock of 11 September and the Doha Development Round', *International Spectator* 37(1): 5–10.

Haass, R. N. (1999) (ed.) *Transatlantic Tensions: the United States, Europe, and Problem Countries* (Washington: Brookings Institution).

Haftendorn, H. (2002) 'NATO III', *Internationale Politik* 3 (Spring): 29–34.

Hassner, P. (2002) *The United States: the Empire of Force or the Force of Empire?* (Paris: Institute for Security Studies), Chaillot Paper No. 54.

Henly, J. Younge, G. and Paton Walsh, N. (2003) 'France, Russia and Germany harden stance', *The Guardian*, 6 March (available at <http://www.guardian.co.uk/print/0, 3858,4619206,00.html>, accessed 18 May 2003).

Henning, C. R. and Padoan, P. C. (2000) *Transatlantic Perspectives on the Euro* (Washington DC: Brookings Institution).

Hill, C. (1998) 'Closing the capabilities-expectations gap?' in Peterson, J. and Sjursen, H. (eds) *A Common Foreign Policy for Europe? Competing Visions of the CFSP* (London and New York: Routledge).

Hill, C. (2002a) '11 September 2001: perspectives from international relations', *International Relations* 16 (2): 257–62.

Hill, C. (2002b) 'EU foreign policy since 11 September 2001: renationalising or regrouping?', First Annual EWC Guest Lecture, University of Liverpool, 24 October.

Hoffmann, S. (2001) 'The United States and International Organizations' in Leiber, R. J. (ed.) *Eagle Rules? Foreign Policy and American Primacy in the 21st Century* (New York: Prentice Hall).

Holbrooke, R. (1998) *To End a War* (New York: the Modern Library), revised edition.

Howorth, J. (2000a) 'Britain, France and the European Defence Initiative', *Survival* 42 (2): 33–55.

Howorth, J. (2000b) *European Integration and Defence: the Ultimate Challenge?* (Paris: WEU Institute for Security Studies), Chaillot Paper No. 43.

Howorth, J. (2001) 'European defence and the changing politics of the European Union: hanging together or hanging separately?', *Journal of Common Market Studies* 39 (4): 765–89.

Howorth, J. and Keeler, J. T. S. (2003) (eds) *Defending Europe: the EU, NATO and the Quest for Autonomy* (New York: Palgrave).

Hunter, R. E. (2002) *The European Security and Defense Policy: NATO's Companion—or Competitor?* (Santa Monica CA: Rand).

Hurd, D. (2001) 'Europe must respond to the arc of danger', *Financial Times* 28 March: 23.

ICG (International Crisis Group) (2001a) 'Macedonia: war on hold', *Balkans Briefing* Skopje/Brussels: International Crisis Group, 15 August 2001 (available at <http://www.intl-crisis-group.org>, accessed 29 August 2001).

ICG (2001b) 'Macedonia: Filling the Security Vacuum', *Balkans Briefing* Skopje/Brussels: International Crisis Group, 8 September 2001 (available at <http://www.intl-crisis-group.org>, accessed 16 October 2001).

ICG (2001c) 'The wages of sin: confronting Bosnia's Republika Srpska', 17 October 2001 (available at <http://www.intl-crisis-group.org>, accessed 17 October 2001).

ICG (2002) 'The continuing challenge of refugee return in Bosnia and Herzegovina', 13 December 2002 (available at <http://www.intl-crisis-group.org>, accessed 14 January 2003).

Ignatieff, M. (2000) *Virtual War: Kosovo and Beyond* (London: Chatto and Windus).

IISS (International Institute for Strategic Studies) (2001) *The Military Balance 2001–2002* (London: Oxford University Press).

Ikenberry, G. J. (2000) *After Victory: Institutions, Strategic Restraint, and the Rebuilding of Order After Major Wars* (Princeton NJ: Princeton University Press).

Ikenberry, G. J. (2001) 'Getting hegemony right, ' *The National Interest* 63 (Spring): 17–24.

Jacobson, H. K. (2002) 'Climate change: unilateralism, realism and two-level games' in Patrick, S. and Forman, S. (eds) *Multilateralism and US Foreign Policy: Ambivalent Engagement* (Boulder: Lynne Rienner).

Jaffe, A. M. and Manning, R. A. (2001) 'Russia, energy and the west', *Survival* 43 (2): 133–52.

Joffe, J. (2001) 'Who's afraid of Mr. Big?', *The National Interest* 64 (Summer): 43–52.

Joffe, J. (2002) 'The alliance is dead. Long live the new alliance', *New York Times* 29 September: A3.

Judah, T. (2001) 'Greater Albania?', *New York Review of Books*, 17 May: 37–42.

Judt, T. (2002) 'Its Own Worst Enemy', *New York Review of Books*, 15 August: 12–17.

Kagan, R. (2002) 'Power and Weakness', *Policy Review*: 113 (available at <http://www.policyreview.org/JUN02/Kagan_print.html>, accessed 10 November 2002).

Kagan, R. (2003) *Of Paradise and Power: America vs Europe in the New World Order* (New York: Knopf).

Kahler, M. (1995) *Regional Futures and Transatlantic Economic Relations* (New York: Council on Foreign Relations Press).

Kay, S. (2002) 'The Prague Summit: beginning or end for NATO?', *Eisenhower Institute Personal Perspectives* (available at <www.eisenhowerinstitute.org>, accessed 27 January 2003).

Keohane, R. O. (1984) *After Hegemony* (Princeton: Princeton University Press).

Keohane, R. O. (2002) 'Ironies of sovereignty: the European Union and world order', *Journal of Common Market Studies* 40 (4): 743–65.

Kindleberger, C. (1973) *The World in Depression, 1929–1939* (Berkeley: University of California Press).

Klare, M. (1995) *Rogue States and Nuclear Outlaws: America's Search for a New Foreign Policy* (New York: Hill and Wang).

Krasner, S. D. (1985) *Structural Conflict: The Third World Against Global Liberalism* (Berkeley: University of California Press).

Krueger, A. (1995) *American Trade Policy: a Tragedy in the Making* (Washington DC: American Enterprise Institute).

Legro, J. W. and Moravcsik, A. (2001) 'Faux realism', *Foreign Policy*, July–August, 81–3 (available at <http://www.foreignpolicy.com/issue_julyaug_2001/legro.html>, accessed 17 January 2001).

Levy, D. L. and Newell, P. (2000) 'Oceans apart: business responses to global environmental issues in Europe and the United States', *Environment* 42 (9): 8–20.

Lewis, F. (1996) 'Politics is bad for foreign policy', *International Herald Tribune*, 22 September: 6.

Light, M., White, S. and Löwenhardt, J. (2000) 'Russian perspectives on European security', *European Foreign Affairs Review* 5 (4): 489–505.

Lindley-French, J. (2002a) 'In the shade of Locarno? Why European defence is failing', *International Affairs* 78 (4): 813–30.

Lindley-French, J. (2002b) *Terms of Engagement: the Paradox of American Power and the Transatlantic Dilemma post-11 September* (Paris: Institute for Security Studies) May, Chaillot Paper 52.

Lundestad, G. (1997) *'Empire' by Integration: the United States and European Integration, 1945–97* (Oxford: Oxford University Press).

McCartney, R. J. (2003) 'Chirac, Schroeder go on defensive', *Washington Post*, 11 April: A37.

McGonigle, R. M. and Zacher, M. W. (1979) *Pollution, Politics and International Law: Tankers at Sea* (Berkeley: University of California Press).

Malcolm, N., Pravda, A. and Light, M. (1996) *Internal Factors in Russian Foreign Policy* (Oxford and New York: Oxford University Press).

Martin, L. L. (1993) 'The rational state choice of multilateralism' in Ruggie, J. G. (ed.) *Multilateralism Matters*: 91–121.

Massari, M. (2000) 'US foreign policy decision-making during the Clinton administration', *The International Spectator* 35 (4): 91–105.

Matthews, J. (2001) 'Estranged partners', *Foreign Policy*, November/December: 48–54.

Mayer, F. W. (1998) *Interpreting NAFTA: the Science and Art of Political Analysis* (New York: Columbia University Press).

Mearsheimer, J. J. and Walt, S. M. (2002) 'Can Saddam be contained? History says Yes', CIAOnet essay (available at <http://www.ciaonet.org/specialsection/iraq/papers/was01/was01.html>, accessed 18 May 2003).

Mearsheimer, J. J. (1990) 'Back to the future: instability in Europe after the Cold War', *International Security* 15(1): 5–56.

Miller, S. E. (2002) 'The end of unilateralism or unilateralism redux?', *The Washington Quarterly* 25 (1): 15–29.

Missiroli, A. (2002) (ed.) *Enlargement and European Defence after 11 September* (Paris: Institute for Security Studies), Chaillot Paper no. 53.

Moïsi, D. (2001) 'The more influence, the greater the divide', *Financial Times*, 27 August 2001: 11.

Monar, J. (1998) (ed.) *The New Transatlantic Agenda and the Future of EU–US Relations* (London and Cambridge MA: Kluwer Law International).

Moynihan, D. -P. (1978) *A Dangerous Place* (Boston: Little, Brown and Company).

Netherlands Institute of War (2002) *Srebrenica – a 'Safe' Area: Reconstruction, Background, Consequences and Analyses of the Fall of a Safe Area* (The Hague) (available at <http://www.srebrenica.nl/en/a_index.htm> accessed 14 January 2003).

Nicolaïdis, K. and Howse, R. (2002) '"This is my Utopia": the EU, the WTO, global governance and global justice', *Journal of Common Market Studies* 40 (4): 767–89.

Nye, J. (2002) *The Paradox of American Power: Why the World's Only Superpower Can't Go It Alone* (Oxford and New York: Oxford University Press).

O'Hanlon, M. E. (2002) 'A flawed masterpiece', *Foreign Affairs* 81 (3): 47–63.

Parmentier, G. (2000) 'Après le Kosovo: pour un nouveau contrat transatlantique', *Politique Etrangère* 66 (4): 765–810.

Parmentier, G. (2002) 'NATO: lost opportunities' in Brenner, M. and Parmentier, G. (eds) *Reconcilable Difference: US–French Relations in the New Era* (Washington DC: Brookings Institution).

Patten, C. (2002) 'Jaw-jaw, not war-war', *Financial Times* 15 February: 16.

Peel, Q. (2002) 'Transatlantic ties after 9/11: a European view', *Internationale Politik* 3 (Fall): 19–24.

Perl, R. (2001) *National Commission on Terrorism Report: Background and Issues for Congress*, Congressional Research Service Report for Congress, 6 February (Library of Congress, Washington DC).

Petersmann, E. -U. (2001) 'Dispute prevention and dispute settlement in the EU–US transatlantic partnership' in Pollack, M. A. and Shaffer, G. C. (eds) *Transatlantic Governance in the Global Economy* (Oxford and Lanham MD: Rowman and Littlefield).

Peterson, J. (1996) *Europe and America: the Prospects for Partnership* (London: Routledge) 2nd edition.

Peterson, J. (1998) 'Introduction: the European Union as a global actor' in Peterson, J. and Sjursen, H. (eds) *A Common Foreign Policy for Europe?* (London and New York: Routledge).

Peterson, J. (2001a) *US and EU in the Balkans: 'America Fights the Wars, Europe Does the Dishes?'* (San Domenico di Fiesole, Italy: European University Institute, Robert Schuman Centre for Advanced Studies) RSC no. 2001/49.

Peterson, J. (2001b) 'Shaping, not making – the impact of the American Congress on US–EU relations' in Philippart, E. and Winand, P. (eds) *Ever Closer Partnership: Policy-Making in US–EU Relations* (Brussels: PIE-Peter Lang).

Peterson, J. (2001c) 'Get away from me closer, you're near me too far: Europe and America after the Uruguay Round' in Pollack, M. A. and Shaffer, G. C. (eds) *Transatlantic Governance in the Global Economy* (Lanham MD and Oxford: Rowman and Littlefield).

Peterson, J. (2002) 'Europe, America and the war on terrorism', *Irish Studies in International Affairs* 13: 23–42.

Peterson, J. and Bomberg, E. (1999) *Decision-making in the European Union* (Basingstoke and New York: Palgrave).

Peterson, J. and Ward, H. (1995) 'Coalitional instability and the multi-dimensional politics of security: a rational choice argument for US–EU cooperation', *European Journal of International Relations* 1(2): 131–56.

Pfaff, W. (1998–99), 'The Coming Clash of Europe with America', *World Policy Journal* 15 (4): 1–9.

Philippart, E. (2001) 'The New Transatlantic Agenda: an overview', presentation to workshop on 'The New Transatlantic Agenda at five: a critical assessment', European University Institute, Florence.

Philippart, E. and Winand, P. (2001a) 'Deeds not words? Evaluating and explaining the US–EU policy output' in Philippart, E. and Winand, P. (eds) *Ever Closer Partnership: Policy-Making in US–EU Relations* (Brussels: PIE-Peter Lang).

Philippart, E. and Winand, P. (2001b) 'Ever closer partnership? Taking stock of US–EU relations' in Philippart, E. and Winand, P. (eds) *Ever Closer Partnership: Policy-Making in US–EU Relations* (Brussels: PIE-Peter Lang).

Pollack, J. (2002) 'Saudia Arabia and the United States', *Middle East Review of International Affairs* 6 (3) (available at <http://meria.idc.ac.il/journal/2002/issue3/pollack.pdf>, accessed 11 November 2002).

Pollack, K. M. (2002) 'Next stop Bagdhad?', *Foreign Affairs* 81 (2): 32–47.

Pollack, M. A. and Shaffer, G. C. (2001a) (eds) *Transatlantic Governance in the Global Economy* (Boulder CO and Oxford: Rowman and Littlefield).

Pollack, M. A. and Shaffer, G. C. (2001b) 'Transatlantic governance in historical and theoretical perspective' in Pollack, M. A. and Shaffer, G. C. (eds) *Transatlantic Governance in the Global Economy* (Oxford and Lanham MD: Rowman and Littlefield).

Pollack, M. A. and Shaffer, G. C. (2001c) 'The challenge of reconciling regulatory differences: food safety and GMOs in the transatlantic relationship' in Pollack, M. A. and Shaffer, G. C. (eds) *Transatlantic Governance in the Global Economy* (Boulder CO and Oxford: Rowman and Littlefield).

Pryce-Jones, David (1999) 'Bananas are the beginning', *National Review*, 5 April: 34–6.

Purdum, T. S. (2003) 'The brains behind Bush's war policy', *New York Times*, 1 February, (available at <http://middleeastinfo.org/article1845.html>, accessed 18 May 2003).

Quinlan, M. (2001) *European Defense Cooperation: Asset or Threat to NATO?* (Washington DC: Woodrow Wilson Center).

Ramet, S. P. (2001) 'The USA: to war in Europe again' in Weymouth, T. and Henig, S. (eds) *The Kosovo Crisis: the Last American War in Europe?* (London and New York: Reuters for Pearson Education).

Ramet, S. P. (2002) 'The United States and Europe: toward greater cooperation or a historic parting? An idealist perspective' in Ramet, S. P. and Ingebritsen, C. (eds) *Coming in from the Cold War: Changes in US–European Interactions since 1980* (Boulder CO: Rowman and Littlefield).

Ramirez, J. D. and Szapiro, M. (2001) 'The EU: old wine from new bottles' in Weymouth, T. and Henig, S. (eds) *The Kosovo Crisis: the Last American War in Europe?* (London and New York: Reuters for Pearson Education).

Reddaway, P. and Glinski, D. (2001) *The Tragedy of Russia's Reforms* (Washington DC: United States Institute of Peace Press).

Reich, R. (1990) 'Who is US?', *Harvard Business Review* 68 (1): 53–64.

Rice, C. (2000) 'Promoting the National Interest', *Foreign Affairs* 79 (1): 45–62.

Rieff, D. (1999–2000) 'A second American century? The paradoxes of power', *World Policy Journal* 16 (4): 7–14.

Ringius, L. (1999) 'The European Community and climate protection: what's behind the empty rhetoric?', *Cicero Report*: 8.

Risse, T. (2000) '"Let's argue!" Communicative action in world politics', *International Organization* 54 (1): 1–39.

Roberts, A. (2002) 'Counter-terrorism, armed force and the laws of war', *Survival* (44) 1: 7–32.

Rodman, P. (1999) 'The fallout from Kosovo', *Foreign Affairs* 78 (4): 45–51.

Rodman, P. W. (1999) *Drifting Apart? Trends in US–European Relations* (Washington DC: The Nixon Center).

Rodrik, D. (1997) *Has Globalization Gone Too Far?* (Washington DC: Institute for International Economics).

Rohde, D. (1997) *Endgame: The Betrayal and Fall of Srebrenica* (Boulder CO: Westview).

Rubin, J. (2000a) 'Countdown to a very personal war', *Financial Times*, 30 September–1 October: I, IX.

Rubin, J. (2000b) 'The promise of freedom', *Financial Times* 7–8 October: I, IX.

Rudig, W. (2002) 'Between ecotopia and disillusionment: Green parties in European Government', *Environment* 44 (3): 20–33.

Ruggie, J. G. (1993) (ed.) *Multilateralism Matters: the Theory and Praxis of an Institutional Form* (New York: Columbia University Press).

Schake, K. (2002) *Constructive Duplication: Reducing EU Reliance on US Military Assets* (London: Centre for European Reform).

Schmid, A. (1996) 'The links between transnational organized crime and terrorist crimes', *Transnational Organized Crime* 42 (4): 67–8.

Schmitt, B. (2000) *From Cooperation to Integration: Defence and Aerospace Industries in Europe* (Paris: Western European Union – Institute for Strategic Security), Chaillot Paper no. 40.

Schmitt, B. (2001) *Between Cooperation and Competition: the Transatlantic Defence Market* (Paris: Western European Union – Institute for Strategic Security), Chaillot Paper no. 44.

Schott, J. J. (1996) 'Reflections on TAFTA' in Stokes, B. (ed.) *Open for Business* (New York: Council on Foreign Relations Press).

Sloan, S. (2000) *The United States and European Defence* (Paris: Western European Union – Institute for Security Studies), Chaillot Paper no. 39.

Sloan, S. (2002) *NATO, the European Union and the Atlantic Community. The Transatlantic Bargain Reconsidered* (Lanham MD and Oxford: Rowman and Littlefield).

Sloan, S. and van Ham, P. (2002) *What Future for NATO?* (London: Centre for European Reform).

Smith, C. S. (2003) 'Chirac scolding angers nations that back US: "New" Europe bristles at call for quiet on Iraq', *New York Times*, 1 February: 1, 10.

Smith, M. (1998) 'Competitive co-operation and EU–US relations: can the EU be a strategic partner for the United States in the world political economy?', *Journal of European Public Policy* 5 (4): 561–77.

Smith, S. (2002) 'The end of the unipolar moment? September 11 and the future of world order', *International Relations* 16 (2): 171–83.

Solana, J. (2003) 'America's trusty partner', *Financial Times*, 21 May: 15.

Spiro, P. (2000) 'The new sovereigntists: American exceptionalism and its false prophets', *Foreign Affairs* (November–December): 9–15.

Stevenson, R. W. and Preston, J. (2003) 'Bush meets Blair amid signs of split on UN war role', *New York Times*, 1 February: 1, 10.

Stewart, R. B. (1992), 'Environmental law in the United States and the European community: spillovers, cooperation, rivalry, institutions', *University of Chicago Legal Forum*: 41–80.

Survival (2001), special issue of *Survival* vol. 42/3.

Szabo, S. F. (2002) 'After Prague: American views of the new NATO', *Radio Free Europe/Radio Liberty*, 4 (24), 4 December.

Talbott, S. (1999) 'America's stake in a strong Europe', Speech to Royal Institute of International Affairs, London, 7 October.

Talbott, S. (2002) 'From Prague to Baghdad: NATO at risk', *Foreign Affairs* 81 (6): 46–57.

Tertrais, B. (2001) *US Missile Defence: Strategically Sound, Politically Questionable* (London: Centre for European Reform).

Testimony of J. O'Neill, Counter Terrorism Section, FBI, to Permanent Select Committee on Intelligence (1996), US House of Representatives, July, 104th Congress (Washington DC: US Government Printing Office): 10.

Thomas, J. (2000) *The Military Challenges of Transatlantic Coalitions* (International Institute for Strategic Studies), Adelphi Paper 333.

Travers, D. (2001) 'The UN: squaring the circle' in Weymouth, T. and Henig, S. (eds) *The Kosovo Crisis: the Last American War in Europe?* (London and New York: Reuters for Pearson Education).

Trenin, D. (2000). 'Russia–EU partnership: grand vision and practical steps', *Russia on Russia* 1, Moscow School of Political Studies and Social Market Foundation, February.

Trenin, D. (2001) 'Russia and the future of nuclear policy', in Schmitt, B. (ed.), *Nuclear Weapons: A New Great Debate*, Chaillot Paper no. 43 (July): 103–26.

Triantaphyllou, D. (2001) 'The Balkans after 11 September – quo vadis?', *Institute for European Studies Newsletter* (Western European Union) 35, October: 6.

UK House of Commons (2000) 'Future strategy for Kosovo and the Balkans', memorandum submitted by the Foreign and Commonwealth Office, Select Committee on Foreign Affairs, Minutes of Evidence (available at <http://www.parliament.the-stationery-office.co.uk/cgi-bin/htm_hl?DB=ukparl.../9111813.htm>, accessed 18 October 2001).

US State Department (2001) 'US response to communication of the Commission of the European Communities, "Reinforcing the Transatlantic Relationship"', 28 March, Washington DC (mimeo).

Vaicbourdt, N. (2001) 'Réflexions sur l'avenir du lien transatlantique' in Bossuat, G. and Vaicbourdt, N. (eds) *États-Unis, Europe et Union Européenne: Histoire et Avenir d'un Partenariat Difficile (1945–1999)* (Brussels and New York: PIE-Peter Lang).

van Ham, P. (2002) 'Can Europe save NATO from irrelevance?' in (with S. Sloan) *What Future for NATO?* (London: CER).

Viguier, L. L., Babiker, M. H. and Reilly, J. M. (2001) *Carbon Emissions and the Kyoto Commitment in the European Union*, MIT Joint Program on the Science and Policy of Global Change Report no. 70.

Vogel, D. (2001) 'Ships passing in the night: the changing politics of risk regulation in the United States and the European Union', European University Institute, RSCAS Working Paper no. 2001/16.

Wallace, W. (2001) 'Europe: the necessary partner', *Foreign Affairs*, vol. 80/3: 16–34.

Wallace, W. (2002a) 'As viewed from Europe: transatlantic sympathies, transatlantic fears', *International Relations* 16 (2): 281–6.

Wallace, W. (2002b) 'American hegemony: European dilemmas' in Freedman, L. (ed.) *Superterrorism: Policy Responses* (Oxford and Malden MA: Blackwell).

Wallace, W. and Allen, D. (1977) 'Political cooperation: procedure as substitute for policy' in Wallace, H., Wallace. W. and Webb, C. (eds) *Policy-making in the European Communities* (New York: John Wiley).

Wallander, C. A. (2000) *The Dynamics of US–Russian Relations: A Critical Perspective*, Program on New Approaches to Russian Security Policy Memo Series. Memo no. 111, PONARS.

Walt, S. (1998–99) 'The ties that fray', *The National Journal* 54 (Winter) 3–11.

Webber, M. *et al.* (2002) 'The Common European Security and Defence Policy and the "third-country" issue', *European Security* 11/2: 75–100.

Wedel, J. R. (1998) *Collision and Collusion: The Strange Case of Western Aid to Eastern Europe 1989–1998* (Basingstoke: Macmillan).

Weiler, J. H. H. (1999) *The Constitution of Europe* (Cambridge: Cambridge University Press).

White House (2002) *National Security Strategy of the United States of America* (available at <http://www.whitehouse.gov/nsc/nss.html> accessed 12 May 2003).

Wiener, J. B. and Rogers, M. D. (2001) 'Comparing precaution in the United States and Europe', Duke Center for Environmental Solutions Working Paper 2000/01 (August 2001).

Wolf, M. (2002) 'Gender and America's agenda', *Financial Times*, 3 April: 23.

Woodward, B. (2002) *Bush at War* (New York: Simon and Schuster).

Yost, D. (2000) 'The NATO capabilities gap and the European Union', *Survival* 42/4.

Zakaria, F. (2001) 'Holing up inside fortress Europe', *Time*, 28–32.

Zielonka, J. (2000) 'Transatlantic relations beyond the CFSP', *International Spectator*, 35 (4 October–December): 27–40.

Index